RECONFIGURING THE NIGERIAN EDUCATION SYSTEM

A Historical Reappraisal and Cultural Renaissance

Charles Ikechukwu Anemelu MA, EdD

Lumen Educational Publications

Copyright © 2018 by Charles Anemelu

All rights reserved. No part of this publication may be reproduced, distributed, or transmitted in any form or by any means, including photocopying, recording, or other electronic or mechanical methods, or by any information storage and retrieval system, without the prior written permission from the copyright owner.

Paperback
ISBN – 10: 0-9980275-0-2
ISBN – 13: 978-0-9980275-0-0

Cover Design:
Courtesy of Strumdigi Services International
Lagos, Nigeria

Dedication

I dedicate this book to all Nigerian educationists and students
— past, present and future.

Acknowledgements

Grateful acknowledgements to my editors, publishers and all volunteer proofreaders. I am also grateful to a few educational referees for their expert advice and useful suggestions. I remain eternally grateful to my dear deceased parents. The same applies to my siblings, close relations, friends, superiors, fellow priests, teachers and educators who never ceased to become strong sources of inspiration to me throughout my academic journey both in Nigeria and in the United States.

Above all, I am deeply grateful to the Almighty God for inspiring me with unmerited vision and foresight that led to the conception of this project. I owe Him a debt of profound appreciation for His help, support and guidance that were indispensable throughout this elaborate and literary trip.

TABLE OF CONTENTS

Preface ix

Introduction 1

Chapter One: The Nigerian Education System 12
    The Concept of Education 15
    Historical Backdrop 17
    Pre-Colonial Education System 19
    Teaching and Learning 21
    Intellectual Training 21
    Vocational Training 22
    Politics and Leadership 23
    Islamic Education 23
    Western and Colonial Education System 25
    A Glance at the Education Ordinances 29
    The Impact of the Education Ordinances 32
    Administrative Approach and Education 36
    Education Ordinance 1916 36

Chapter Two: The Current Education System 40
    Educational Reforms 45
    The Education System's Structure 46
    Duration of Basic Education 47
    Psycho-Cultural Factors 50
    Persistent Challenges 50
    Illiteracy 52
    Poverty and Unemployment 54
    Moral Decadence 62
    Industrial Actions and Strikes 63
    Gender Inequality 66
    Commentary and Recommendations 70

Chapter Three: Policymaking and Implementation   74
    The Colonial Era (1842-1959)   75
    The Post-Colonial Era   78
    National Policy on Education   82
    Hindrances to Education Policy Implementation
        in Nigeria   83
    Instability and Changes in Government   84
    Political Factors   86
    Financial Constraints and Overinvestment   87
    Conflicts of Interest   88
    Prejudice and Discrimination   88
    Cultural Considerations   89
    Commentary and Recommendations   91

Chapter Four: International Models and Eye Openers   95
    Singapore   99
    Hong Kong   100
    Japan   102
    Taiwan   105
    South Korea   107
    Macau   109
    Finland   112
    Estonia   115
    Shanghai   118
    Commentary and Recommendations   122

Chapter Five: Integrating Technology into Curriculum   127
    An Overview   127
    Implications of Digital Education   129
    Barriers to Technology Integration   133
    Poverty of Power Supply   133
    Insufficient Computer and Technology Training   134
    Funding and Financial Challenges   135
    Finding a Balance   135
    Psycho-Cultural Appropriateness   137
    Commentary and Recommendations   140

Chapter Six: Children and Youth Education   143
    School Climate and Culture   150
    Dropouts, Absenteeism and Truancy   153
    Monitoring and Boosting Attendance   156
    Incentives and Rewards   158
    Excursions and Field Trips   159

Chapter Seven: Infrastructural Investments and Education   164
    Public Infrastructure   165
    Roads and Transportation   166
    Security Infrastructure   172
    Power and Electricity   174

Chapter Eight: The Importance of Competition   177
    Competition vs. Collaboration   179
    Competition in Education   181
    Competition and Curriculum   182
    The Nigerian Situation   186

Chapter Nine: Education and the Nigerian Culture   189
    Culture and Education   190
    Diversity and Fraternity   194
    Dynamism and Resilience   196
    Democracy and Freedom   198
    Curriculum and Culture   202
    Language of Instruction   204

Chapter Ten: Education and Quality of Instruction   207
    Teacher Training and Classroom Instruction   208
    Quality of Teaching and Instruction   211
    Pivotal Subjects and Teaching   212
    Division of Labour   213
    Recruitment of Teachers   215
    Remuneration and Rewards   217
    Teacher Evaluation   219
    Retired Teachers   222
    Commentary and Evaluations   223

Chapter Eleven: Endemic Challenges and Investments   225
    The Nature and Causes of Corruption   226
    Corruption in Education   226
    Negative Impacts   229
    A Positive Foundation   230
    Solutions and Recommendations   231
    Additional Comments   233
    Investigations and Transparency   235
    Economy and Education Funding   236
    Education Budgets   240
    Corporate Investment   244

Chapter Twelve: Reconfiguring Nigerian Education   247
    Lessons from Colonialism   247
    Later Progress in Education and Scholarship   250
    The Colonial Time's Educational Status in Europe   252
    The Way Forward for the Nigerian Education   254
    Culture and Tradition   255
    Ability and Aptitude   257
    Creativity and Resourcefulness   259
    Capacity-Building and Development   261
    Managing Nigeria's Education System   263
    Continuity   263
    Uniformity in Practice   265
    Originality of Structure   266
    Summary, Evaluation and Conclusion   267

Epilogue   274

References   283

LIST OF TABLES

1. Earliest Secondary Schools in Nigeria and Years Established — 28
2. Student Population (Primary, Secondary and Government Assisted Schools) by Gender from 1888 to 1890 — 33
3. Relative Poverty Headcount from 1980 to 2010 — 55
4. Citizens Living in Extreme Poverty in 1990 vs. 2013 — 58
5. The World's 2018 Extreme Poverty Statistics — 60
6. Colonial Era's Education Ordinances, Commissions, and Reports — 75
7. The Six Oldest Tertiary Institutions /Universities in Nigeria — 78
8. Post-Independence Educational Acts, Commissions/ Reports, & National Constitutions — 80
9. Total Budget vs. Educational Sector Budgets and Percentage Equivalents from 1999-2016 — 243

LIST OF FIGURES

1. The Current Nigerian Education System in a Pyramidal Framework — 12
2. Nigeria's Unemployment Rates in Statistics from 2014 to 2017 — 61
3. Elements and Benefits of excursions for students — 160
4. A Framework of Some Elements of Competition in Education — 193
5. A Framework of Components and Offshoots of Human Culture — 193
6. A Conceptual Framework for Reconfiguring the Nigerian Education System — 255
7. A conceptual depiction of robotic revolutions — 270

Preface

A seminal moment in my study of the Nigerian system of education came in 2014, barely two years after I completed my doctoral programme in Education Leadership, Management and Policy (and final graduation) at Seton Hall University, South Orange, New Jersey in the United States of America. My research on the psycho-cultural adjustment challenges of foreign-born students at community colleges in the north-eastern United States deepened my knowledge of some foreign nations' education systems and strengthened my resolve to trace the challenges faced by Nigeria's education system slightly from the same psycho-cultural perspective. The same doctoral research gave this current work the much-needed immediacy and momentum.

Reconfiguring the Nigerian Education System: A Historical Reappraisal and Cultural Renaissance represents a major attempt in print to delve into the challenges bedevilling the current Nigerian system of education. This book traces different policy mistakes and oversights that have given rise to some of the issues in the nation's education system and puts forward fresh proposals and potential resolutions to these issues. It is written to meet the requirements of the Nigerian citizenry and the complex needs of our environment.

It is my wholehearted purpose to make an important contribution in the life journey of education in my fatherland. I am making this volume available to encourage an awareness and understanding of the nation's education system and process. Nigerians and their families cannot appreciate, cherish, preserve, or jealously guard their own education system, despite its many decades of existence, if they do not either understand how the sector works or become aware of its challenges.

Currently, it seems that many students and university graduates in Nigeria lack the ability to apply their knowledge and skills in everyday societal life. Therefore, this book is written in such a way as to propose an educational process that supports the development of thinking skills and inculcates tradition-based teaching and learning techniques along with other noble values. The hope is to achieve these goals in order to produce well-balanced citizens who can contribute to the harmony and prosperity of a nation and its people. Also, it will equip Nigeria's policymakers, educators, teachers, stakeholders, students and their families with the basic knowledge of the challenges facing the nation's education system and the possible way forward.

Although many excellent books have been written and literary works produced on the general principles, theories, concepts and specialised aspects of the Nigerian education system and the challenges facing it, there is paucity of literature on the potential bases of these challenges, let alone the availability of possible and workable solutions relative to the nation's basic psycho-socio-cultural environment. Almost no research has been conducted on the subject. This present book, therefore, attempts to review the Nigerian system of education and its challenges from a different perspective. It offers a literary update on the country's education system and methodology as education experts grapple with challenges that did not exist about three decades ago but now have become significant.

This book intends to highlight the following points:
- That the future of Nigeria's education system is bright, in conjunction with the ability of its children and young people.
- That school attendance could be sustainably encouraged and dropouts, truancy and illiteracy reasonably curbed.
- That Nigeria's education system could be anchored or based on certain elements of its traditional heritage and even on some aspects of its historical education systems that were characteristically inclusive, vocational, self-reliant and pragmatic enough to address the needs of the immediate environment.
- That Nigeria can always learn from international education system models to consolidate its own existing education system.
- That technology could be used (but not depended upon) to enhance teaching and learning in Nigerian schools.
- That effecting a balance in the use of technology for teaching and learning should be considered paramount in its integration into curriculum.
- That teacher effectiveness could be bolstered with decent rewards, incentives and timely remunerations.
- That the education sector could be drastically improved with sufficient funding and by effectively cutting out its endemic problems and challenges.

While writing this project, one of the greatest difficulties was to ascertain available materials and verify them for accuracy of historical dates and statistical data, as I found a few of them either irregular or conflicting. Thankfully, the literature on the nation's education system was not bulky. Also, while writing this volume, I have often been reminded of the need to make education in Nigeria flexible enough to capture rapid advancements in science and technology but also to substantially accommodate the traditional methods of teaching and learning. Ever since building a sustainable system of education in Nigeria became the central theme of discussions among educators, education stakeholders, policymakers, administrators and communities, a need has been felt for a book of this nature.

This book makes a keen attempt to be useful, interesting and worth reading. Leaving out irrelevant materials, attempts were made to discuss and share essential facts with direct links to what are practicable and workable in Nigeria. This objective and vision will not be achieved unless one gains a better understanding of what caused these problems in the nation's education system and what lessons from history and international education models can inform the country's future education policies, programmes and services.

Efforts were made to clearly explain the challenges facing the country's education system. The works, books, resources and literatures that I consulted in the process of this writing are either acknowledged or cited in the bibliography. It is noteworthy that in some chapters, the words "system" and "structure" are used interchangeably to describe levels of education.

This volume, which I consider timely, based on a decade of study and reflection, presents a brief but in-depth portrait and basic analysis of the current state of the Nigerian education system. It is not about criticising the nation's education system or that of any other nation or continent. Instead, it provides us with an all-round but non-exhaustive view of education in Nigeria from the viewpoint of a Nigerian who is deeply interested in education and the overall unity, peace and progress of Nigeria as a nation.

I hope that this book will be useful for Nigeria's education stakeholders, policymakers, educators, administrators, principals, teachers, students and their families. The same applies to other readers whom, I believe, may benefit from learning bits of the history of Nigerian education that were gleaned and compiled from a variety of sources. These sources were quite insightful and valuable. They also point to other sources that are not discussed directly in this book. Any suggestions and feedback to promote its further improvement will of course be gratefully acknowledged and possibly incorporated into the next edition and revision.

Charles I. Anemelu (MA, EdD)
Charleston, West Virginia
November 20, 2018

Introduction

A fair assessment of the Nigerian education system would immediately present some quantitative progress over the past four decades, especially in the boost of school enrolment. Onwuameze (2013) aptly notes that following the introduction of education policies and programmes, growth in enrolment at the primary and secondary levels has largely been sustained. To be specific, enrolment of pupils in primary schools increased from 3,515,827 in 1970 to 14,383,487 in 1985 and to 20,080,986 in 2010. As at 2015, UNESCO's review of Nigeria's education system found that enrolment at the primary and junior secondary levels had greatly increased since the year 2000. Nonetheless, transition and completion (graduation) rates remained below 70%. Enrolment rates increased by 130% for secondary education in the period from 2000 to 2013 but decreased by 4% for the primary level (Centre for Public Impact, 2017).

Even though some progress has been recorded and a few intervention strategies adopted over the years in the country's education system, the citizenry does not yet appear to be convinced that the problems in that sector have been or will ever be fixed. Various concerns voiced, and articles written by both educationists and non-educationists alike seem to be pointing not towards high academic performance, turnout of college graduates, or acquisition of degree certificates but to the sector's systemic inadequacy, perceived inefficiency, dysfunctionality and non-pragmatic constitution. Of course, any nation's system of education that is demonstrably unable to address or supply its own basic needs and that of its citizenry in a sustainable fashion could be characterised by the negative features listed above. A strategically well-structured education system, for instance, should be able to address the problems of unemployment, poverty, insecurity, illiteracy and disease (to name just a few) in any given nation that is interested in true development.

Public opinion suggests that many citizens of Nigeria still lack confidence in the leadership, governance and management of the nation's education system, especially in policy formulation, development and implementation. This brief but profound review of the Nigerian education scheme would undeniably reveal a beleaguered system. On the upside, its future prospect looks promising and unlimited. Despite this optimism, the Nigerian education system seems to be tending towards a downward plunge. Essentially, the nation's still- struggling education system appears to be headed for collapse if the trajectory of its present journey is unchanged or the system itself not restructured to be more need-based and pragmatic.

In a 2010 study, the United Nations Educational, Scientific and Cultural Organisation (UNESCO) reported that, with approximately 10.5 million children of primary school age out of school in the entire nation, Nigeria dominated 12 other countries as it accounted for 47% of the global out-of-school (OSC) population. This study also indicated that Nigeria was among the four countries that had experienced the highest dropout rates since 1999 (Abdulrahman, 2013). Perhaps UNESCO's report will do a service with this discomforting disclosure by bringing more attention to the Nigerian education sector. Nigeria's OSC population could even be compared to the populations of some countries in Africa and across the globe. The population of Libya, for instance, is about 7 million, while the population of Liberia is about 5 million. Has Nigeria's unsettlingly large number of out-of-school children made the burden of education either overwhelming or unbearable for it?

Recognising the scope and size of the problem, an updated report from the Permanent Secretary of the Federal Ministry of Education, Adamu Hussaini, at the 62nd National Council on Education (NCE) in Kano state indicated that Nigeria had the highest percentage of out-of-school children in the world (Adewale, 2017). Of recent, the Universal Basic Education Commission (UBEC) has claimed that the population of the nation's out-of-school children has increased from 10.5 to 13.2 million (Alake, 2018). This is not exactly good news. Could this alarming report be signalling a broader loss of momentum in the governance and management of Nigeria's education sector?

No single person should take the blame for the state of the nation's education system. Emphasis needs to be put on the fact that many children were never granted the opportunity to receive formal education in the first place rather than on the high dropout rates. Most of the Nigerian children who are not in school today have never set foot in any classroom at all. From both a psycho-cultural and psychosocial standpoint, the likelihood that children will either never start school or simply drop out as they advance in age cannot be ignored. On an extended note, people should also be mindful that, in the African culture and even in other cultures, it is often suggested that children or adolescents who are advanced in age are more likely to drop out of school than their younger counterparts. This should be a growing concern of the Nigerian education policymakers and critical stakeholders in the country.

Further, on a different but related note, the release of the May/June 2015 result of Nigeria's West African Senior School Certificate Examination (WASSCE) revealed that, out of 1,593,442 candidates that sat for the examinations, only 616,370 (38.68%) obtained credits in five subjects or above including English language and mathematics. In a bid to highlight the slight improvement from previous years, the head of the Nigerian WASSCE office in Lagos stated that the total number of candidates who obtained five credits in English language and mathematics in 2013 was 639,760 (38.30%); in 2014, the number was 529,425(31.28%).

However, in 2015, the exam body is reported to have withheld 118,101 results over alleged exam malpractices (Adesulu, 2015; Mohammed, 2015). Commenting on cheating and exam malpractices, the West African Examinations Council (WAEC) stated that Nigeria had the highest number of cheating incidents of all five countries in which the Council operates. In 2016, WAEC ceased to recognise 113 Nigerian secondary schools that were implicated in examination malpractice and annulled the results of 30, 654 candidates who sat for 2012 SSC exams (WENR, 2017).

Nevertheless, the 2016 results saw a significant improvement in the WASSCE students' academic performance. Of the 1,552,758 students that sat for the May/June exams, 878,040 candidates (52.97%) obtained credits in five subjects or more including English language and mathematics. The examination's body announced that it withheld the results of about 137,295 candidates because of either cheating or exam malpractices, representing 8.89% of those who took the examinations (Okonkwo, 2016).

The WASSCE results for 2017 indicated yet another improvement in the candidates' scores. Out of 1,559,662 candidates that sat for the examination, 923, 486 candidates (59.22%), obtained a minimum of five credits or more including English language and mathematics. This represents a 7% improvement from the previous year. Nevertheless, 214,952 candidates' results were reported as withheld (Adedigba, 2017).

Recently, the West African Examinations Council released the 2018 May/June West African School Certificate Examination (WASCE) results. It registered an achievement decline in comparison with previous years. According to the report, 786,016 out of 1,572, 396 candidates (49.98%) obtained five credits or more in English language and mathematics, while 858,424 candidates (54.59%) obtained credits in a minimum of five subjects including English but without mathematics.

In summary, a total of 1,213,244 candidates (76.84%) obtained credits in a minimum of any five subjects, with or without English language and/or mathematics (Olowolagba, 2018). Certainly, the 2018 results (49.98%) showed a significant decline in comparison with the results in both 2017 and 2016, during which 59.22% and 52.97% of the candidates, respectively, obtained credit passes in a minimum of five subjects including English language and mathematics.

There is a general conviction among policymakers that feedback from the performances of candidates in public examinations not only provides information about the educational progress of learners in a systematic way but is also indicative of the quality of teaching and learning that take place in the classroom (Obioma, Junaidu & Ajagun, 2013).

Admittedly, academic performance can be a sign of either a strong or poor education system, depending on the quality of teaching and learning. The preceding three consecutive May/June results of the West African Senior School Certificate Examination, though eclectic, have at least shown that academic performance or improvement in academics is not necessarily the major problem in the Nigerian education system. Even though this performance relatively represents a positive stride, it is still not essentially the yardstick with which to measure the strength of the structure and functionality of the nation's education system, taking its lingering challenges, reliability foibles and other emerging problems into account.

The drawbacks in Nigeria's education system have been judged as partly or entirely the product of culpable or inculpable negligence, incompetence, greed, corruption, laissez faire attitudes, ineffectiveness, faulty, distorted, or non-implementation of policies and other unfavourable factors, traceable to a handful of heads of educational agencies and institutions along with some affiliated stakeholders in the Nigerian education system. Common critics also believe that blame, to some degree, should be apportioned to disinterested and illiterate parents, nonchalant student learners, irresponsible teachers and academic staff members, ignoble education leaders and administrators. Nevertheless, these circumstances, whether factual or not, look more like the symptoms of the underlying problems than the potential cause.

Could those problems have been wholly the result of how the entire education system was structured? It does not seem likely. Just as no single factor listed above is entirely to blame, the bottlenecks in Nigeria's education system cannot be completely attributed to the perceived inefficiency of the system's structure, although they certainly depend partly on how its curriculum of studies is designed.

Reasonable circumstances might sometimes call for a commonly approved review or a solid restructure of a given education system and its curriculum. Nevertheless, an inherently helpful cultural conservatism, which presupposes and promotes continuity, should always sound this serious caveat: Do not alter any given education system frequently, arbitrarily, or at whim. A few signs of underdevelopment in the Nigerian education system may have exposed the weakness of its infrastructure coupled with the lack of preparedness to compete intra-continentally, much less internationally. Nonetheless, since the state of the country's educational development is deemed increasingly desperate, there is no justification for complacency. Rather, there is an acute need for a thorough systemic review and strategic modification of the entire education sector.

Finding solutions to the problems facing the education sector in Nigeria today would always require a rough start. Certainly, there is no known quick-fix method or detailed scientific outline to achieve immediate success when it comes to reliable progress in any nation's education system. However, various strategies could be copied and deployed to chip away at potential hindrances and improve upon what has worked in the past.

Therefore, the first step in reconfiguring the Nigerian education system is to gain a well-balanced and informed knowledge of the system, retracing its evolution to appreciate relevant and useful elements. When properly directed, this might lead to a more consolidated education legacy and a system that could survive the exigencies of an increasingly dynamic and changing world.

No one can claim monopoly of knowledge on how to address the persistent crises in the education sector; therefore, lingering challenges should be addressed with concerted effort from all and sundry to resolve the opposition and resistance that would normally be expressed by a variety of individuals. The entire Nigerian citizenry should be familiarised with the modus operandi (mode of operation) of the current education system while policymakers endeavour to redefine its nature, character, importance, indispensability and practical relevance in this new millennium. Additionally, it is vital that people try to reposition and reshape the education system's intellectual and vocational threads to fit the fabric of the schools' (and institutional) curriculum; teaching contents and learning methods towards a need-based and pragmatic end. These objectives will be discussed in a much more detail in the 12 chapters that follow this introduction. The contents of each of these chapters and this work are summarised below.

The introductory section sets the context for the rest of the book. In an assessment, it seeks to give a panorama of the Nigerian education system and offer us an optimistic summary review of its current position. This critical section lays emphasis on the fact that the nation's education remains progressive despite its struggles.

Chapter 1 delineates this work's definition of education as a concept, offering us a historical backdrop of Nigerian education that stretches back to its inception; various types of teaching and learning plus vocational trainings are explored. Also, this chapter notes that the Nigerian system was subject to both pre-colonial and colonial pasts, during which the European missionaries and colonialists managed the education sector in the regions and protectorates that were later amalgamated to become Nigeria in 1914. Prior to and a few years after this, the desire of the colonialists to strike a balance and meet the needs of the people in their educational offerings led to various policy reforms that produced the education ordinances of 1882, 1887 and 1916.

Chapter 2 attempts to provide the context of the current Nigerian education system and structure and explore how this resulted from further policy reforms, after Nigeria gained independence, which brought about the Universal Primary Education (UPE). This chapter also objectively identifies persistent challenges in the country and against the education sector, such as illiteracy, poverty and unemployment, moral decadence and gender disparity and examines the psycho-cultural factors that underlie these challenges.

Chapter 3 explores in detail how education policies were formulated during the colonial era and after. This leads to an elaboration of the factors that hinder Nigeria's education system, such as instability in government, political forces, financial challenges, conflicts of interest, cultural considerations, prejudice and discrimination.

Chapter 4 serially documents nine international education models in countries and cities around the world. These include Singapore, Hong Kong, South Korea and Finland, among others and each example offers a clue as to what a totally integral approach to education and a balanced curricular model could provide for us and why Nigeria's education system needs a technical overhaul.

Chapter 5 discusses the importance of technology and how it could be judiciously integrated into the nation's curriculum to support, enhance, guide and expand learning objectives. The chapter also examines barriers to integrating technology into the classroom. These include unsteady power supply, insufficient computer skills and the necessity of technology training. The same applies to funding and financial constraints.

Chapter 6 delves into the current state of child and youth education in Nigeria, which is pivotal for any societal development. It discusses excursions and field trips as among the most effective methods of experiential teaching and learning.

Chapter 7 considers the critical nature of public infrastructural investments and education. It places road accessibility, transportation, electricity and security infrastructure as vital elements of the learning environments in both schools and universities. The same applies to their potential impacts on students' academic progress.

Chapter 8 examines the importance of competition in the Nigerian education system. It explores the difference between competition and collaboration and what they mean to the education sector, investigating how they could be taken into consideration when formulating education curriculum.

Chapter 9 takes an in-depth look at education in relationship to the Nigerian culture. In this chapter, the nature of the Nigerian education system is further explored in relation to the cultural concepts of diversity and fraternity, dynamism and resilience, democracy and freedom in addition to the national curriculum and language of instruction.

Chapter 10 reviews the facets of high-quality education and instruction while touching upon the bases of teacher training and classroom instruction. The importance of decently rewarding and remunerating teachers for effectiveness is highlighted in this section.

In addition to this bottom-line issue of teacher evaluation, the chapter addresses division of labour in teaching and proposes associations of retired teachers. School culture and climate, as well as dropouts, absenteeism and truancy, are dealt with in detail. Finally, an analysis of how to monitor and improve attendance is provided.

Chapter 11 discusses the endemic challenges of corruption and fraud in the Nigerian education system as well as encourages investment in education. It explores the nature and possible root causes of corruption, proffering solution and recommendations on how to address this prevalent issue. Despite the problem of corruption, this chapter still encourages providing vital educational funding and corporate investment.

Chapter 12, which serves as the last chapter of this book, reviews and describes ways in which the Nigerian education system can be reconfigured and properly realigned relative to its culture, tradition, ability, aptitude, creativity and resourcefulness. The same applies to capacity-building and development. It further advocates how to manage Nigeria's education system when considering factors, such as continuity, uniformity and originality of structure. The section ends with a summary, an evaluation and a conclusion of the discourse in this work.

Chapter One
The Nigerian Education System

Nigeria, as a country, operates a federated system of government with 36 states and a Federal Capital Territory (FCT), Abuja. These states and the FCT have a total of 772 local governments. Nigeria's education system and structure (besides kindergarten [K] or pre-basic education) comprises 6 years of primary school education, 3 years of junior secondary school, 3 years of senior secondary education and a 4-year undergraduate programme, if desired. This 6-3-3-4 system can also be broken down into the categories of the Universal Basic Education (UBE), post-basic (or senior secondary) education and tertiary education (9-3-4).

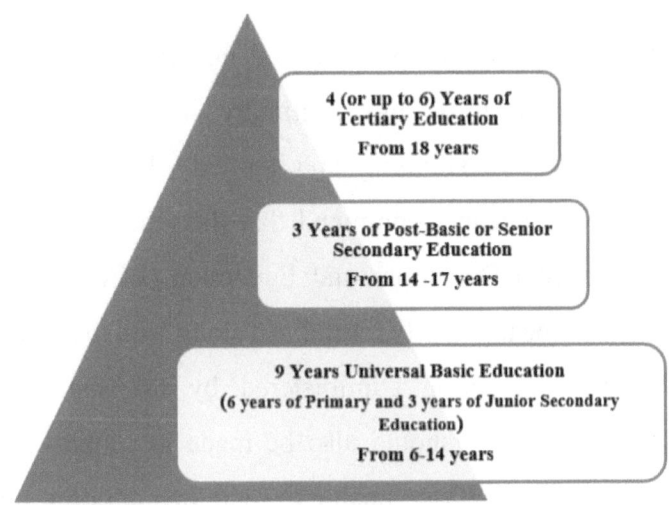

Figure 1. The Current Nigerian Education System in a Pyramidal Framework.

This structure was designed to broaden the nation's education system's relevance, accessibility, inclusivity, functionality and quality. In this education system and formal education journey, basic education, which covers 9 years of schooling (6 years of primary and 3 years of junior secondary education) is considered compulsory (National Policy on Education, 2004).

This education system is largely administered by the federal, state and local governments, with the Federal Ministry of Education assuming centralised responsibilities, such as overall education policy formulation, development, implementation and evaluation. The same applies to quality control as well as checks and balances with the federal government primarily involved in tertiary educational institutions. States take responsibility for secondary and high school education, while the local governments are responsible for primary and elementary school education.

For various psycho-socio-cultural and foundational reasons, which include uniformity and continuity in human educational formation, smooth transitioning and an easy linkage to primary schools, it is pertinent to recommend that the kindergarten or Early Childhood Care and Developmental Education (ECCDE), although rightfully private, be ultimately formalised along with the higher levels of the Nigerian education administered by the state and local governments. Provisions should also be made to support and assist parents and guardians who are unable to send their children and minor dependents to formal kindergarten education owing to cost, poverty, or general non-affordability.

According to a report from the Nigeria Federal Ministry of Education, the number of public ECCDE centres across the country was 20,693 in 2009 (35% of 58,595 total primary schools). This increased significantly to 30,901 in 2013 (50% of 61,305 total primary schools). This 25% increase has positively affected the number of pupils enrolled in ECCDE programmes (Federal Ministry of Education, 2015a).

Although the current condition of the nation's education system seems to underscore the reality that it may crumble if its mission is left unreconstructed, the future could still be bright for Nigeria as a country. Experts have even suggested that effectively forming and implementing positive education policies could boost the economy and help it prosper. Because education is essentially linked to any nation's economy, it might be easier to negate the claim of a failing education system if Nigeria gains a large and prosperous economy in comparison with other countries in Africa and, by extension, the world. Excitingly, the result of an updated Gross Domestic Product (GDP) for Nigeria, a preliminary projection released by the Federal Government, indicated that the Nigerian economy had outclassed and surpassed South Africa's economy by the mid-2015 to become the largest economy in the entire African continent, with the potential to emerge as a strong economy globally. The nation occupied the 21st position globally in GDP, given its purchasing power parity (PPP) and internally generated revenues (IGR). This report, however, would be more beneficial if the citizens made it a criterion of remedy for the Nigerian education system and development. Despite this sudden leap in Nigeria's GDP from 2013 to

2015, the quality of life of the nation's citizenry has not changed, owing to its huge population, among other factors.

For Nigeria to achieve economic development, creativity and productivity, Nigerians need a substantial investment in human capital that begins with public formal education. Public formal education lays the foundation and sets the pace for sustainable economic growth and expanded opportunities. It is one of the top priorities of any civilized nation or society. Even though the common view of public education in Nigeria has never been gloomier than it appears today, Nigeria still aspires to educate its students to global standards.

The Concept of Education

In sum, education helps members of a society to acquire a suitable appreciation of their cultural heritage and to live more satisfying lives through the acquisition of desirable skills, knowledge, habits and values for people living in the society.

Oji (1982) defines education as a process by which people acquire knowledge, skills, habits, values, or attitudes that allow them to become useful members of the society. Okere (1990) defines education as a process of developing the individual morally, socially, emotionally, physically and aesthetically to promote his and the society's welfare. Education has also been described as the process of acquiring knowledge, skills, attitudes, interests, abilities, competence and the cultural norms of a society to enrich the society's perpetual development (Babafemi, 2000). It is a process of acquiring skills and obtaining relevant knowledge and aptitudes (Adunola, 2010). Additionally, Omotoso (2010) captures the concept and essence of education as intertwined with emancipation in a logical crisscross.

This intersection produces justice as the summation of education and emancipation by implication. She also presents a clear picture of education as an emancipation that results from a primordial search for enlightenment and survival.

Chukwusa (2011) suggests that education has to do with systematic development and cultivation of the mind and other natural powers. In a similar vein, Garba (2012) attempts to expound on education as not only central to development and instrumental in the acquisition of appropriate skills and abilities, both mental and physical competence and the necessary equipment for individuals to live in and contribute to the development of society, but also as a treasure that every human being should heavily invest in and pursue.

The essence and big picture of education support the idea of training students who will transform societies and, by extension, the world. Fortunately, education in Nigeria has always been considered a public enterprise and a transformational instrument aimed at achieving national development. Suffice it to observe that in line with this trend, the National Policy on Education in Nigeria, launched in 1977, was directed towards self-realisation, individual and national efficiency, national unity and so forth as well as geared towards achieving social, cultural, economic, political, scientific and technological development (Amaghionyeodiwe & Osinubi, 2006).

In summary, education could be further defined as the process of transmitting and receiving information that is relevant for psychological, physical, intellectual, emotional and moral training based on the participants' internal and external cultural, historical and social environment and aimed towards the total development, maintenance and ultimate sustenance of target individuals, communities, or societies. It imbues learners with the skills and abilities to personally survive and contribute to other groups' survival in the broader world.

At present and without doubt, Nigeria deserves a stronger, wider and more consistent educational foundation. To aid in achieving this, this work will retrace its steps to the past with a short history of the country's educational development. Investigators into the Nigerian education system need an accessible pool of historical data to enable them to glean valuable information regarding the trend of educational development in Nigeria from pre-colonial times to the present.

Historical Backdrop

Any nation that is ignorant of its past will probably charge into the future blindly, as it lacks the foundation and antecedents to give directions. In this context, blindness about the past leaves the future blurred. Without a doubt, certain historical precedents could positively impact Nigeria's educational planning, policymaking and administrative efforts. Irrespective of what may have wrongly transpired in the nation's education system since independence and how imperfectly it might have been comported, Nigerians should still hold on to the successes of the past. Ignoring the beautiful, functional and pragmatic ingredients in Nigeria's traditional education system would only be disrespectful to its children, grandchildren and other future generations. The citizens still cherish and relish many aspects of the nation's cultural and traditional past. Historical evidence testifies that its education system has colonial as well as pre-colonial pasts that are rich in various ways.

Re-exploring the country's educational and psycho-socio-cultural history as a nation, when constructively and meticulously done, might offer us some helpful clues to a better progress as well as exert some positive effects on the relevance of the education system today. The re-exploration and re-examination of the past might nostalgically call for possible experimentation, re-contextualisation, reintegration and incorporation of some of the nation's primordial education heritage into the current system but in the light of modern science and technology. Primarily, taking these steps will familiarise members of the new and younger generations with their background, helping them to understand their basic and physical environment to enable them to successfully shape their own future. Familiarity with the history of a nation can also play a useful role in prescribing a desirable direction for its better and more stable educational future.

This re-examination of relevant educational elements in the past is not suggestive of an imprudent retrogression to the stone and dark ages. Of course, that type of unexamined roll-back could constitute an impediment to an individual's natural and independent growth. A revisit to the past will lay a solid foundation and set the stage for further development based on one's background, functional cultures and traditions of learning. It is of interest to note that existing solutions to complexities in problem solving and conflict resolution can often be found in one's positive cultural and traditional problem-solving methods. Such beneficial aspects in human cultures and traditions could be considered pragmatic because they provide useful, reliable and workable solutions to problems.

Great nations often confidently roll back to their constitutional, democratic and historical traditions whenever important decisions on public affairs and policymaking pose a daunting challenge. In the same vein, a re-enactment of relevant elements in Nigeria's primordial and cultural education traditions, though with some limitations, might provide its current education system with some creative and efficient adjustments.

The existing literature on this subject has classified Nigeria's pre-independence education traditions as (a) Pre-colonial, Indigenous, or Traditional (b) Islamic and (b) Colonial (Western). The following sections will examine each of these areas in detail.

Pre-Colonial Education System

Prior to the advent of European colonialism, education in major parts of the African continent was mostly community-based and indigenous. It was a subsistent type of education, geared solely towards the common good, that is, the survival and well-being of a people. Nigeria's pre-colonial education system was not only functional, practical and creative, it was also progressive in orientation.

It was an informal and purely traditional education system. It normally began with induction ceremonies. Induction was an educational initiation process whereby the members of a given society within the continent were introduced into certain values, norms, social activities, philosophies, principles of life and modes of thought that were considered beneficial to the general society. It was often carried out in special ceremonies. The procedures of induction ceremonies could vary according to tribal and ethnic groups. Africa was illustrious for its rich cultural heritage and moral values that were transmitted through the ages.

Owing to the preliterate nature of such an education system, it was mostly run without school buildings or infrastructure. The lessons and classes were typically conducted in small village playgrounds, fields, tree shades, town centres and arenas. Of course, there were no professional teachers. Learning was done more by apprenticeship with adult members and elders of the society playing the roles of teachers, masters and mentors for the inductees. Initiations were often conducted according to certain age groups, referred to as age grades. In this case, members graduated from lower to higher age grades. Due processes were followed, and customary rules were abided by. What made this traditional education system rich and remarkable were the practical, functional and creative aspects of its nature coupled with the productive efficiency of its philosophy. Its curricular contents, though largely undocumented, were comprehensive and elaborate, embracing virtually all segments of human development and profoundly affiliated with the general workforce expectations of the larger society.

Esu and Junaid (2010) listed the curricular contents of this education system as mental broadening, physical fitness, moral uprightness, religious deference, good social adjustment and interactions. Children and the youth participated in activities, such as wrestling (grappling), dancing, drumming and acrobatic displays. Emphasis was laid on mastery learning, which is characteristic of the contemporary educational process. The same was applicable to hard work, productivity, self-reliance and collective orientation towards the maintenance of the existing social order. Individuals were encouraged to learn the virtues of honesty, respect for rights, lives and property, respect for elders and the dignity of manual labour. The main objective of this education system was to inculcate in the members a certain sense of social responsibility within the community and to produce individuals who would become useful members of society.

Teaching and Learning.

Action learning (or learning by doing) and storytelling were employed effectively in teaching local history to adolescents. Inculcating an in-depth knowledge of the ethics and principles of traditional medicine, carpentry, sorcery, or cultism was reserved for certain families and the training in this regard was undergone strictly by apprenticeship. Services, such as leather work, truck pushing, building trades and sundry indigenous crafts were also handed down in families as well as by apprenticeship. Apprenticeship, studentship or a training period was indeed a common practice for most occupations. For experimentation, practical objects were handled by learners during their training. There was continuous assessment of learners' performances, a practice that is still in vogue in the contemporary education system. For the final examination, a practical test, relevant to the learner's experiences and level of development, was normally given.

Intellectual Training

Mental or intellectual training comprised the study of the local history, myths, legends, storytelling, moonlight story-relaying, poetry, folktales, reasoning, riddles and proverbs. People who excelled in these areas were highly revered, as their expertise was of tremendous benefit to their societies. An individual's intellect was trained and developed in these directions to enable him to fit into such valued professions as rainmakers, herbalists, hunters, local judges, arbitrators, orators, cult leaders and traditional priests. To provide intellectual, rational and critical-thinking skill training to the boys, they were required to attend meetings along with their fathers where they would just sit quietly, listen attentively and observe in order to learn the community meeting processes and gain leadership skills.

The traditional education and training provided by the community were comprehensive and elaborate about character, intellectual, physical, social and vocational development. Nevertheless, their shortcomings were obvious. In the absence of writing, people depended on the power of their minds to facilitate the retention and transmission of learned ideas for future generations. Since memory can fail and the custodians of useful information pass away, or skills killed, all the treasures in the same connection would be lost in consequence (Garba, 2012; Mkpa, 1997; Oyeleke & Olajumoke, 2013).

Vocational Training

In pre-colonial Nigeria, vocational training was the major form of education. Children and youths were taught farming, fishing, weaving, wine tapping, trading, cooking, carving, knitting, cattle rearing, blacksmithing, house-building, making and forging local farm implements. This training was geared towards helping the new generation achieve self-sustenance as well as contribute to their communities and societies.

Cultural exigencies highly treasured gender discrimination in vocational training. Boys were trained in vocations that were considered male-appropriate, such as tree climbing, palm wine tapping, grappling, hunting and archery. Besides these skills were the duties of adulthood that they fulfilled by playing minor roles in the community. Girls, by contrast, were required to stay with their mothers at homes and were trained in cooking, cleaning, weaving, knitting and other skills that were considered female-appropriate. Because of the widespread nature of vocational trainings, researchers have recorded only few cases of unemployment during the pre- colonial era.

Politics and Leadership

Various societal well-being issues constituted the traditional political education. In this instance, the youth were primarily taught rules and regulations governing the family, villages and human relationships among members of society. Attendance of village and community meetings to acquire leadership and political skills was essential because ideas were exchanged at such meetings.

Islamic Education

According to Garba (2012), Islam arrived in Nigeria through the Wangarawa, a migrant Muslim community of scholars and traders whose leader was Adbulrahman Zaite. Today, most or their descendants are respected as imams and teachers across the northern part of Nigeria, especially in Bauchi, Bornu and Zaria (Kaduna state). Citing Fafunwa (1974), Garba suggests that Islam was first accepted in northern Nigeria in the later part of the 11th century by a Kanem Bornu ruler known as Umme Jilmi (1085-1097). Later, in the 13th and 14th centuries, it was accepted by both Dunama I and Dunama II.

Mukhtar (2016), states in a scholarly presentation that, by the end of the 15th century, Islam had already started becoming a state religion in some Hausa states, especially in Kano during the reign of

Muhammad Rumfa (1466-1499). Furthermore, the role of the migrant Muslim communities like the Wangarawa, Fulani and Kunta migrants into the region contributed immensely to the spread and consolidation of Islamic education among the various peoples of Central Sudan.

In 1804, the Jihad conducted by Shehu Usman (Uthman) Danfodio was believed to have helped revive, spread, strengthen and even extend Islamic studies and education to women. Islamic education received tremendous support from some northern leaders. For instance, Abdullahi Bayero (Emir of Kano) reportedly built an Islamic school that later became Bayero College, Kano. This same college today is Bayero University, Kano, upgraded following its continued growth and expansion in scope. Over the years, institutions for Islamic education were established in many parts of the country. However, their delimitation was the emphasis on the Arabic language which is not the central language of education and communication in Nigeria as a whole.

In the northern part of the country, Islamic education was one of the components of being religious and spiritual. For most people, Islamic education was delivered informally under the tutelage of scholars with specialty in teaching and learning. Those teachers and scholars were also referred to as mallams or ulamas. Children memorised chapters of the Quran prescribed by the local mallams or religious teachers before they reached the age of 6. Additionally, the Arabic language was typically required for prayers. Therefore, religious training included drills on the Arabic alphabets as well as the ability to write, read and copy texts in Arabic. In those days, Islamic instructions were provided in the houses of the mallams, a local mosque, or under an umbrella tree on a thoroughfare.

The primary school level is believed to have been the most popular. Later, young and intellectually disposed Muslims, who came from well-to-do families, would examine the meanings of the Arabic texts. Arithmetic, algebra, grammar, syntax, jurisprudence, logic, theology and rhetoric were also introduced, taught by special teachers at the advanced level. Students who graduated at this level advanced for studies in famous Islamic learning centres.

A few formal Muslim schools were also established and administered in almost all major northern Nigerian cities, but most notably in Kano, where the Islamic Brotherhood developed an outstanding number of schools. These schools trained children and young people from devout and affluent families who wished to have their own education, following European learning styles but kept within a strictly Islamic religious context. Such schools operated as local private institutions of learning that strongly upheld the pre-eminence of religious values within a modern school system. Government takeover of private and parochial schools in the mid-1970s deprived such institutions of certain privileges until they were reinstated as independent schools in 1990 (Ajah, 2015).

Western and Colonial Education System

Modern influences on Nigeria's education came in the form of Western education, primarily introduced by the early Christian missionaries in 1842, which positively transformed as well as gave colourful hues to the nation's indigenous education system. This development took place after the suppression of the slave trade (in 1807) that lingered for decades. The first mission school in the form of Western education was officially founded by the Methodist Church (or the Wesleyan Mission) in 1843. This school was located in the border town of Badagry, an area of Lagos along the Atlantic Coast. It was originally named Nursery of the Infant Church, perhaps later taken over and renamed St. Thomas's Anglican Nursery and Primary School by the Anglican Church through the Church Missionary Society (CMS) in 1845. Subsequently, the Anglicans (CMS), Baptists and Presbyterians established schools, followed by the Roman Catholic Church.

In 1853, while the CMS and its affiliates opened a school in Ibadan, the Baptist church was founding one at Ijaye. In 1865, the Anglican missionaries founded the Bishop Crowther LGA Primary School in Lokoja, Kogi state, courtesy of the instrumentality of the then Bishop Samuel Ajayi Crowther, as its founder and the first African Anglican Bishop. Even though the Portuguese commerce and trade expedition, with their attendant efforts to informally introduce Catholicism to their trading partners and customers by building a few churches and schools between the end of the 15th and early 16th centuries, failed because of the slave trade, the Roman Catholic mission impact was soon felt again with the arrival of Padre Antonio in Lagos, where he started the work of evangelisation in earnest by building a school in 1868. Owing to the previous efforts of the Portuguese, the Roman Catholic Church did not have many problems in resuscitating the creed (Sulaiman, 2012, p.90).

Education at this time, at the primary level, was built on the philosophies of the respective Christian missionaries. Based on their constraints and needs in facilitating evangelisation, the curriculum of studies of these early mission schools primarily included reading, writing, arithmetic and religion. Nevertheless, the same Western form of education was later promoted by the colonial administration in such an essentialist way as to suit its purpose of colonisation (Abdulkareem, 1992, p.139; Garba, 2012). Favourable changes and reforms in the colonial government's education policies positively influenced the introduction of secondary schools in Nigeria by the Christian missionaries.

June 6, 1859 saw the establishment of the first secondary level education by the Anglicans (CMS): the CMS grammar school in Bariga, a suburb of Lagos in Lagos state. This school began with only six students who were destined to become clergymen. They lived in a small single-story boarding house known as Colton House. The curriculum of studies included English language, arithmetic, Greek, Latin, Bible knowledge, geometry, history, geography and logic. The first and pioneer principal of the school from 1859 to 1878 was a man known as Babington Macaulay (1826-1878), the father of Herbert Macaulay (1864-1946), the surveyor and nationalist. On the next page is a table list of the oldest secondary schools in Nigeria and the years they were founded:

Table 1

Earliest Secondary Schools in Nigeria and Years Established.

Name of School	State	Year Founded
1. CMS Grammar School, Lagos	Lagos	1859
2. Gregory's College, Lagos	Lagos	1876
3. Methodist Boys High School, Lagos	Lagos	1878
4. Methodist Girls High School, Lagos	Lagos	1879
5. Baptist Academy, Lagos	Lagos	1885
6. Hope Waddel Training Institute, Calabar	Cross River	1895
7. St. Anne's School, Ibadan	Oyo	1896
8. St. Andrew's College, Oyo	Oyo	1896
9. Baptist Training College, Ogbomosho	Oyo	1898
10. The Old Wesley College, Elekuro, Ibadan	Oyo	1905
11. Abeokuta Grammar School, Ogun	Ogun	1908
12. Kings College, Lagos	Lagos	1909
13. Alhuda College, Zaria	Kaduna	1910
14. Ijebu-Ode Grammar School, Ogun	Ogun	1913
15. Eko Boys High School, Lagos	Lagos	1913
16. Ibadan Grammar School, Ibadan	Oyo	1913
17. Government Secondary School, Ilorin	Kwara	1913
18. Government College, Katsina-Ala	Benne	1914
19. Etinan Institute, Etinan, Akwa Iborn	Akwa Ibom	1914
20. Baptist Boys High School, Abeokuta	Ogun	1915
21. Barewa Training College, Zaria	Kaduna	1921
22. Methodist College (former Ibo Boys Institute, Uzuakoli	Abia	1923
23. Dennis Memorial Grammar School, Onitsha	Anambra	1925
24. St. Gregory's College, Lagos	Lagos	1928
25. Government College, Ibadan	Oyo	1929
26. Government College, Umuahia	Abia	1929
27. Aggrey Memorial College, Arochukwu	Abia	1931
28. Igbobi College, Yaba	Lagos	1932
29. Christ the King College, Onitsha	Anambra	1933
30. Christ's School, Ado Ekiti	Ekiti	1933
31. Holy Rosary College, Enugu	Enugu	1935
32. Government Secondary School, Owerri	Imo	1935
33. Edo College, Benin City	Edo	1937

Record shows that there were more secondary schools in Nigeria than in the other British colonies. By 1939, there were presumably over 40 secondary schools in Nigeria; established through the efforts of the Christian missionaries, colonial government, local communities and private individuals, yet there was limited access in the spread of secondary education because of the size and population of the country. Moreover, the secondary level of education was so scarce, competitive and selective that about 75 percent of students who completed their primary education were not admitted into those secondary schools. It was partly for this reason that thousands of children of secondary school age across Nigeria were leftout.

Notably, because of the comparatively high school fees, financially poor parents were both unable and reluctant to send their children to secondary schools. This state of affairs lingered for some decades with unfavourable implications. For instance, in 1941, many students withdrew from Edo College, established in 1937, owing to a hundred percent increase in school fees. This was a great impediment because it was the only secondary school in Benin City, Nigeria that made secondary education accessible to many Edo students. Nevertheless, a few students who could afford the fees, attended secondary education in Lagos and other parts of the country (Gabriel, 2015).

A Glance at the Education Ordinances

Later in 1882, the British colonial government promulgated an education ordinance aimed at gaining absolute control over the education sector in Nigeria, 10 years after their financial provisions (in 1872) to the Christian missionary societies in support of education. The ordinance covered all of the British West African territories: Lagos, Gold Coast (present Ghana), Sierra Leone and Gambia.

The focus of this ordinance was on the promotion, assistance and support of education in the Gold Coast colony. The Gold Coast colony comprised the present-day Ghana and the entire Lagos in the western part of Nigeria. Lagos and Gold Coast were jointly governed at that time. This ordinance was similarly extended to other African colonies, namely Gambia and Sierra Leone. It was chiefly intended to usher in the colonial administration's enterprising involvement in the education of the natives. Its intention was to prepare them for the new (meagre) roles they would play in the colonial administration. This ordinance initiated joint participation and collaboration in the Nigerian education system between the colonial government and the missionaries as well as private individuals and voluntary organisations.

Collaboration between the government and the missions started even prior to the enactment of the 1882 ordinance, the first of its kind that had great impact on the Gold Coast colony, to which Lagos belonged until 1886 when it was made a separate colony and protectorate. With this ordinance, a General Board of Education was established for the first time in the history of British colonialism in West Africa. This Board included the Governor himself, members of the executive council and not more than four nominated members (Aissat et al, 2012, p. 10).

The contents of the curriculum of the mission schools were reported as irrelevant and unrelated to the background, customs and values of the citizens. Likewise, the products of those schools were criticised as grossly inadequate, inept and unskilled as well as inefficient by the British Trading Companies that employed some of them. In keeping with European education culture, assessments, examinations, academic performance, examination results and rankings of students became the major emphasis of the colonial education system in Nigeria. These criteria constituted the yardsticks and benchmarks by which intelligence was assessed, certificates issued or earned, promotions made, and employment offered. Instructively, this European educational culture (portions of which are essentially good) has survived into the present-day Nigerian system of education. It offers both lasting advantages and major disadvantages as well as shortcomings.

Invariably, no provisions were made in the 1882 ordinance for the teaching of the vernacular. According to clause 10 section 5 of the ordinance, grant from the government would be paid for English language and not for the vernacular (Fajana, 1972). Because the curricular contents, methodology and the language of communication were unfamiliar to the Nigerian children, this Education Ordinance was destined to fail. This unsuccessful and disappointing development led to the provision of a new ordinance in 1887, which later proved effective. It was the first effort of the colonial government to administer education, especially in some of the cities in Lagos. The importation and employment of foreign teachers were largely encouraged, and financial support was given to missions, private individuals and voluntary agencies to establish more schools.

The 1887 Education Ordinance was issued after Lagos was separated from the Gold Coast colony in 1886. This ordinance, though primarily meant for the Lagos colony (covering Lagos Island, Badagry, Ebute-meta and Yaba), consequently affected Nigeria as well. Even though this new (1887) ordinance offered some amendments to the education system provided by the 1882 ordinance, it remained imperfect. Major amendments were further made in the roles that missionaries played in the leadership, organisation and management of non-governmental schools. The missionaries replaced the local school boards set up by the 1882 ordinance, though, the Board of Education still maintained and conducted the inspection of schools, including issuing certificates to teachers. Also, the Board recommended schools that needed financial assistance and grants from the government. Such recommendations had to be supported by relevant data (Aissat et al., p.12).

This new ordinance advocated schooling for all children irrespective of ethnicity, tribe, or religion. Financial aids and grants were offered based on the number of students in attendance, which needed to average 20 and the curriculum that was intended for each standard (Aissat et al., p.13). Grants and incentives were strategically offered to schools and individual students to encourage strong academic performance or withdrawn to discourage poor academic performance. Schools that offered optional subjects could receive grants. Grants were also given to the missions based on their various student populations and capacities. The new ordinance also encouraged industrial and vocational training in schools. The same was applied to practical and manual skills, such as handicrafts and household works.

The Impact of the Education Ordinances

The 1887 ordinance was more successful than the ordinance of 1882 because its prescriptions were practicable and pragmatic. In short, they were workable to the extent that the education system experienced much progress as well as improvement in its overall quality. New subjects were both encouraged and introduced into the basic curriculum. The benefits of this education ordinance, flexibility in inspections and examinations, accessibility and affordability, were then extended to most parts of the colony. This trend saw huge increases in the number of students that attended both primary and secondary government and assisted schools between 1888 and 1890. See the following table for illustrations:

Table 2

Students' Population (Primary, Secondary and Government Assisted Schools) by Gender from 1888 to 1890.

	1888		1889		1890	
Denominations	Male	Female	Male	Female	Male	Female
Catholic	150	57	303	71	297	59
German Mission	931	375	976	383	1,078	441
Government	626	160	638	177	512	153
Wesleyan	1,067	124	1,071	109	1,183	129
Total	2,774	716	2,988	740	3,070	782

Source: Aissat & Djafri, 201, p.14

Sulaiman (2012) suggests that the British colonial policies on education were formulated and implemented in Nigeria between 1882 and 1926 when it became apparent that the missionary education was not solving the education problems of the natives. It was within this long stretch of time that the 1887 ordinance was enacted. According to Sulaiman's observation, the colonial governments concentrated on governing the country and left the education sector in the hands of the missionaries until they determined that the education offered by the missionaries could not sufficiently serve the needs of the colonial masters and the newly evolving nations. The colonial government then had to intervene in the education of the colonies by enacting education laws and edicts to guide the educational practices of the existing schools and their proprietors, and these formed the foundation upon which the education systems of most African nations are built today (Sulaiman, 2012).

Even though schools were indiscriminately established because of the high value given to education, as a means of evangelisation, little or no attention was initially paid to science, engineering and technology by the missionaries, which in the later century prompted concerns about their willingness and readiness to prepare the citizens for eventual independence, freedom, liberty and autonomy. Arguably, one might strongly contend, sufficiently and justifiably so, that it was not the primary responsibility or part of the core objective of the early European missionaries to prepare Nigeria for independence but to initiate the citizens into the Christian faith with a type of primary level education needed at that time, given the existing status quo coupled with the challenges of differences in languages, dialects, customs, values and inherent complex cultures among peoples, tribes, colonies and protectorates. The same limitation applied to their guiding ethos and principles of evangelisation; strictly based on the separation of "religion and government", which underpinned both the missionary objectives and activities. The colonial government's primary responsibility was to provide civil and secular education to the citizens of Nigeria and to their other African colonies. Morally, they were entrusted with a civilising mission, while the missionaries were entrusted with an evangelising mission.

The level of education introduced by the missionaries would enable them to train new Christians who could in turn assist the missionaries in their work as catechists, lay readers and teachers (Onyebamiji & Omordu, 2011). Even though education was an instrument that could eventually lead to nationhood and self-reliance, it is still pertinent to note that the missionaries were primarily sent to Nigeria by various Christian denominations for evangelisation, not colonisation or to prepare Nigeria for independence as a country. Without discounting the idea that education was one of the most effective tools for both evangelisation and colonisation, people still needed to focus on the primary purpose of the Christian missionaries, which was to curb slave trade and convert pagans, heathens and, if possible, people in general to Christianity. Moreover, a clear majority of the Nigerian populace, before the advent of the missionaries and the British colonialists, were pagans and heathens, especially in the East, West and the South. Therefore, the focus of the missionaries' education was spiritual, biblical and theological rather than secular, which would have incorporated the sciences, engineering, technology, politics, law, architecture, medicine, humanities and liberal arts. Their aim was to train communicators, interpreters, church readers or lectors, pastors, biblical teachers and evangelists.

Apparently confusing the British colonialists' education system with that of the early Christian missionaries, Garba (2012) argues that the colonial brand of education was essentialist by orientation, aimed only at the spiritual purification of the learner and was irrelevant to the needs and interests of Nigerian learners and society.

Administrative Approach and Education

Nevertheless, it was the sole responsibility of the British colonial government to prepare the citizens for eventual independence, ideal nationhood and necessary self-reliance. Rather, it employed (or resorted to) the Indirect Rule System, which recognised only the existing traditional administrative structure to control the Lagos colony along with the southern and northern protectorates. These regions later became Nigeria, by amalgamation, in 1914. It was an administrative strategy that enlisted the help of traditional rulers as middle men between the colonial masters and the people. The Indirect Rule System's policy, which was introduced by the British colonial government in West Africa, impacted the whole of Nigeria. It was a policy that restricted the extension of both Christianity and Western education to the northern protectorate, which apparently explains the basis for the chasm in the level of educational development between the northern and southern parts of Nigeria today. The consequences of this initiative still have some enduring implications for Nigerian education policy planning, formulation and implementation.

Education Ordinance 1916.

Following the 1914 amalgamation of the northern and southern protectorates that formed Nigeria, the then Governor General, Lord Frederick Lugard, formulated the ideas that shaped a large part of the

1916 ordinance, which intended to standardise education across the whole country. The recognition that education was also related to good conduct and usefulness to both oneself and the society largely informed this ordinance, which tried to reorganise Nigeria's school and education system. According to Fabunmi (2005), the 1916 ordinance recommended that grant-in-aid be offered in the following percentages:

- Tone of the school, discipline, organisation and moral instruction —30%
- Adequacy and efficiency of the teaching staff—20%
- Periodical examination and general progress — 40%
- Buildings, equipment and sanitation —10%

This ordinance created an initiative for the government's financial participation in education and cooperation between the government and the missions.

To convince the northern Nigerian leaders that Western education would not affect their Islamic culture and tradition, Lugard met with them, representing the entire North, which had resisted the introduction of Western education as a cultural intrusion for quite a long time. His endeavour finally yielded a positive result. Garba (2012) reports that, prior to this successful exploit, Lugard established government schools for the sons of chiefs and mallams in 1904. He intended that these mallams be educated in English and that readings and writings of Hausa language be done in Roman characters without prejudice to Islam (p. 56).

Garba (2012) contends that, with the advent of Christian missionaries and subsequent colonisation of Nigeria by the British colonial masters, essentialism was imposed on the Nigerian education system, with education viewed as a central body of the essential knowledge that must be transmitted to all who came to school. In this type of education, the Nigerian teacher was expected to be strict, disciplined and well-behaved to the extent that he would be considered a model for emulation. Additionally, the student was expected to learn what the teacher taught him by memorisation and reproduction of the same on the examination day (Garba, 2012, p.53).

The form of education and education policies adopted by the colonial administrators was ultimately considered incompatible with the existing traditions and aspirations of the citizenry. It also contradicted the true philosophical principle of essentialism, which holds the view that children ought to be educated, using ideas and methodology considered crucial to the prevalent culture. The colonial ruling system and the political climate were oligarchic and moderately despotic, with the practice of true democracy relatively non-existent. It is noteworthy, therefore, that while the positive effects from the British colonialists' education system were greatly appreciated by the citizens, some of them conflicted with the local cultures. Even though the impacts of colonialism and the European colonialists' essentialist (but non-progressive) education system still linger, well-educated and right-thinking Nigerians have variously indicated that it was high time we moved on. It is reasonable to hold that the education system, which the colonial masters introduced in Nigeria was not essentially or necessarily ill-willed. However, some critics would prefer to fully uphold the negative impacts of colonialism even in the 21st century.

According to Garba (2012), the Europeans' aim at introducing Western education in Nigeria was to make the ordinary individual useful in his environment and to ensure that exceptional individuals would use their abilities for the advancement of the community, not to its detriment or to the subversion of any constituted authority. Some of the aspects of their education system conflicted with Nigeria's indigenous values (and natural human eagerness plus tendencies towards unhindered progress). As circumstances would have it, the progressive trajectory — dimension and direction — of the purpose of education in Nigeria later changed towards forming and moulding individuals who would contribute greatly to the development of the nation in anticipation of the sovereignty and self- governance that materialised in 1960.

Chapter Two
The Current Education System

Before and during the early years after independence, the Nigerian education system was judged to be parochial, archaic, sluggish, unprogressive and irresponsive to the needs of the citizenry, inadequate, elitist, unsatisfactory; inconsistent with the goals, objectives and aspirations of the nation (Nduka, 1964; Fafunwa & Aisiku, 1982; Obayan, 1982).

Given this existing status quo in the Nigerian education system's development, efforts were made and intensified by the then federal government to adopt a system of education that would be considered best suited for the entire nation's development. Consequently, it spelt out the core philosophy and objectives of education as contained in its revised national education policy implementation's official document: "Education goals in terms of its relevance to the need of the individual and the kind of society desired in relation to the environment and realities of the modern world and rapid social changes should be clearly set out"(National Policy on Education, 1981, p.5).

Suffice it to reiterate that the education system in Nigeria is managed, controlled and funded at the federal, state and local government levels. Public and private institutions are the providers of education in Nigeria, with the Federal Ministry of Education playing a major role of regulating the education sector, policy development and the maintenance of quality control.

Pre-independence Nigeria witnessed series of educational reforms, some of which were rolled out as ordinances. As at 1954, the education system in Nigeria, with reference to levels, was 8-6-2-3; that is, 8 years of primary school, 6 years of secondary school, 2 years of higher school certificate and 3 years of university education. From 1954 onwards, the education system was changed to 6-5-2-3. This new system reduced 8 years of primary education to 6 years and 6 years of secondary education to 5. Two years of higher school certificate education remained constant, as did 3 years of university education. This change in policy was a patriotic attempt to reform the education system for the common good of Nigerians. It was a reform by the colonial administration that was apparently precipitated by anticipated demonstrations for independence and self-governance by the citizenry.

Invariably, there was a great boost in hope and optimism that the post-independence Nigerian climate would engender tremendous and favourable reforms in the country's education sector. Nigerians were indeed hungry for genuine development and progress. In 1969, participants at the National Curriculum Conference in Lagos, having criticised the colonial education system as both devoid of relevance and vitality, advocated change in the nation's education. This recommendation was made with the expectation that the cherished privilege of independence would empower the country towards the path of vocational, scientific, technical and technological advancement. It was in this 1969 National Curriculum Conference, considered a major landmark, that the first idea of changing the system from 6-5-2-3 to 6-3-3-4 was raised. It existed only as a proposal at this point, seriously under consideration and would be the first major reform in Nigeria's post-independence education system, if implemented. This innovative idea was aimed at fostering national unity, raising the quality of education, injecting pragmatism and functionality into the nation's school system and producing graduates who would be able to make use of their hands, heads and hearts (Omolewa, 1986; Babafemi, 2003). This 6-3-3-4 national proposal on education policy was reportedly explained in 1980 during a seminar in Bagawda, Kano. The explanation went as follows:

> The new senior secondary school proposed in the Federal Republic of Nigeria national policy on education is an innovation, indeed a transformation of the present system which is a five-year course followed by a 2-year higher school certificate course, neither of which is employment oriented. Both aspects appear to prepare students for the higher institutions in several disciplines providing university graduates with no supporting intermediate personnel, therefore limiting their productivity. Further, the range of discipline the student could pursue in the university is equally restricted and particularly deficient in mathematical, scientific, technological and agricultural disciplines. To redress the situation both at the higher institutions and the secondary school, the 3-3 structure has been proposed to channel junior secondary school pupils into the senior secondary school as well as into teacher-training and craft (Adamu, 1994).

For various logistical reasons, the 6-3-3-4 education levels proposal was not immediately implemented and did not start in 1982, at least when the first beneficiaries of the ambitious 6-year Universal Primary Education (UPE) programme, reintroduced in 1976, would have completed their primary school levels of education. Nevertheless, by 1985, Anambra and Kano states had started applying the new system. According to Adamu (1994), the *New Nigerian* of March 12, 1985 reported that "almost all the other states have either delayed their own implementation of the policy or made some changes in format as a result of shortage of funds, teaching staff, workshops and the needed equipment". The full implementation of this education system's reform appeared to have been somewhat chaotic and non- uniform. Notably, prior to 1985, the structure of the Nigerian formal education system levels was still basically 6-5-2-3: 6 years of primary school, 5 to 7 years of post-primary school (comprising a 5-year secondary school education and a 2-year teacher training college education) and 4 to 6 years of tertiary education in colleges of education, polytechnics, colleges of technology, or and universities. Primary education in Nigeria typically begins at the age of 6.

Even though the idea of the 6-3-3-4 education system in Nigeria is traceable to the 1969 National Curriculum Conference and the International Literacy Day, this bold step taken by the Federal Government certainly expedited the implementation of this policy initiative beginning in 1985. It was also popularly orchestrated and finally consolidated, nationwide in 1989 by the Hon. Minister of Education, Professor Babs Fafunwa, who apparently had pioneered its initial proposal two decades earlier in 1969. This newly approved Nigerian system of education is widely believed to have a structurally striking resemblance to the United States' system, which Japan adopted in 1945 with great success. The 6-3-3-4 system of education was considered a laudable programme capable of ushering in a positive educational revolution and a bright future regarding Nigeria's technological development. It was a system generally intended to give citizens the chance to submit their own quota of usefulness to the nation's development according to individual abilities and worth. Instead, the system was interpreted differently, muddled up and left suffering from poor and shoddy implementation without achieving the intended result (Babafemi, 2003; Gusau, 2008).

In 1999, following the election of President Olusegun Obasanjo, the UBE programme was conceived, eventually signed into law in 2004. It was also designed and enacted in a bid to achieve the Education for All (EFA) goals. This educational reform's scheme was aimed at eradicating illiteracy by the year 2010 as well as increasing the adult literacy rate from 57% to 70% by 2030. Thus, the existing education system with four levels (6-3-3-4) was restructured into the three major levels (9-3-4) of Universal Basic Education (Amaghionyeodiwe, & Osinubi, 2006; Federal Republic of Nigeria, 2000). According to the Centre for Public Impact, as at 2015, Nigeria ranked 103 out of 118 nations in UNESCO's Education for All (EFA) Development Index. This ranking takes universal basic education, adult literacy, quality of education and gender parity into account.

The basic levels of primary school and junior secondary school are now composed of 9 years. Post-basic or the senior secondary school level has 3 years and the tertiary level of education comprises 4 to 6 years, depending on the programme of study. Today, basic education includes 6 years of primary school and 3 years of junior secondary school (JSS). The first and unbroken 9 years of UBE is (said to be) mandatory, free and the right of every child in Nigeria (Gusau, 2008).

According to Sule and Bawa (2012), in the 21st century, the goals of education include improving the future workforce, developing individuals' cognitive skills, removing barriers to participation and raising awareness about social responsibility. This is what the 9-3-4 school curriculum intends to achieve by implementing sound and effective education. These changes in the Nigerian curriculum are also intended to be more effectively aligned with policy goals.

Educational Reforms

According to Onuigbo (2009), educational reform is a lengthy process that always begins with identifying, studying and analysing problems, then evaluating and possibly terminating the programmes. Also, it involves the development of alternative policies, experimentation, implementation, reviews and reports. Imoke (2011) observes that educational reforms are representatives of conscious advancement of policy plans that have the potential of bringing an important transformation to the sector. In sum, the basic idea (and common intent) of policy reforms is to make it more responsive to the needs, longings and expectations of the people in a given society.

Various educational reforms, introduced by the Nigerian Federal Ministry of Education since independence, were designed and intended to reform and improve the nation's education system to meet the needs of the citizenry. Maximum efforts appear to have been put in so far, but they seem to have yielded minimum results with individual and national development. In sum, those reforms were aimed at promoting the common good as well as addressing some deficiencies and limitations of the citizens, such as illiteracy, poverty, unemployment and insecurity, among others. The success or failure of a nation's education system will be determined by how effective and efficient it has proven itself in either addressing those problems or alleviating those needs.

The Education System's Structure

Even though the problems of Nigeria's education system do not necessarily lie in its structure or configuration, one can still investigate these for possible shortcomings. Policymakers tend to prioritise international policies and requirements for eradicating illiteracy when structuring and operating the nation's education system. However, there are potentially relevant questions to ask before building any education structure for any nation. First, is the nation looking for a system and structure that will improve or diminish it? Second, how will the structure and configuration of a nation's education system help in solving existing societal problems: social, cultural, political and economic? Third, how was the nation faring before the introduction and implementation of the new system? Fourth, what is the country's population (not just the population of the illiterate)?

Regarding the Nigerian context, what was the situation of things in Nigeria when we were running the 6-5-2-3 system (introduced in 1954) compared to the situation today? Is it likely that the colonialists suspected and probably became persuaded that they would leave the nation and, therefore, implemented a poor education system? This author believes that to be logically unlikely. This point will be explored later. What, then, was the quality of education and how useful were the products of that system in comparison with the products of today's Nigerian education system, notwithstanding the invention of the internet and computer technology? Based on standards, is a first degree in today's Nigerian university not equivalent to a secondary school certificate in the 1980s? If the answer is yes, then modelling the nation's education structure after the colonialists' might be the best and strongest way to reform its education system, but with its roots planted in the common and positive aspects of its culture and tradition. Comparatively, one might suspect that the current system looks essentially laden with a few but obviously strong shortcomings. Those shortcomings are explored in the following section.

Duration of Basic Education

Before (or while) reformulating the section of the education policy that gave us the 9-3-4 tiers of education, Nigeria's education policymakers might have been influenced by some international requirements aimed at eradicating illiteracy. Nevertheless, it is difficult to tell if they considered the people's culture, psychology, social values and traditions in the process of this reform. A case in point: Except for the 3 years of senior secondary and 4 years of post-secondary, one might easily consider nine years of basic education to be unnecessarily long. Not only is it unusually long, it is also made mandatory, thereby making it more onerous. In response to opposing views, pundits have severally defended the 9-3-4 system as an improvement upon the 6-3-3-4 system. Some others argue that it is simply a better face of the (6-3)-3-4 system, produced by adding 6 to 3 to make it a basic 9-year education system. However, the arrangements seem to be two different schemes with different curricula, as the "necessary" gap between the primary and secondary levels has been eliminated. Could any policy that considers Common Entrance Examinations obsolete, for instance, be responsible for closing this "much-needed" gap? Does it justify eliminating a desirable break that followed what was previously the country's distinctively primary (or basic) education system? Does it not look or sound like a misplacement of priority?

The rationale associated with policy reforms that gave us the 9-3-4 school system may not be able to fully convince or change the mindset of the people in that regard whether culturally or psychologically. Nigerians should not forget that it was the demonstrations for independence and by implication a better system of education that eventually brought about the change from 8-6-2-3 configuration (that is, 8 years of primary school, 6 years of secondary school, 2 years of higher school certificate and 3 years of university education system) to a 6-5-2-3 structure in 1954. This change was apparently the best policy reform that the colonial master could give us. One would be curious to know what the population of Nigeria was at that point. Of course, the population was much smaller than the number the country has today.

Common reasoning contends that the 6-5-2-3 education structure, which the colonialists gave us following protests for independence must have been a type whose impact would end up convincing the citizens that they really intended to help Nigeria. Perhaps, they were aiming to relax agitations from the citizens, thereby enabling them to stay longer or remain permanently in the country. It seemed that the British did not want to vacate Nigeria, especially when they discovered the level of both natural and human resources in the country and the potentially huge amount of financial gains accruable to them after the amalgamation in 1914. At the very least, the citizens' clamour for independence brought the British colonial government and

Nigerian political leaders together between 1951 and 1954 into meetings and deliberations to give Nigeria a draft of a new Federal Constitution in 1954 (Dike, 1980). As at 1954, when the British government was still in control, the then current education system emphasised decentralisation, a policy that remained in force until independence in 1960. I would like to speculate that, perhaps because of pressures from both within and outside of Nigeria, the colonialists finally decided to do what was right for us. It is unlikely that the previous 8-6-2-3 education structure, which could keep learners in the basic or primary schooling level "forever", was a better option. Anyone can compare the two structures to see the strength of this reasoning considering the citizens' psycho-socio-cultural values and needs.

Would the British colonialists (or imperialists) have given us the "best" education system if they were certain that they would never leave? One could consider the first structure (8-6-2-3) as seemingly opportunistic and imperialistic while the second structure (6-5-2-3) could be viewed as circumstantial and placating. This seemed so because the British must have been situationally compelled, both internally and externally, to do what was right for Nigeria before their exit. But why would Nigeria resort to a system that either mimics or looks like the first education system, even with its almost unbridled growth in human population? Compare the difference in population between 1954 and 2017. Without disapproving or undervaluing the 9-3-4 system outright, I would advocate either a reversion to the 1954-1985 system, which I consider better, or simply the maintenance and sustenance of the 6-3-3-4 system, which was fully adopted by all the states in Nigeria by 1989.

Psycho-Cultural Factors

Being mostly non-individualistic and communalistic by culture as well as naturally affable, Africans, although in many ways like the Europeans, Asians, Middle Easterners and others, have distinct psycho-cultural factors that need to be considered significant. For instance, most Africans are culturally open, competitive, dynamic and gregarious (Makhubele, 2008). Like every other group, they may not like staying in one place for a very long time, especially when confined, limited, or restricted. Similarly, duration may be very important to them in their commitments and engagements. It is still a critical part of their progressive cultural mentality, which perhaps they share (in common) with Europeans, Asians and some Middle Easterners. Moreover, anything, place, or situation that isolates, lasts "too long" or "too late" may not resonate so well with African persons, especially when separated from their families, friends, peers, colleagues, or contemporaries. This is also applicable to other people, especially those whose cultures are either collectivistic or communalistic. Therefore, "adult education", although tolerable and useful, may not be quite convenient or suitable for a typical African person. The same applies to staying too long in school or in the classroom.

Persistent Challenges

Given the above psycho-cultural factors in the African mind-sets and values, how would one convince or persuade illiterates and dropouts in Nigeria that education is good for them with the 9-year mandatory basic education? Upon first sight, this is a complex challenge. While the world is advancing, who would imagine himself or a family member remaining in a segment of an education system for 9 years? With strikes and industrial actions complicating issues in the country, moreover, a 4-year duration at a Nigerian university could stretch over a period of 7 years. Imagine if this situation were applied to the 9-year basic education system. If the normal age to complete secondary school is 16, then it would be 19 with the new system (9-3-4), an age when some students are doing their bachelor's degree programs or even, in some exceptional cases, master's degrees in Europe and the United States. With the current 50% illiteracy level in Nigeria, the implementation of this new system and its greater demands might even push the percentage higher. In the United Kingdom, undergraduate degrees are completed in 3 years, excluding law, medicine and other major science programmes.

Does the number of years in the 9-year basic education structure improve classroom academics or learning? Not necessarily. For instance, if a school did not have an English or mathematics teacher in a primary 3 classroom, a situation that might last into primary 6 when the structure was 6-3-3-4, how was it guaranteed that the situation would change (that is, the employment of needed teachers) with the 9-3-4 system? Are there no institutions in Nigeria today that are administered even under the type of academic situation being discussed here? This is a question, which suggests that it is not necessarily by changing the structure that an education system is made more efficient or functional but by doing what is imperative: implementing and enforcing workable policies to improve schools and students' academic performance. But does there exist any correlation between change in the structure of education and the employment, or the availability or the efficiency of teachers in schools? How does one account for high school graduates who cannot speak or write correct sentences in English or even solve simple arithmetic problems?

Indeed, there are also other persistent needs and problems that indicate that Nigeria is still far from having a perfect education system. These problems and challenges could be summarily broken down into:

1). Illiteracy

2). Poverty and Unemployment

3). Moral Decadence

4). Industrial Actions and Strikes; and

5). Gender Inequality.

Illiteracy

No doubt, the cost of illiteracy with its consequences in any nation is far more than the cost of encouraging and introducing literacy, which comes in the form of knowledge and formal education. Also, an educated workforce is a vital component of a dynamic economy. As a crisis, illiteracy is likely to give rise to poverty and unemployment and has a measurably negative impact on a nation's Gross Domestic Product (GDP). Hence, illiteracy is considered adversarial to human development both at the individual and societal levels.

It must be admitted that, despite various actions taken by the Nigerian government, non-governmental organizations (NGOs), educators, schools and stakeholders to address existing illiteracy coupled with some remarkable improvements in the nation's education system, illiteracy has continued to remain a problem with some alarming statistics. In 2010, a National Literacy Survey conducted by the National Bureau of Statistics reported that the adult literacy rate in Nigeria stood at 56.9% with huge variations between states (with Lagos at 92.0% and Borno at only 14.5%), regions (urban 74.6% vs. rural 48.7%) and sex (male 65.1% and female 48.6%). Moreover, statistics from the Federal Ministry of Education indicate that only 500,000 of the 40 million adult illiterates are enrolled in adult learning classes. There are 3.5 million nomadic school-aged children, with only 450,000 of them accessing any form of schooling (United Nations Educational Scientific Cultural Organisation, 2012). These statistics came at a time when the world's illiteracy level was approximately 20%, making that of Nigeria comparably troubling. In the same vein, the Country Comparison Index of Literacy Level by country in 2012 testified to the worrisome literacy situation in the country, showing that Nigeria ranked 161 out of 184 countries with a 66% literacy rate. This implies that, as at 2012, Nigeria belonged to the mainstream of the world's most illiterate countries.

During the 2013 International Literacy Day, the then Minister of State for Education, Chief Nyesom Wike, disclosed that 35 million adult Nigerians aged 15 and above were illiterate, compared to 25 million in 1997. In the flag-off of the 2014 International Literacy Day, as a former Minister in the Education Ministry, Wike further reported that the number of illiterate adults in the country was estimated at 60 million (Ogunbiyi, 2015). If these statistics are correct, then the number of illiterates that the nation accumulated between 2013 and 2014 alone bears an eloquent testimony to the failure of Nigeria's education policies and programmes.

According to a UNESCO survey, 65 million of Nigerians were illiterate in 2015, while 59.6% (35 million) of adult Nigerians (age 15 and above) were literate, indicating an increase from 56.9% in 2010.

Recently, the estimated number and percentage of Nigerian children reported to be not registered in school remain embarrassing. Given the current situation, one can comfortably affirm that the goal of meeting the national projection of reducing illiteracy by 50% by 2015 was neither attained, nor will the Millennium Development Goals (MDG's) be attained anytime soon if the current unfavourable trend of illiteracy in the country is not urgently checked.

Poverty and Unemployment

Poverty and unemployment have been identified as among the challenges and crises that have not been addressed by the current education system. They are practical problems that constantly clamour for redress. It is a bit embarrassing that after 59 years of Nigerian independence, the discovery of vast oil riches and decades of eclectic educational reforms, the basic standard of living in the country has not improved. In other words, a large population of Nigerians still live in abject penury.

As at January 2012, the National Bureau of Statistics (NBS) reported that about 112.5 million, which represented 69% (of the relative poverty measure) of Nigerians lived below poverty baseline. Alternatively, according to NBS, 112.47 million Nigerians out of the estimated total population of 163 million lived below poverty level in 2010. This is represented in the Nigeria Poverty Profile table, in summary. See the next page:

Table 3

Relative Poverty Headcount from 1980 to 2010

Year	Poverty Incidence (%)	Estimated Population (Million)	Population in Poverty (Million)
1980	27.2	65	17.1
1985	46.3	75	34.7
1992	42.7	91.5	39.2
1996	65.6	102.3	67.1
2004	54.4	126.3	68.7
2010	69.0	163	112.47

Source: National Bureau of Statistics, 2010

It is paradoxical that the preceding poverty profile and report emerged when the Central Bank of Nigeria (CBN) revealed in its Annual Report that growth in the country's economy remained relatively strong in 2011, with the real Gross Domestic Product (GDP) growth rate recording a marginal growth of 7.4%. This was lower than its growth by 8% in 2010. Nevertheless, it was higher than the annual average of 7% growth over the period of 2007 to 2011 (Central Bank of Nigeria, 2011, p.142).

These poverty-related figures, as deplorable as they appear, do not reveal the profoundly negative implications and impacts of human poverty across the entire nation. Poverty restricts access to basic education, which results in illiteracy and can pave the way for potential involvement in societal crimes and criminality. It also inhibits its victims from gaining access to quality healthcare in Nigeria. A huge number of the citizenry are susceptible to preventable cases of hunger and mental and physical illnesses. They are also, sometimes, subjects of human rights abuses, social exclusions, alienations and homelessness.

In 2016, a United Nations (UN) report on Nigeria's Common Country Analysis (CCA), partly described Nigeria as follows:

> Nigeria, with a population of over 175 million, is the most populous nation in Africa and the seventh most populous in the world. Its population will be approximately 200 million by 2019 and over 400 million by 2050, becoming one of the top five populous countries in the world…. Nigeria is one of the poorest and most unequal countries in the world, with over 80 million or 64% of its population living below poverty line. The situation has not changed over the decades but is increasing. Poverty and hunger have remained high in rural areas, remote communities and among female-headed households and these cut across the six geo-political zones, with prevalence ranging from approximately 46.9% in the South West to 74.3% in North West and North East…Youth unemployment which is 42% in 2016 is very high, creating poverty, helplessness, despair and easy target for crime and terrorism. Over 10 million children of school age are out of schools with no knowledge and skills (Opejobi, 2016).

A similar report from the United Nations Human Development (UNDP, 2016) ranked Nigeria as 152nd out of 193 countries in the latest Human Development Index (HDI), followed closely by Cameroon as number 153 and Zimbabwe in the 154th position. The same report places Nigeria's neighbouring and sister country, Ghana, at 139 — far above Nigeria. Nevertheless, it reveals some positive elements of

Nigeria, at least for recording a 13.1% increase in human development in the 10 years between 2005 and 2015. This type of report is largely determined by the number of people with access to education and other basic amenities. HDI is a composite statistics of life expectancy, expected years of schooling and per capita income indicators that are used to rank countries into four tiers of human development. Human development, in this context, is undertaken by expanding levels of freedom to enable all human beings to pursue choices they find valuable.

According to the World Bank's 2017 Atlas of Sustainable Development Goals, 35 million more Nigerians were living in extreme poverty in 2013 than in 1990. Extreme poverty means living on less than $1.90 (then approx. ₦300) a day. The World Bank Atlas tracks the positive changes and progress made by various countries to meet the 17 development goals set out by the United Nations Organisation (UNO). The areas of progress include reduction of poverty, economic inequality and illiteracy rates and an increase in the use of clean energy. This data reveals that, among the 10 countries measured; Bangladesh, Brazil, China, Ethiopia, India, Indonesia, Mexico, Pakistan and Russia, Nigeria recorded an increase in the population of citizens living in extreme poverty between 1990 and 2013. See table on the next page:

Table 4

Citizens Living in Extreme Poverty in 1990 vs. 2013

People living in the extreme poverty (less than $1.90 per day)		
Country	**1990**	**2013**
China	756 million	25 million
India	338 million	218 million
Indonesia	104 million	25 million
Pakistan	62 million	12 million
Nigeria	51 million	86 million
Bangladesh	45 million	18 million
Brazil	31 million	10 million
Ethiopia	29 million	20 million
Mexico	9 million	4 million
Russia	3 million	0.04 million

Source: World Bank, 2017

According to this data, the number of Nigerians living in extreme poverty rose from 51 million in 1990 to 86 million in 2013, implying that the nation added 35 million people to its poverty population. Extended data from the World Bank Atlas show that this population was 51 million in 1990, 71 million in 1996, 87 million in 2002, 83 million in 2008 and 86 million in 2013. While the nation's population surge (from 96 to 174 million people between 1990 and 2013) can be somewhat linked to these increasing numbers, it is unlikely that it also explains the persistence (and even near-consistency) in the country's reported poverty level. All other participants, the most highly populated nations of the world, also experienced and recorded population increases over the same period, with some of them dwarfing Nigeria both in population increase and in their already existing populations.

The preceding data show that poverty population in the country diminished from 87 to 83 million between 2002 and 2008, indicating a reduction by 4 million within 6 years. This begs several questions. What transpired within that period that made this huge positive difference? Who were responsible for making this significant difference? How were they able to accomplish such a difficult feat? Should Nigeria not enlist their expertise and consultations in the future life of the nation? If, for instance, what they did impacted only a few sections of the nation more than others, why would the government not replicate and extend the same strategy to the remaining parts of the country?

The latest report from the United Nations' 2018 Atlas of Sustainable Development Goal presents Nigeria as having overtaken India, a country seven times larger in population, with the largest extreme poverty inhabitants numbering 86.9 million. This huge and rising population represents approximately 50% of Nigeria's estimated 180 million, making the nation the current poverty capital of the world (Kazeem, 2018). See table on the next page:

Table 5

The World's 2018 Extreme Poverty Statistics

People living in the extreme poverty (less than $1.90 per day)	
Country	2018
Nigeria	86.9 million
India	71.5 million
Dem. Republic of Congo	60.9 million
Ethiopia	23.9 million
Tanzania	19.9 million
Mozambique	17.8 million
Bangladesh	17.0 million
Kenya	14.7 million
Indonesia	14.2 million
Uganda	14.2 million

Data Source: Quartz Africa, 2018

Because of the problems of poverty and unemployment, some Nigerians, especially young ones, seem to have ditched morality and decent human values in a bid to break those presumed jinxes (poverty and unemployment). Some have decided to indulge in fraudulent activities and crimes, deceit, cheating, corruption, embezzlement, systematic stealing, cultism, gang affiliations, prostitution, thuggery, robbery, kidnappings, cybercrimes and other lucrative but nefarious acts. Nigeria's unemployment challenge, moreover, has not shown any sign of slowing down, as demand for employment keeps outstripping supply. The majority of those most affected are those within the age range of 15–25 years, with 21 as the age median.

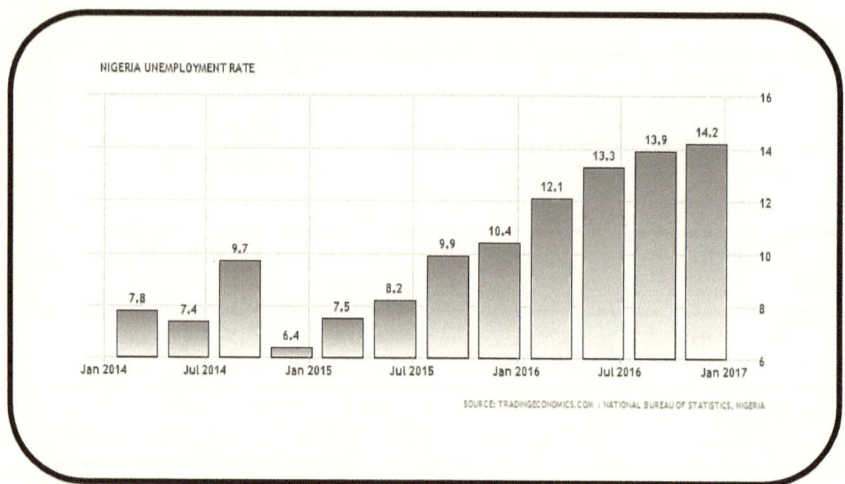

Figure 2. Nigeria's unemployment rates in statistics from 2014 to 2017

In the mid-2014, during the World Environment Day programme, the CBN, through its Special Assistant on Sustainable Banking, Dr Aisha Mahmood, declared that unemployment has remained a serious challenge to the Nigerian economy. While delivering a paper on the Nigerian Sustainable Banking Principle, she said:

> In Nigeria, there is the issue of youth and employment. Seventy percent of the 80 million youths in Nigeria are either unemployed or underemployed. We are all witnesses to what

happened recently during the immigration recruitment exercise and this is simply because 80% of Nigerian youth are unemployed. (Mahmood, 2014)

The crisis of poverty and unemployment in Nigeria today cannot be overemphasised. Recent data published by the National Bureau of Statistics (NBS) places unemployment rate in Nigeria at 14.2% in the last quarter of 2016, up from 13.9% in the preceding quarter. That was the ninth consecutive quarter that the nation's unemployment rate had increased (National Bureau of Statistics, 2017).

Moral Decadence

There is no gainsaying the level of moral decadence in Nigeria, despite the primary designation of the nation's education programme to promote morality. This is cause for great concern. Disrespect for elders by the youth, for instance, seems to be rampant across states and the same applies to isolated involvements in sociopathic and antisocial behaviours detrimental to the progress of a civilised society. Nigerians are supposed to share discipline and moral values that cut across religions, traditions and cultures in common. This apparently rapid spread of immorality has been attributed to young people's tendency to consider their indigenous culture outdated and their traditions obsolete. Therefore, they queue up to embrace Westernisation in its totality, abandoning the nation's indigenous cultures and traditions and thereby losing their identity (Abba, 2015).

Many families, parents, guardians and teachers in Nigeria seem to have abandoned their traditional roles and responsibilities of teaching children and promoting positive religious, moral and societal values. According to Abba (2015), children need training and orientation in values, such as compassion, respect, tolerance and understanding. Naturally, education begins at home. These are the values that should be taught primarily at home and reiterated in both primary and secondary schools. Without good family upbringing, students can be corrupted by peers who have little or no home training of their own, so re-emphasising common ethics in schools is crucial. In this instance, the families, parents, guardians and teachers should not take the entire blame for this problem, since it has become systemic, based on unmoderated and unregulated contemporary social values.

Moreover, even though Nigeria's education system is sympathetic to moral and societal values, it has not yet fashioned a holistic approach to battling poverty, which leads to illiteracy and potentially to a certain lack of ethics on its own.

Industrial Actions and Strikes

Nigeria has a long history of industrial actions by the Academic Staff Union of Universities (ASUU) in its endless contractual disagreements with the federal government. Sometimes, days, weeks and even months of their memorials or anniversaries are either celebrated or simply commemorated by their advocates, especially whenever similar strikes commence or are carried out. Indeed, strikes and industrial actions by ASUU and other entities, such as the Nigerian Labour Congress (NLC), the Nigerian Union of Teachers (NUT), the Nigerian Medical Association (NMA), the Non- Academic Staff Union of Universities (NASU), the Academic Staff Union of Polytechnics (ASUP), the National Association of Medical Doctors

(NARD) and the Trade Union Congress (TUC) have become almost an important part of Nigerian customs. They have gained much notoriety to have been branded by some as the "Nigeria's Yearly Festivals" (NYFs).

Admittedly, industrial actions and protests, in non-violent forms, might constitute necessary means and useful toolkits by which significant negotiations can be initiated and agreements reached. Nonetheless, when they become incessant, any nation's general economy can be heavily and negatively impacted. Arguably, any frequent industrial actions, protests and strikes that involve schools or tertiary institutions are signs and symptoms of a dysfunctional, deficient and inefficient education system. For decades now, the Nigerian education sector and system have been badly impacted by frequent industrial actions and strikes. These developments with their attendant stress, inconveniences, disruptions, distortions and drawbacks in the nation's educational industry have increasingly gained recognition in the same sector.

Tertiary institutions in Nigeria — colleges of education, polytechnics and universities — have variously embarked on strikes. According to Adavbiele (2015), the first notable strike in Nigeria was held in 1945; and ever since, different groups and unions have been embarking on strikes and industrial actions across the sectors of the economy. Citing Olakunle (2011), Adavbiele notes that evidence points towards the fact that, among all sectors, the education sector has received the greatest hit (Adavbiele, 2015, p. 134). The experiences of many students in the universities and tertiary institutions have been prolonged unnecessarily because of these types of protests. Between August and November 2000, the universities were on strike. The same situation occurred between March and September 2001 and December 2002 to around June 2003. The Academic Staff Union of Universities (ASUU) and the Academic Staff Union of Polytechnics (ASUP) embarked on strikes in 2013, while the Colleges of Education Academic Staff Union (COEASU) engaged in the same strike actions in 2014. In 2016 alone, both academic and non-academic staff of the University of Ibadan and Obafemi Awolowo University, Ile Ife, were reported as having embarked on strikes. Another tertiary institution, Ladoke Akintola University of Technology, known for its history of industrial actions, had its staff embark on a protracted strike that lasted from June 2016 into 2017.

Industrial actions and strikes have huge implications for Nigeria's educational institutions and for the country. Institutions' academic programmes are distorted during strikes because of abrupt cessations of teaching and learning. Students are left with half-baked literacy and mediocre academic statuses. Expectedly, there are also resultant delays in both students' admissions into and graduations from the NCEs, ONDs, HNDs, bachelor's, master's and doctoral degree programmes.

Further development, research, regular institutional education process and the use of acquired scientific, vocational, technical and technological knowledge and skills are disrupted, altered, or simply stunted. Prolonged strikes could dampen the morale and resourcefulness of the academic and vocational staff as well as the students of the affected institutions. Instead of using those timeframes for volunteering, offering community services, committing to group inventions, or any organised security advocacy and surrogacy, especially during the most prolonged periods of strike actions, some students (and even some lecturers) get involved in various forms of social crime and criminality that include corruption, sexual harassment, robbery and, in recent times, kidnapping for ransom. This is where moral decadence and its offshoots show up. People should be mindful of the dictum: Idleness is the devil's workshop. This type of chaotic and disorderly situation compromises the future of the nation's educational, social, political and economic integrity.

Despite the negative effects of strikes, various groups and unions have continued to embark on pickets, protests and industrial actions across the country. Often, many students, teachers and staff are involved in these actions, which could have resulted from some major administrative or policy issues, such as the violation of agreements and provisions, non-payment of salaries, inadequate or deplorable infrastructure, protests for salary increases and allowances or protracted lack of institutional support, underfunding, or some other forms of apparently unfair conditions and treatments.

Frequent striking actions have disrupted the implementation of essential education policies and programmes as well as diminished the quality of education in various schools and tertiary institutions in the country. How would one rather work to end the causes of strikes and give Nigerians quality education programmes instead?

Gender Inequality

As at September 1, 2018, the population of Nigeria was estimated to be 198,100,000 people. Out of this vast population, women constituted about 98,000,000, that is, about 49.5%. Nonetheless, in Nigeria's overall human and economic development, vast gender inequalities exist in educational opportunities and in the distribution of education across different groups. In major instances, this problem can be traced back to the African cultural values and traditions that emphasise women's connection to the home and domestic responsibilities. These traditions have influenced and limited women's choices of occupation, education, vocational trainings and areas of developmental interest in Nigeria for centuries. In consequence and for centuries, women's roles, abilities, skills and competencies have been historically regarded as stereotypically gender-based and restricted. These cultural constraints, social pressures and environmental factors create feelings of inferiority in many Nigerian women (Oniye, 2010).

Modifications in the National Policy of Education over primary education in 1998 laid much emphasis on the significance of "education for all citizens". For a more impactful change to take place, women need to be more systemically and strategically encouraged to develop interest in all academic programmes and disciplines, not only in art but also in science and technology. The same applies to administration.

According to Johnson and Markham (2004), education and gender inequality in Nigeria have focused on a variety of physical, social and cognitive contexts. Over the years, authorities have changed their theoretical platforms. This change has resulted in continuous discrimination against women and widened socio-economic inequalities in the country with disastrous effects. It has not only fuelled national and social problems, but it has also retarded development and political empowerment. In short, gender inequality has set in motion educational disparity and low employment among women and has limited their potential for sustainable economic development.

Notably, some progress in enrolment has been made over the decades on this challenge. But the nation still needs to do more to increase women's visibility and make sure that their impact is felt in society at large. According to the Federal Ministry of Education (2000), in the 35 years from 1960 to 1995, Nigeria recorded a sizeable improvement in women's involvement in the field of education, especially at the primary school level. This data indicates that the total number of females who enrolled in primary schools in Nigeria in 1960 was 1,083,147, while 7,134,682 enrolled in 1995. The total number of male registrations in 1960 by contrast was 1,829,471, while a total of 8,729,421 enrolled in 1995. Also, the same source provides data showing some improvements in their enrolments in the secondary school level of education in Nigeria from 1990 to 1995, all in comparison to the enrolment of men. This data indicates that the total number of female students that enrolled in secondary schools in Nigeria as at 1990 was 1,240,525, while a total of 2,094,279 females enrolled in 1995. The total number of male registrations in 1990 was 1,661,468, while a total of 2,354,713 enrolled in 1995 (Federal Ministry of Education, 2000). One might be curious to know how many of the females (both in population and percentage) made it to graduation or to the tertiary level of education.

Additionally, about a decade later, reports from states' Ministries of Education suggest that enrolment into primary schools in the country increased. The proportion of girls enrolled in primary schools increased from 45.7% in 2010 to 48.6% in 2015. Completion rates for girls in primary and secondary schools increased from 46.7%

and 47.1% respectively in 2010 to 48.3% and 47.9% respectively in 2015. The proportion of girls enrolled in secondary schools increased slightly from 45.3% in 2010 to 45.7% in 2015. Nevertheless, this report indicates that enrolment into tertiary institutions across the country was still male-dominated, on average. However, the same reports show that female teachers constitute most of the primary school teachers in Nigeria (Federal Ministry of Education, 2015b).

Overall, while the preceding statistics reveal some positive progress in girls' enrolment, they give us a glimpse and some predictions of the future as well as facts about the dropout rate, which remained substantial over the years. Moreover, these statistics make it clear that Nigeria had (and perhaps still has) challenges in retaining its pupils and students for long stretches of time in schools.

Nigeria seems to have made an unimpressive achievement in the implementation of the gender equality programmes. With various factors considered, statistical data from the 2012 Gender in Nigeria Report, published by the British Council Nigeria (2012), suggests that Nigeria ranked 118 out of 134 countries in the Gender Equality Index. The United Nations Development Programme (UNDP), in the 2015 global Gender Inequality Index (GII), ranked Nigeria low in human development, occupying the 152nd position out of 188 countries across the globe.

The World Economic Forum (WEF), furthermore, ranked Nigeria 122nd out of 144 countries in the 2017 Global Gender Gap Report. This report, as one of the most recent from WEF, clearly indicates that Nigeria as a nation has not been able to close the gap of gender inequality for decades now. For the sake of the general progress and development of the nation, the government can still do something more for the country's education culture and tradition by rapidly addressing gender inequality. Scholars have been able to establish that inequalities and discrepancies in socioeconomic status (SES), of which gender is an element, can influence the education system, academic performance and outcomes among industrialised nations.

Thus, making concerted and sustained efforts to close the gaping gender gap in the Nigerian education sector, the health sector and labour markets can be a great resource in the continued effort to eradicate poverty and hunger in the country. Promoting gender equality and empowering women in an inclusive human development scheme could go a long way towards a healthy development by addressing the issue of low human development and advancing economic growth.

Commentary and Recommendations

For some time now, Nigeria appears to have dragged its feet so much in addressing major issues in its education system and development that the situation now requires urgent attention. Any more years spent failing to squarely address pressing issues in Nigeria's education sector could spell greater economic risks, engender socio- political disruptions and possibly make the problem almost futile to manage in the future. It might also deprive the nation's future generations of their rights to a strong and reliable education system. It will certainly be far more expensive to maintain compared with steps taken now to tackle those problems.

Any attempt to overhaul Nigeria's beleaguered education system will inherently be a tumultuous venture. No matter how constructive and data-driven the approach, it will rarely receive full support. Initiators of the reform would clash with the teachers' unions and the college and university unions. Teachers, college professors and university faculties and their unions might hold rallies, pickets and industrial actions in protest across the states of the federation. Thorny issues with these groups have hovered on the horizon for decades. Negotiating with the Nigerian Union of Teachers is certainly a good idea, as it would enable the government to work out programmes that would augur well with everyone including the students.

Nigeria must redirect the system of education that it is practicing today towards a more formidable modern enterprise that is culture friendly and consolidated with digital advancement. This author believes that the traditional as well as the inherited education system is destined for a towering global significance, if properly harnessed and integrated into the modern digital technology. One can envision the level of the nation's education system's performance as equal to or eclipsing that of South Korea in about a decade, if strong and positive policies were well-implemented.

Even though John Dewey maintained that knowledge and the entire educational process are a continuous reconstruction and reorganisation of experience, picking and dropping potentially workable education policies and programmes without a complete implementation is never a good idea in any nation's broader educational development. The same suggestion applies to any haphazard approach to reforms. Persistent policy gymnastics in the education sector have not been of any help to the nation. While education policy formulators need to be more consistent and decisive, policy implementers are being called upon to become more alive to their responsibilities in a more patriotic fashion.

Policies impact peoples' lives in the long-term and therefore should not be casually made by one or two people over a cup of tea. Instead, they need to be crafted conscientiously and with a high degree of reliability. This responsibility is about improving the system and standard of the nation's education sector. People should be careful not to be confused or inadvertently twist the whole thing. The idea is to solve Nigeria's problems, not modify them. Simply modifying them would be like a debtor who previously wore *agbada* or *dashiki* now wearing a suit, so no one, including his creditor, will recognise him. Do students get consulted before policies are implemented in the Nigerian education system? Policymaking should be democratic, evidence-based, pragmatic, with extensive consultations made. Otherwise, the impact can become minimal or ruinous.

Concerning gender disparity, gender stereotypes, even though not always obvious, are a huge part of the Nigerian culture. But the issue of gender is also affiliated with the subject of diversity, which remains a great asset in every nation's political, economic, social and cultural development. An improved knowledge and awareness of the huge advantages in gender diversity in the society could impel all Nigerians to create a climate where both men and women are always appreciated and respected. Diversity, which involves differences in gender, enriches decision making, problem solving and policymaking in all spheres of life and in any given human society. It brings to the fore varied opinions, positions, ideas, views, talents and perspectives that could be usefully integrated into shared knowledge. It generates inclusive initiatives and healthy competition that could easily usher in progress.

Therefore, the involvement of women in important societal issues and decision making is a resource that could breed excellence. Such an initiative could also usher in a period of increased productivity, expertise and sustainable development. Nonetheless, to achieve a certain degree of gender balance in the Nigerian education system, there must be some considerable improvement in gender parity both in schools and tertiary institutions' enrolments.

Chapter Three
Policymaking and Implementation

Since scientists, scholars, educators and administrators globally pay so much attention to education policymaking processes and call for the consideration of more systematic, functional and pragmatic bases in that regard, this chapter endeavours to delineate education policymaking, its processes and adoption in the Nigerian education system. The overarching rationale guiding this study aims to deepen the conceptual and descriptive understanding of the process by which education policies are determined, developed and adopted. It will also explore and explain policy process's inherent hindrances, inadequacies and dysfunctionalities, especially in the Nigerian context. Why does and would an education policy, programme, or system change? Why would it be altered, modified, or even rejected?

How did education policymaking and its implementation start? Education policy formulation, along with its implementation in Nigeria today, is retraceable both to the colonial times (when the British government was the colonialist) and the post-colonial era, after Nigeria attained its independence and sovereignty. The British education policies did not sufficiently meet the local needs of local people, nor did the colonialists consider indigenous involvement in the formulation of salient policies to be necessary.

The Colonial Era (1842-1959)

The British colonial administrators adopted the British system of education and administered it in Nigeria using certain education codes, laws, guidelines and ordinances, such as the 1882, 1887, 1916, 1926, 1948 and 1959 education ordinances. At that time, the indigenous people were not actively involved in the formulation of the education laws and policies that guided the administration of education in the protectorates. These Nigerian education laws, ordinances and policymaking bodies (in the form of commissions and reports) are outlined in the table below:

Table 6

Colonial Era's Education Ordinances, Commissions and Reports

Ordinances and Commissions	Year
Education Ordinance	1882
Nigerian Education Ordinance	1887
Education Ordinance	1916
Phelps-Stokes Commission	1922
Education Ordinance	1926
Education of African Communities' Memorandum	1935
Mass Education in African Societies Imperial Memorandum	1943
Elliot Commission	1943
Phillipson Report	1948
Ashby Commission	1959

The focus of the tabulated education laws, ordinances and codes was to provide guidelines on how to administer education in the colony. In fact, modern day policies, laws and techniques of educational administration in Nigeria are based on those ordinances and codes (Fabunmi, 2005; Ijaduola, 1998 & Ogunnu, 2000). The colonialists occasionally modified and re-authorised established education laws, guidelines and education ordinances with a view to meeting the exigencies of the changing times. The aim of these laws, ordinances and commissions initiated by the colonial government was to provide an across-the-board education system that would meet the needs of Nigerian citizens, especially at the primary and secondary levels. There was indeed a certain sense of consistency, pragmatism and order that drove and empowered their method of educational administration, management and policies. Undoubtedly, their system of educational administration was regulated by well-organised, solid, systematic and consistent education guidelines and blueprints. It is noteworthy that the education policies proposed, formulated and implemented by various commissions set up by the Nigerian government, both pre- and post-independence, were responsible for the country's major educational and even economic developments.

In 1955, one year after Nigeria constitutionally became a country of three regions with the federal capital in Lagos and 7 years after 1948, when the Philipson Commission recommended a universal, free, compulsory primary and secondary education in Nigeria, the Western Region, with the promulgation of the Education law in that same year (1955), introduced the UPE. It was launched in the eastern region in 1957 and the Lagos education ordinance was initiated that same year. In 1958, the northern government resolved to make the provinces accountable for the organisation of primary education. However, UPE was not introduced in the north until after independence owing to financial problems, teacher-supply difficulties and insufficient data-collection procedures coupled with religious and cultural influences (Taiwo, 1980, Obidi,1988, Fafunwa, 2004, Fabunmi, 2005 & Imam, 2012).

The Ashby Commission, set up by the British colonial government in April 1959 to study post-school-certificates and higher education in the country, submitted its report to the Nigerian government in September 1960, a month before independence. This Commission was made up of nine members: three Americans, three British and three Nigerians and its purpose was to predict Nigeria's educational needs of up to 1980. In fact, it was the recommendations of the Ashby Commission's report that saw the establishment of some of the pioneering universities and advanced level teacher-training colleges in Nigeria. This commission recommended the establishment of four Federal Universities in the country that taught education-vital courses. Following this recommendation, five universities were established instead of four. They are: University of Nigeria, Nsukka (1960), Ahmadu Bello University, Zaria (1962), University of Ife (now Obafemi Awolowo University), Ile-Ife (1962), University of Lagos, Lagos (1962) and University of Ibadan, first founded as University College in 1948. This was a real investment in education in general and the bedrock of the development of higher education in Nigeria.

Notably, before independence, there were only two major tertiary institutions in the country: Yaba Higher College, founded in 1932 and University College, Ibadan (UCI) founded in 1948. Members of the commission also recommended that the cost of training teachers should be borne by the regions along with the necessity and indispensability of the UBE for the nation's economic development.

Table 7

The Six Oldest Tertiary Institutions / Universities in Nigeria

No.	Name of Institution	State	Year Founded
1.	The Yaba Higher College, Yaba*	Lagos	1932
2.	University of Ibadan*	Oyo	1948
3.	University of Nigeria, Nsukka	Enugu	1960
4.	Obafemi Awolowo University, Ile Ife	Osun	1961
5.	Ahmadu Bello University, Zaria	Kaduna	1962
6	University of Lagos	Lagos	1962

*The Yaba Higher College was later upgraded from University College to University of Ibadan in 1948 (after it was relocated and renamed).

The Post-Colonial Era

The quest for educational freedom, progress and reforms continued to grow after Nigeria gained independence from the colonialists. Nigeria was still divided into four regions: Eastern, Western, Northern and Mid-Western. One of the most immediate but poignant education policy developments of this period was the takeover of schools from missionaries and voluntary agencies and the reduction of the 8-5-2-3 levels of education to 7-5-2-3. The first level was for primary education, the second level for secondary education, the third for high school certificate and the fourth for university education. At the final stages, students sat for external examinations and received performance-based certificates. Also, to set the stage for the need-based national policy on education that finally arrived in 1977, there was massive government funding of education that included tuition-free university education.

Higher education, that is, everything other than primary or secondary education, was the responsibility of the premiers in the regions and the Prime Minister in Lagos. Post-independence Nigeria was a crucial time for the political, economic and educational development and growth of the nation. During that period, there was an overwhelmingly popular consciousness about the poor standards of education at all levels and the urgent need for a reform. Notably, the recommendations of the Ashby Commission did not totally address all the challenges facing the Nigerian education sector, especially at the regional levels. Therefore, to fill this gap, the regional governments set up commissions to study and address some specific issues and aspects of the Nigerian education system. All these commissions, as represented in the table on the next page, critically highlighted the poor quality, non-functionality, inadequacy and lack of relevance of the nation's education in relation to the needs of the citizenry.

Table 8

Post-Independence Educational Acts, Commissions/Reports, & National Constitutions

Laws and Commissions	Year
The Nigerian Constitution	1960
Archer Report	1960
Banjo Commission	1960
Oldman Report	1962
Ikoku Commission	1962
Dike Commission	1962
Ajayi Commission	1964
Asabia Commission	1967
Taiwo Commission	1968
Somade Commission's Report	1969
National Policy on Education	1977
Nigerian Constitution	1979
Nigerian Constitution	1999
Universal Basic Education Act	2004

To illustrate, in 1960, the western regional government set up a commission under the chairmanship of the Rev. Canon S.A. Banjo to review the entire education system in western Nigeria. In 1961, the Banjo Commission, given the needs of that era, recommended that the modern schools in the western region be converted to junior secondary schools (JSS). It was a time to experiment with this education system in Nigeria, as was already the case in Liberia, a system that worked out successfully in the United States.

In 1962, the first National Development Plan was inaugurated. Because of political impediments and hindrances, it ended up being unsuccessful. In that same year (1962), the concept of "comprehensiveness" was introduced in the Nigerian secondary education. In the post-colonial era, the federal (and especially the military) and state governments enacted decrees and edicts, respectively, for the administration, management and regulation of education in the nation. Also, with the coming of the civilian administration, education laws were promulgated. The edicts mandated the government takeover of schools from individuals and voluntary agencies. Of interest is Decree No. 14 of 1967, which saw the creation of 12 states out of the four previously existing regions in the country.

According to Fabunmi (2005), education administration decrees were also enacted by the future federal military governments in Nigeria from 1966 to 1979. The same was applicable to the states, which promulgated edicts for the regulation of education, its management and provisions. Examples include East Central State's Public Education Edict No. 5 of 1970, Lagos State's Education Law (Amendment) Edict No.11 of 1970, South Eastern State's Education (School's Board) Edict, No.20 of 1970 and Mid-Western State's Education Edict, No.5 of 1973. Each state amended its education laws when necessary. All the edicts had common features, such as the state takeover of schools from individuals and voluntary agencies and the establishment of school management boards and unified teaching services (Fabunmi, 2005).

National Policy on Education

The historical and educational antecedents of both the pre-colonial and post-colonial eras in Nigeria had brought about the first indigenous National Policy on Education in 1977, 4 years after the federal government of Nigeria inaugurated a seminar of distinguished experts in 1973 to deliberate it as a truly national education policy. This resulted in a consolidation of the National Curriculum Conference convened in 1969 to review the education system and its goals. It also identified new national goals for Nigeria that would determine the future and direction of education in the country (Nigerian Educational Research Council, 1972; Imam, 2012, p.188). It was aimed at solving relevant educational problems, addressing the needs, aspirations and challenges of the citizenry and developing education policies that would meet the developmental needs of Nigeria as a nation. With changes in the education system and programmes as well as socio-political developments in the country, this policy has undergone several revisions.

The National Policy on Education (NPE) in Nigeria is the followed national guideline for the effective management, administration and implementation of education at all tiers of government. There has been significant revolution in the education sector in Nigeria and there definitely needs to be national policy reforms to align with the current trends) in the sector to ensure proper and efficient execution of the Board of Education's guidelines and regulations. The NPE in Nigeria is a statement of the government's regulations, anticipations, expectations, goals, requirements and standards for quality education delivery in Nigeria (Federal Republic of Nigeria, 2004).

Policymaking requires careful planning, analysis, formulation, implementation, monitoring and subsequent evaluations of policy outcomes. For decades now, education policymaking seems to give the impression that there is indeed an overall willingness to tackle educational issues in Nigeria. In recent years, new policies appear to have spread, but this outlook seems to be an illusion, since such developments are being outrun by rapid growth in the conflicts of general political interests as well as among some educational leaders and administrators.

Accurate information and data are indispensable in measuring the strengths and weaknesses of a given nation's education system. The absence of reliable data makes educational planning and other forms of planning in Nigeria virtually unproductive. Additionally, follow-up questions need to be asked regarding specifics, such as how education policy discretions could be exercised, coupled with the reasons behind each decision.

Hindrances to Education Policy Implementation in Nigeria

It is admissible that the Nigerian education system has undergone decades of policy overhauls and amendments. These overhauls and amendments, among other reforms, include regulating the minimum pay for teachers employed in assisted schools, evaluating teachers based on students' performance in examinations, expanding school attendance options, providing supervision and inspection of schools and instituting free compulsory and universal primary education (Fabunmi, 2005; Osokoya, 2002). Additionally, various governments have made major efforts and undertakings focused on helping especially traditional public schools, colleges and universities.

Despite these undertakings, Nigeria's present education standard remains at odds with its aspirations and those of the founding fathers, namely: to produce one of the best-educated and competitive workforces across the globe.

The poverty of policy implementation in the Nigerian education system is attributed to several factors, both familiar and unfamiliar, in the nation's journey towards the development of an integrated education. These factors can be broken down as follows:

Instability and Changes in Government

Frequent changes in government coupled with political, economic and social instability hinder the progress of any institution, organisation or country in many ways. Policy epilepsy and changes in the Nigerian education sector have been largely attributed to the country's longstanding political instability and frequent changes in the federal and state governments.

According to Azike (2013), between 1979 and 1983, education was free in some states but not in others. This disorderly situation might have led the military government to suspend the UPE programme and subsequently introduce UBE in 1999. In 1979, before the civilian government was formed, the ruling military regime promulgated Decree No.33 to establish federal polytechnics, describing the role of the polytechnic councils under Section 5. In 1983 and beyond, following the military takeover of power with the attendant decline in the country's education and teachers' working conditions, several further decrees were enacted to control, guide and regulate the nation's education sector. With Decree No.19 of 1984, the federal government closed all private-owned universities and abolished the establishment of the same.

Decree No. 16 of 1985 authorised the Federal Ministry of Education to establish the national minimum standards, approve courses and programmes and launch educational institutions based on assessments and accreditation by the National Universities Commission (NUC). In 1986, Decree No.20 introduced a change in the nation's school academic calendar from January to December to from October to September as well as implementing the 6-3-3-4 system of education. Decrees No.26 and 31 of 1988 proscribed the Academic Staff Union of Universities (ASUU) from taking part in trade union activities and amended the provisions of the National Primary Education Commission. In 1990, Decree No.36 revoked the proscription of ASSU and abolished the National Primary Education Commission that established the 1988 minimum standard of primary education. Nevertheless, this Commission was re-established in 1993.

In short, between 1991 and 2007, which comprised both military and civilian regimes, the nation's education policymakers and administrators functioned under approximately nine ministers and commissioners of education at the federal and state levels. With the reform and reintroduction of the Nigerian constitution in 1999, the National Policy on Education was reviewed and the UBE re-inaugurated, plus prepared for re-authorisation in 2004. Under such eclectic scenarios, inconsistencies, indecisions and policy rigmaroles, the presence of crisis in the nation's education system and policymaking should not be a surprise. Of course, under such a status quo, it would be difficult if not impossible to productively maintain an existing education policy.

Political Factors

Experience and expertise are the qualities needed to properly run any country's education system. This was evident even in pre-colonial times when the education system was characteristically pragmatic and functional in the sense of having reasonably flexible logistics. Even though the public education of any given nation is necessarily an extension of its political system, the education system of any nation ought not to be politically manipulated by weighing the partisan political ramifications of every single education policy despite how unpopular and irrelevant (those ramifications are). Likewise, education policymaking should not be controlled by a presumed superiority that is borne out of inexperience or non- expertise. This type of misguided initiative, if tolerated, could render a nation's education system and policymaking corrosively non-progressive or simply leave the system with a type of bureaucracy or policies capable of stifling effective reforms and important innovations.

For the Nigerian education system to progress, there is the need to honour expertise and experience in such a way that they drive leadership and management. It would be inadvisable, for instance, to ask the president of a country, by virtue of his office, to direct the affairs of an education system's development and reform. Chances are that he is not well-suited to run schools, any more than he is well-suited to run his office or govern his nation. There is the likelihood that when an educational issue arises, such an executive might cling to ideological solutions without primarily identifying and verifying the problems. Should people expect a different or positive result in Nigeria's education system and education policymaking outcomes if such a method was to be perennially deployed in its educational leadership and administration?

Financial Constraints and Overinvestment

Inadequacies in the funding of education policies and programmes can become a major hindrance to the implementation of major education policies and necessitate their reconsideration and possible alteration, if not withdrawal. Underfunding can also result in major education policy failures. As an illustration, the innovative programmes and policies that saw the introduction of the UPE in various parts of the country and the establishment of modern prevocational schools to absorb the products of UPE were not successful because of huge financial constraints and implications. The UPE was aimed at giving free primary education to all children age 6-12. To help curb illiteracy, address educational inequality, bring about some level of expansion and increase in school enrolment, these programmes were inadequately planned, owing to poor data and financial underestimations, thereby resulting in an overwhelming project, an unanticipated investment. For instance, it was reported that when the schools opened to register the pupils for the school year, 2.3 million children were expected; instead, 3 million arrived for registration (Fafunwa, 2004). This development would affect the provisions of infrastructural facilities and the necessary number of teachers, classrooms and school materials.

Conflicts of Interest

Policymakers, administrators and education leaders of varied descriptions have diverse interests and roles that are both personal and professional. Often these stakeholders in education permit their interests to get in the way of those of their colleagues. Conflicts of interest could emerge when the interests and primary objectives of the stakeholders are "different" from or clash with those of their educational institutions and organisations. Conflicts of interest could also arise when any of these educational leaders or administrators' duties and responsibilities are influenced by other duties, roles and responsibilities they hold. These responsibilities could take the form of business involvements, partnerships, or financial commitments, family or sundry affiliations and party or social club memberships. Attachment to commitments and individual situations can impede their ability to perform their duties without some compromise to diligence, honesty, accountability and transparency.

Prejudice and Discrimination

Unbridled preference for some peculiar religious values, tribalism, nepotism, clannishness and unhealthy cultural complexities may have also contributed to the decline of education in Nigeria. Any urge to confine the borders of any nation's public education policies to values, traditions, or cultures that are characteristically callous should be re-evaluated or resisted. Public education policies should not be tailored to any religion, cultural values, or preferences. At all times, competence, ability, quality, professionalism and excellence should be encouraged instead of bigotry, ethnicism, nepotism, clannishness and tribalism, not only in the education sector but also in all sectors.

Moreover, the analysis, formulation and implementation of any education policy should be strictly based on and geared towards true freedom, liberty, guided by broader democratic values. The need for a genuine gesture of brotherliness, friendship and fellowship cannot be overemphasised.

For Nigeria to be able to finally formulate an education system, programmes and policies that are solid and resilient, there is the need to embrace dialogue and peace across all the nation's cultural, political, religious and social sectors. These two factors are antidotes, best options and resolutions to both covert and obvious conflicts as well as unnecessary tensions and disruptions in the nation's overall development. Of course, for anything to work in Nigeria, Nigerians need a peaceful co-existence devoid of unchecked ethnic, regional, cultural, social and religious preferences or unhealthy discriminations. The nation needs to constantly encourage and build upon positive mutual tolerance.

Cultural Considerations

In every analysis, formulation and implementation of education policies, attention should be paid to the inherent and prevalent culture. Culture, in this perspective comprises but is not limited to relevant religious values and environmental, ethnic and tribal factors. Efforts must be continuously made to ensure that education policies adapt to local conditions. Policy planning involves investigating the educational needs of the people, their pertinent religious, economic, social and environmental conditions. Doubtless, religious, ethnic and tribal differences sometimes hinder education policy planning, development and implementation; if threatening and divisive values are not properly reconciled with unifying options and positive alternatives carefully amalgamated. Nigeria, like most of the nations on earth, is culturally conservative, socially progressive and politically democratic. This cultural conservatism will always conflict with education policies that are incompatible with the sociocultural and psycho-cultural lives of the people.

The primary-secondary-tertiary school structure and system of education introduced by the British colonial administration seemed compatible with Nigeria's collectivist culture and values; therefore, it has survived to this day. Subjectively speaking, the education structure of 6-5-4 seemed to have allied well with the nation's collective culture for many years. Whether the 6-3-3-4 education system, which was also viable, was fully implemented before the introduction of the current 9-3-4 structure (UBE) remains a big question.

It should not be overlooked that the consequences of the indirect rule system's policy introduced by the colonial government, which somewhat and unfortunately separated the citizens based on regions, religion, ethnicities and tribes still exerts a latent impact on the Nigerian educational development and its attendant policy implementations. The policy's primary restriction of the extension of both Christianity and Western education to the northern protectorate not only explains the basis for the imbalance in the educational development between the north and south but also has some enduring implications for education policy analysis, formulation and implementation in today's Nigeria.

Commentary and Recommendations

If there is any recent growth in the approval ratings of the progress of education leadership and management in Nigeria, it could probably be partly attributed to improvements on how education policies have been carried out in various states across the federation. Education policymakers, leaders and administrators are generally well-meaning, but the problem often lies in the misplacement of priorities, conflicts of interest and the inability of education leaders to sufficiently plan, formulate and subsequently implement education policies. Under a functional education system, Nigeria should not have much difficulty advancing a potent succession of policies and reforms that would permit it to achieve universal accessibility and rapid enrolments.

As a follow-up, enrolment, admission and transition into tertiary institutions in the country might need a review by moderating potential excesses in the rigours, standards and levels of academic requirement for prospective candidates especially in the entrance examinations. In a nutshell, even though entrance exams for tertiary institutions need to be demanding and rigorous, they do not have to necessarily look like or become premature equivalents of a master's degree level examination. By Decree No. 2 of February 13, 1978, the Federal Military Government of Nigeria established the Joint Admissions and Matriculation Board (JAMB). Its function is to coordinate the conduct of tertiary-level institutions' entrance examinations as well as to place successful candidates into the appropriate institutions. These institutions include the universities, colleges of education and polytechnics. Today, JAMB organizes and conducts annually the Unified Tertiary Matriculation Examination (UTME).

While the effectiveness of JAMB in coordinating the conduct of examinations for candidates seeking admissions into universities and other tertiary institutions for some years now must be applauded, some of its methods, policies and procedures could still be reviewed or revised in the process of reconfiguring Nigeria's education system. Among a few issues that have arisen in recent years, several candidates have failed the UTMEs not because they were not intelligent enough to pass them, but because they lacked the basic knowledge on how the computer-based tests work. Moreover, the effectiveness and impact of the longstanding cut-off mark policies along with the quota system regulations have neither been objectively tested nor have the tertiary institutions' general admission's processes been methodically evaluated.

Consistently granting admissions only to a comparatively few candidates consequently reduces the prospects of the nation's workforce, with a hugely negative impact on its economy, let alone its internal security. This observation calls for more flexibility in establishing cut-off marks and admission requirements by JAMB and the tertiary institutions, respectively. This type of flexibility or "circumstantial concession" should be prudently and judiciously exercised more, especially whenever the nation's economy tends towards a recession or its unemployment rate rises.

In a period of national economic decline or high unemployment rate, for instance, more UTME candidates who did not reach the prescribed cut-off marks for certain academic programmes could be invited for oral or written interviews, and those who are successful, considered for possible switches to related programmes that require lower cut-off marks or suit the candidates' academic abilities and inclinations. In making these determinations, tertiary institutions' officials could review the candidates' accumulated secondary school academic GPAs and general school performance. Additionally, oral or written interviews could help them confirm those candidates' suitability for necessary concessions. There have been cases where candidates who were demonstrably intelligent and academically clever at the secondary level, ended up not being successful in the UTME, even after several attempts. Some of these unsuccessful candidates have wound up becoming either worthless or burdens to the society.

One might ask the following questions: In practice, will a candidate who scored 163 in UTME be able to study theatre arts in any university in Nigeria? Will a candidate who scored 189 be able to gain admission for medicine or pharmacy in any university in Nigeria? Will a candidate who scored 177 be able to study law in any university in Nigeria? While this section is not advocating the admission of every candidate who takes the UTME into the nation's tertiary institutions, a more diligent review of relevant JAMB and tertiary institutions' policies might be beneficial to more candidates and, by extension, to the nation's economy and its internal security.

For education policymaking to work in Nigeria, the Federal Ministry of Education should be able to produce substantial, correct and reliable statistics that are not only acceptable to the Nigerian policymakers, planners, educators, researchers and agencies but also suit the standards of both continental and international educational organisations. Education statistical data should not be arbitrarily developed or subjectively determined. The collection, processing and analyses of educational data by the Federal Ministry of Education and its allied agencies, such as the State Ministries of Education (SME), the Joint Admissions and Matriculation Board (JAMB), the National Universities Commission (NUC), the National Bureau of Statistics (NBS), the National Board for Technical Education (NBTE), the National Teachers' Institute (NTL), the National Youth Service Corps (NYSC), the West African Examination Council (WAEC), the National Examinations Council (NECO) and the United Nations Educational, Scientific and Cultural Organisation (UNESCO), are expected to be detailed, objective, comprehensive, reliable and informative. Such data should essentially include numerical information on the status of students' enrolment, retention and graduation in individual institutions. The same should be made applicable to demographics as well as the population of students, staff, teachers and academic staff.

Chapter Four
International Models and Eye Openers

Education leaders and Nigerian students today are not oblivious of the various international assessment programmes aimed at testing the aptitudes and progress of students in education. Although they may not tell the whole story about any nation's academic ability, these tests and assessments can reveal a lot and shed great light on the progress, improvement, or decline of a country's education system, compared to their international counterparts. The Programme for International Student Assessment (PISA), first administered in 2000, tests the proficiency of almost a million 15-year-olds across the globe, in mathematics, science and reading.

PISA is administered in every 3 years by the Organisation for Economic Cooperation and Development (OECD). Trends in International Mathematics and Science Assessment (TIMSS), which was instituted in 1995, is administered to fourth and eighth graders every 4 years to determine how well they have learned mathematics and science curricula. Even though these two tests are different, they are highly correlated. Both are scored based on a 0-1,000 scale, with the international mean average of 500 and a standard deviation of 100. Any country whose score hovers around or below the mean average of 500 does not look promising. Moreover, both tests have a lot in common with their predictability.

Nevertheless, unlike many other exams, PISA assesses the ability of students to apply knowledge to real-life problems. The examination was first conducted in the early 2000s when a sample of

510,000 students took the exam in 65 countries, representing 80% of the world economy. It is an assessment whose results are anticipated with excitement by schools, students and teachers around the world. It is considered a reliable yardstick to measure individual nations' academic abilities. In this periodic assessment, Asian students have consistently and largely continued to excel and trounce other nations. The Chinese city of Shanghai, Singapore, Hong Kong and South Korea, for instance, have achieved significantly higher scores than other nations and regions.

Catching up with these academically successful societies like China, Singapore, Japan and South Korea is not unattainable now, but it would certainly be more beneficial to have an educationally committed economy. The question is, how would Nigeria perform, compared to other countries, if it were to participate in these international education assessments? Would its performance be disappointing? Could it be sufficiently likened to its recent international soccer (football) and allied sports' performances? Would the outcome expose the apparently weak status of Nigeria's general education system? Can one make ranking predictions that may not seem too complicated or have an embarrassing outcome? Of about 75 nations participating in these tests, how many of them might still outscore Nigeria? For various reasons of practice, commitment, hard work, vision, clear focus and individual sacrifices, the answers to these questions cannot be predicted with certainty. The ground-breaking performance of Nigeria's student girls from Regina Pacis Secondary School Onitsha, Anambra state, who represented both Nigeria and Africa at the World Technovation Challenge in Silicon Valley, San Francisco, California, shows that Nigerian students' intellectual ability and aptitude cannot be underestimated, especially when properly groomed with attention, clear vision and strong support. Technovation is a programme that offers girls around the world the opportunity to learn the programming skills to emerge as tech-entrepreneurs and leaders (Omilana, 2018). One hundred and fifteen countries participated in the qualifiers, but only 12 teams from all over the world were selected as finalists. Nigeria's team, a group of teenagers from Anambra state, developed a mobile application called "FD Detector" to tackle the problem of fake pharmaceutical products in Nigeria. They not only clinched the Gold Medal in this competition but also defeated teams from the United States, Spain, Turkey, Uzbekistan and China. This remarkable performance is testimonial to the amazing progress that some of the nation's children are making in science, technology, engineering and mathematics (STEM). Without a doubt, these teenagers are laying the cornerstone for scientific and technological advancement in Nigeria.

The same recognition applies to another team of five young Nigerian students from secondary schools in Lagos who represented the country at the First Global Robotic Olympiad (GRO) in Mexico. Competitors were expected to solve problems related to energy with the use of robotics and an award would be given to a country or a team with the best engineering design. The Nigerian team made up of four females and one male between ages 15 to 17 competed with 193 teams from 187 countries around the world and won two bronze medals (News Agency of Nigeria, 2018).

Nevertheless, despite these wonderful achievements and performances and even with the hope of joining other nations of the world in making science and technology the bedrock of economic development, Nigeria still needs to learn from other nations' unique teaching and learning techniques, strategic education policymaking and relevant reforms to enable it to consolidate natural abilities plus strengthen its education system in the long term. Even though one is not clamouring for uncoordinated imported systems of education, the suggestion here is still about what Nigeria can learn from the world's high performing education systems. It is also about discovering underlying administrative mechanisms and rediscovering those teaching and learning methods that explain other nations' education systems' consistently positive performances. There is nothing inappropriate in studying other nations when developing curriculum or reconfiguring Nigeria's system of education.

Notably, in the modern world, the ability of students to compete confidently and effectively is often hindered by the poor performance of their education systems. The nation's politicians, business leaders and policymakers should be concerned that the education system in Nigeria has not yet come of age, much less kept pace with some of the nations that participate in the international achievement examinations. This state of affairs should kick-start a debate in the nation's Senate and House of Representatives over which education policy overhaul might be instituted to improve the country's still-struggling education system. This discussion is especially critical because Nigeria faces an urgent need to improve and consolidate its quality to become competitive in the globalised economy, with which most of these participant countries are already closely connected. The following section will explore some of the high-scoring nations and regions with salient reviews. These include Singapore, Hong Kong,

Japan, Taiwan, Finland, Macau, Estonia and South Korea, among others.

Singapore

For over a decade now, Singapore has consistently outscored other countries in both the Programme for International Student Assessment (PISA) and International Mathematics and Science Assessment (TIMSS). These programmes test children's aptitude and abilities in math, science and reading. What is the secret of their persistent success? Amidst various classroom practices in countries across the globe and even among top-performing nations, Singapore runs what I would describe as a "traditional and customised" method of classroom learning. What are their teaching and instructional regimes? Do they have strengths, weaknesses, limitations, constraints, advantages and disadvantages? What are they? Are their education systems transferable to other countries? Are their systems suitable for the 21st century knowledge-based economies? The following factors could be considered:

First, Singaporeans are known for uniformity in their classroom teaching and instructions. They are highly scripted. This applies to all levels of education and disciplines. Their teaching method is coherent, relevant, procedural and pragmatic. They apply any method that has been fruitful or fits a purpose at any time. There is always a priority and focus on covering the prescribed curriculum and recommended syllabus. Instructions are based on facts and procedures and geared towards preparing the students for both the semester, end-of-the-year and other major examinations. Therefore, with emphasis on mastering specific procedures and methods, especially in math and science, there is much reliance on textbooks, workbooks and examples with lots of drills and practice.

Teachers dominate classroom discussions. They make sparing use of "high-stakes" or "high-leverage" teaching practices that are more obtainable and useful in the Western world. For instance, they seldom check a student's prior knowledge, or communicate learning goals and achievement standards. The primary focus of teaching in Singapore is to transmit the conventional knowledge of the curriculum and increase performance in examinations. It is about curriculum, instruction and assessment.

Education in Singapore is believed to be a product of a distinctive and unique set of historical, institutional and cultural influences. These factors go a long way in explaining why the education system is especially effective in the current assessment environment, but they also limit how transferrable it is to other countries (Chua, 2014). Despite the wave of decentralisations of education systems in many countries, especially in many Western countries, Singapore's education system remains centralised, integrated, coherent, flexible and well-funded.

Hong Kong

The education system in Hong Kong, a region in southern China, is both competitive and vibrant. It is modelled after that of the United Kingdom, which colonised Hong Kong from 1841 to 1997. Children begin primary schooling at the age of 6, with a 6-year duration at the primary level. Emphasis is placed on early education for children with a curriculum that creates a sound nursery educational foundation for kindergartners before they move on to primary schools.

In Hong Kong, many primary schools employ Chinese methods of teaching and instruction. Contrary to Western countries, the class population is usually large, between 35 and 45 students. English language, mathematics, physical education, social studies, music, art, science and Chinese are among the subjects that pupils are expected to study at the primary school level.

At the secondary level, all students also have a 6-year duration in education (3 years of junior secondary and 3 years of senior secondary education). Like the Nigerian system, mandatory basic education is 9 years (a compulsory 6 years of primary and 3 years of junior secondary). Public primary and secondary education is free. At the 12th grade which is the end of the senior secondary education, students take the Hong Kong Diploma of Secondary Education (HKDSE) examination in preparation for transitioning to tertiary institutions. The curriculum for the HKDSE is divided into three categories: 1) Core and elective subjective, 2) Applied learning and 3) Other language subjects.

Education at the tertiary level is extremely important in Hong Kong, with students free to choose from eight available universities and other tertiary institutions whose academic statuses are like those in the university setting. Often, openings in universities are fewer than the many students who are ready to continue their university educations. Those who are not admitted into the undergraduate programmes can obtain associate or higher degrees. Others prefer to earn their post-graduate degrees from universities abroad. At the tertiary education levels, Hong Kong encourages, fosters, respects and welcomes talents, academic freedom, academic exchanges, institutional autonomy, independence, diversification and collaboration. It adopts international standards in curriculum design and quality assurance while offering joint international academic programmes. It is crucial to note that Hong Kong authorities built a highly centralised system of education during the 20th century, which at the end of the century moved towards decentralisation.

The Hong Kong Ph.D. Fellowship Scheme was even launched in 2009 to attract both outstanding local and non-local students to pursue Ph.Ds in Hong Kong universities. It provides each successful candidate with a monthly stipend of about 2,600 US dollars besides a conference and research-related travel allowance of about 1,400 US dollars annually for a period of about 3 years.

With Hong Kong, one sees a region that is obsessed with education from the primary to the tertiary level. In that society, education is not an option: it is an expectation. Nigeria can learn a lot from these features, which seem to be the secret of Hong Kong's success in education.

Japan

In Japan's education system, teaching and learning are about quality rather than quantity of lessons. Each class begins with the customary greetings to the teacher. During class, pupils and students are challenged to teach (or discuss problems) what they have learnt with each other; the Japanese believe that, by sharing, a student will retain about 90% of what (s)he learnt. Enough time is given to keep them motivated and the teacher endorses students who solve problems correctly. In some instances, students are permitted to briefly play the role of the teacher in class. While differences in the students' backgrounds, limitations, aptitudes, enthusiasm, interests, skills and cleverness are recognised and accommodated, students are not treated differently or preferentially by the teacher for individual achievements. Integration and the ability to interact with others in class is considered crucial. Indeed, it is an egalitarian education system that rewards efforts rather than achievement. If, for instance, mathematics proved difficult for a student, the teacher would handle it as though it were a language course, such as English language or Japanese to make it easier for young learners to understand.

While the teacher remains the only authority, facilitator, motivator and, in some cases, the only known "dictator" in class, teaching and learning are still considered interactive. The focus of this system of education is on the whole child. Instead of just intellectual development, the curricula include character formation, civil virtues, discipline and moral education, hygiene, table manners, cleaning and social skills. These are all parts of the holistic role of primary level education. They are not considered the primary responsibilities of parents. Lunch is provided and eaten together in the classroom by both teachers and students. This strategy helps teachers and students to develop a good rapport and closer relationships. All efforts are made to ensure that each student has a strong sense of belonging and feels happy, to the extent that students hardly skip classes or come to school late. The average number of pupils and students in a class is a little below 40. The number of students in a Japanese classroom used to exceed 50 because of rapid population growth. Children study Japanese, mathematics, science, physical education, social studies, music, crafts and home economics subjects like sewing skills and simple cooking. They also learn the traditional Japanese art of calligraphy. A growing number of elementary schools have started teaching English language. An average school day lasts for about 6 hours, making theirs one of the known long school days in Asia. Pupils and students are given assignments and homework during vacations. Information technology is used only to enhance education and most schools have internet access.

As in Hong Kong, the Japanese school system includes 6 years of elementary school, 3 years of junior high school, 3 years of senior high school and 4 years of university education. Japan today has one of the world's most educated populations with very high enrolment and almost zero illiteracy. Even though the Japanese education system is qualitative, some of its presumably foreign critics and reform-minded external educators believe that it is breaking down and no longer adapted to societal needs in this era of globalisation. They contend that turning away from egalitarianism and fostering more of individual creativity might help to bring it back on track. Recently, there have also been complaints that the chances of students benefitting from education is gradually dwindling as Japan, like some parts of the world, replaces more and more people with robots and machines. As a result, major corporations are hiring less and many of the highly educated are in menial and part-time employments.

This development is indeed a penetrating revelation from relevant sources. Nevertheless, one has seen how the Japanese education system works along with its essential features and how it differs from some other school systems. Overall, Nigeria can learn a huge lesson from the Japanese education model as it reconfigures its own education system.

Taiwan

Overviewing Taiwan's education system makes it obvious that Taiwan, an island home to roughly 23 million people located in the southern part of China, though independent since 1996, is still influenced by China both politically, economically and educationally. Taiwan is officially known as the Republic of China with its central educational authority as the Ministry of Education of the Republic of China. This Ministry is responsible for developing, implementing and maintaining education policies and managing public institutions of learning across Taiwan. Its education system consists of a mandatory and basic level of education: 6 years of elementary education and 3 years of junior high school education (or secondary level education) and 3 years of senior high schools or vocational school. Higher education and institutions of learning include colleges, universities and institutes of technology, graduate schools and postgraduate programmes. In 2014, in a spate of educational reforms, the Ministry of Education added 3 years of senior secondary education to the curriculum, making it also compulsory. This was a transition from 9-year to 12-year mandatory education in Taiwan. This reform seems to have addressed the widely criticised defects of the previous system by making the curriculum less restrictive, offered high-quality early childhood education and art available to all students and improving vocational education and training programmes, among other factors. At the primary level, students graduate from primary schools with a primary school diploma and are not required to take any tests to enter junior high school.

The official language of instruction is Mandarin Chinese. The academic year runs from September to June. Like Japan, Taiwan has almost a 100% literacy rate. Students graduate from Taiwan with very high scores in mathematics and science when compared with other nations' standards around the world. Nevertheless, this model was criticised for so much concentration on "memorisations or rote learning", which is not unusual for people from that region of the world as well as for graduating candidates who lack the analytical thinking or creativity that is obtainable from education systems with general curricula that are more functional, pragmatic and need-based.

In three decades, Taiwan's higher education system has undergone a rapid transformation from an elite system to a universal one, making it possible for many Taiwanese to earn college and university degrees. When the Taiwanese government approved the creation of new private tertiary institutions in the mid-1980s, new players flooded the sector. There is no doubt that the rapid growth in education impacted both the higher education sector and Taiwan's economy because enrolments, graduations and the number of tertiary institutions rapidly increased, generating concern about the quality and sustainability of that sector.

Moreover, with the decline in birth rate and the nation's population, the higher education sector in Taiwan is facing a big challenge with policymakers contemplating mergers for the universities. The Ministry of Education has also predicted that enrolment will drop by 2023. No doubt, the higher education sector in Taiwan is facing many challenges to remain competitive in a global education market. Recently, budget allocations from Taiwan's government were less than one quarter of the total budgets put into higher education around the world and only one third of this was exclusively spent on education, making it difficult to keep academic and regular staff who were offered more lucrative opportunities in other countries.

It is important to mention that, even though the public preschool education (or kindergarten) which care for children ages 2-6 is not a part of the compulsory education system in Taiwan, it is nevertheless, supported by the government, thereby helping poor families and enabling them to enrol their children. Today, many private preschools not run by the government exist in Taiwan. Some operate under franchise arrangements throughout the country.

South Korea

South Korea is famous for having a very strong education system. It has consistently shown excellence in mathematics, science and reading for over a decade at a level well above the OECD averages. Undeniably, the country's students' results and overall education outcomes are considered good. Also, the government seems to be exhorting students to be more creative and productive by recognising holistic abilities and strengths as well as performance in examinations. For the past decade, South Korea had become the beacon or yardstick whose standards of education, measured by its performance in PISA, are comparable to those of other countries.

Pre-school, which is offered from the age of 3 is optional in South Korea. Families have the option to send their children either to a government-run or private pre-school programme, some with fees. Compulsory schooling, then, begins from the age of 5 or 6. From the primary school (ages 6-12), which is free, pupils move into the middle schools (12-15) and subsequently into high school (ages 15-18). Primary and middle school education is compulsory, while secondary schooling is not. Middle school, in this context, can be considered analogous to Nigeria's junior secondary school (JSS), which covers both compulsory and elective courses, whereas high school is like the senior secondary education level. Curriculum at the middle school level covers math, the Korean language, the English languages, social studies, science and arts, physical and moral education. It is at this stage that education becomes more intensive, putting pressure on the students to get high grades to qualify for entry into reputable high schools. Competition can be quite tense, as students are screened according to individual abilities in various subjects. Additionally, healthcare is very important to the South Koreans; children are offered compulsory but free vaccinations at medical centres to attend schools. Children are also given other healthcare support while they remain in school.

    Students can make a choice for their high schools based on each school's specialty, such as foreign language, art, or music, or for the student's convenience; for instance, the one that falls nearest to their home address or place of residence. At this stage of high schooling, parents can pay for their children's cost of tuition and school meals. On completing high school, students can take the College Scholastic Ability Test (CSAT), which is notoriously rigorous. The typical Korean school is divided into the first semester, running from March to July before the summer vacation and the second semester, which runs from the end of August to the middle of February with a break. This calendar applies more to the state schools than to private and international schools, which may often follow the standard Western calendar. This calendar includes a long summer vacation and Christmas break. South Korea is believed to have in major cities about 45 typical competitive international schools of high standards that teach English and other major world languages. Their syllabus is that of the international baccalaureate or the United States standard curriculum. School fees vary depending on individual schools and the programmes being offered.

Macau

Macau, an autonomous urban city of about 600,000 people and a former Portuguese colony from 1557 to 1999, is considered a special administrative region of the People's Republic of China with a mix of cultural influences. It maintains a different political and economic system than mainland China. A small coastal territory of China, Macau has a Catholic background that stretches back hundreds of years. The Catholic Church provides most of the city's schooling. Macau was the first region in Greater China (Mainland China, Taiwan, Hong Kong and Macau) to provide 15 years of free and compulsory formal education. This includes 3 years of kindergarten, 6 years of primary education, 3 years of junior secondary school and 3 years of senior secondary education. Macau's literacy rate is estimated to be about 94%. Macau had progressed from following its coloniser (Portugal) and neighbouring regions (Hong Kong and Taiwan) to establishing its own education system.

The first wave of education policy reform in Macau took place in the late 80s and early 90s, which led to a more disciplined education system, localised curriculum model, teacher education and universal free education with Chinese as the medium of instruction. In 2006, the second wave of education policy reform began, paying special attention to reconstructing the existing curriculum. Interweaving the past, present and future became a focal point. It is in this context that the education system in Macau can be better understood. Non-tertiary education in Macau was categorised into two parts: formal education and continuing education. The formal but self-reliant education system includes kindergarten, primary schooling, secondary schooling and special education, while the continuing education includes family education, vocational and technical, recurrent and community education as well as other educational activities. Vocational and technical forms of education are offered at the senior secondary school level. To create favourable conditions, the government has reduced the number of pupils for each class from 35-45 to 25-35 students, effective from the 2007/2008 academic year.

This type of education may be implemented either as formal education or recurrent education. While Macau is a tourism and gambling centre with abundant employment opportunities provided by casinos, there is a popular motivation to bring positive change in that environment by improving the education sector, especially in teaching and learning. As at 1999, when Macau returned to Chinese sovereignty, authority and administrative responsibility, it was home for to two universities and two tertiary institutions. Since then, as the casinos flourished, the colleges and other tertiary institutions have grown to about 10. Four of them are public institutions that are managed and controlled by the government. Macau participated in the Programme for International Student Assessment (PISA) for the first time in 2003 and since then has participated regularly in this tri-annual testing programme. Macau occupies one of the leading positions among 72 countries and economies in the leagues of mathematical, reading and scientific literacy performance in the PISA of 2015. It will also participate for the sixth time this year (2018).

Most schools in Macau are private schools. Macau has many cultural, economic and political similarities to Hong Kong, but they differ greatly in their higher education systems. Macau perceives higher education as the major pillar of its economy and aims at developing it by placing increasing and productive emphasis on it. Higher institutions are characterised by "vocationalisation" since their education curriculum is not only training-oriented but also directed towards acquiring knowledge and skills for future occupation and employment. The government supports the autonomy of tertiary institutions but coordinates the development of various institutions to bolster their academic quality.

In 2014, undergraduate applications from China to Hong Kong dwindled, whereas they increased for Macau, with about 7,000 Chinese applications received at the Macau University of Science and Technology, roughly a 30% increase from 2013. Compared to Hong Kong universities, Macau, a city that does not essentially compete with Hong Kong in attracting students from China, saw a dramatic rise in enrolment. Lower fees and cost of living could be implicated as among the major considerations by prospective Chinese undergraduates. The high cost of tuition and lodging as well as a severe shortage of hostels appeared to have kept them from applying to colleges in Hong Kong, among other reasons. While the languages of teaching and learning in Hong Kong are Putonghua and Cantonese, Portuguese (and English Language in some places) is the language of learning in Macau. Additionally, Chinese students not only feel more welcomed in Macau because of Macau's hospitality; they also consider studying in Macau an opportunity to learn a foreign and second language, Portuguese (or English language).

The Macau government generates large amounts of tax revenue and is thus able to increase its funding and investment in higher education and thereby making educational opportunities plentiful. Notably, the government's involvement in and its control over Macau's university system, however, had many unfavourable impacts on its management, curricula, staffing, research and development. It weakens university autonomy considerably. This might provide a big lesson for Nigeria to better manage its education system.

Finland

From the year 2000 through 2009, following Finland's dramatic performance in PISA and progress in its education system coupled with the release of its rankings in science, reading and mathematics, many nations have been curious to know what Finland is doing so well. As at 2006, it was the world's best-performing country. Even though its results have currently diminished, Finland remains one of the top-ranking countries in the world.

Finland's education system is somewhat different from those of other countries around the world, yet it arguably remains the world's best and most successful education system. In a nutshell, Finland understands that the best education begins at kindergarten and stretches all the way into higher education. It stresses the importance of learning not just to do well on tests but to become more knowledgeable and skilful. The emphasis is on lifelong learning. There is uniformity across the country in having the same goals for all students. Finland provides free education from preschool (kindergarten or nursery school) all the way through the university level. This provision applies to every child in the country. During the kindergarten stage, children learn to play, sing and take part in various other games. The implication of these activities is that, before Finnish children learn their times tables, they learn how to be "children", how to play and get along with one another. A lot of emphasis is put on childhood as the basis for lifelong development. Remarkably, all Finnish schools are funded by the government. Students pay nothing to go to the universities and other tertiary institutions. University education, at all levels, is subsidised by the federal government.

Education in Finland includes at least 1 year of preschool or kindergarten (ages1-6), 9 years of basic education and comprehensive schooling (ages 7-16), 3 years of general upper secondary schooling, 3 years of bachelor's degrees, 2 years of master's degree and any further studies for doctoral or licentiate degrees.

Just as Nigeria gained recognition in 2006 as the happiest country on earth, Finland was crowned one of the happiest nations to live in, given its beautiful landscapes, democratic politics, employee-focused work culture and high wages. The country's attitude towards its education system is also qualitative, progressive, welcoming, egalitarian and nurturing for children's needs and development. Equal opportunities, not disadvantaging less privileged families over wealthier ones, enable children from diverse backgrounds to socialise as they grow up to foster positive and successful outcomes in their adult lives. Students, teachers and parents value free time, usually providing 15 minutes of playtime after 45 minutes of teaching to help the children learn social and cooperative skills. In Finland's educational philosophy, competition is not as important as cooperation. The students are trusted to do well without competition. They also have very little homework. All relevant classwork is completed during school hours, leaving the children free to play with their friends and families in the evenings. Moreover, contrary to many other countries in the world, young students in Finland do not take standardised tests. The country discourages mandated standardised testing before the age of 16.

By Finland's standards, a school's team of special educators and decision makers involve a social worker, a nurse and a psychologist. Their education decision and policymaking are usually guided by reliable research conducted by the government or educational agencies in environments devoid of undue politics. If, for instance, research findings reveal the effectiveness of an educational programme, strategy, or technique, then it will be implemented in schools. The government agency personnel who run education in Finland, from national officials to local authorities, are educators rather than businessmen, military leaders, or politicians.

In Finland, moreover, teaching is recognised as an honourable and distinguished profession. To qualify as a teacher in Finland, a candidate must have at least a master's degree as well as the equivalent of the rigorous legal residency programme for law or medical professions, during which the best minds are selected to share their knowledge with the youth. Many schools are small enough that teachers know every student. Additionally, teachers are sufficiently paid. They are trusted to do whatever it takes at any given time to help students learn. Finland takes seriously what works in teaching and learning.

Estonia

Estonia's independence from the Soviet Union was restored in 1991. Often overlooked, this northern European country of about 1.5 million people seems to have gradually joined the ranks of the world's education elite. It could begin to attract the same degree of attention as Finland, South Korea, Singapore and Japan if it retains its education achievement's upward trajectory. With its long academic traditions, world-class higher education institutions and attractive destinations, Estonia is welcoming more and more international students into its universities. In 2012, it ranked 11th in math and reading and 6th in science out of 65 countries that participated in the PISA. Despite tying in certain categories with some other high-performing nations, Estonia had the smallest number of weak performers across Europe.

The structure of Estonia's education system includes preschool or nursery school (age 1.5 to 7), basic education (grades 1-9), upper secondary education and higher education. Estonia's comprehensive and basic school system, which is compulsory covers from age 7 to 17. Acquisition of basic education and transitioning to upper secondary schools (which are divided into general secondary schools and vocational secondary schools) depend on successfully completing the curriculum and passing three basic final examinations. A successful completion of secondary education qualifies a student to continue to higher education, which is also divided into professional higher education (in a vocational school or institution of professional higher education) and academic higher education (in a university). Higher education in that nation retains the traditional Anglo-Saxon structure of academic studies, with the first level as bachelor's study, the second level as master's study and the third level as doctoral study. Estonia has about 20 tertiary institutions across the country: six public universities, one privately owned university, eight state professional higher education institutions and five private professional higher education institutions.

Schools have autonomy, which includes the ability to make decisions on curriculum and to employ or dismiss teaching staff. Governance of education in Estonia is shared between central and local authorities. After its independence from the Soviet Union about 27 years ago, Estonian became the official language of instruction in Estonia's schools. Though culturally diverse, this Baltic nation's strength lies in the uniformity of school instructions and exams and the fact that the education system is based on equity, giving equal opportunities to students of all backgrounds, despite Estonia's sister nations like Hungary and Czech Republic transitioning to systems that suit the needs of their elites. This trend of uniformity and equity is a holdover from the Soviet era education system, which Estonia intends to keep as it strives to reform its education system.

In addition to equity, education is highly valued in Estonia and this positive response informs its better test scores in international tests like PISA. Autonomy as well as respect for teachers in this tiny country is comparatively high. Teachers of the lower secondary level are required to obtain 5 years' initial teacher training, including mandatory teaching practice and continued professional development. Unexpectedly, teachers' salaries are low compared to the OECD average. Despite this disparity, Estonians value and cherish the teaching profession. Also, Estonian teachers stay with the same pupils and students from grades one to three and sometimes to grade six. This continuity helps develop deep relationships between teachers and students. Early childhood education is free, along with free lunch. Higher education is also free. The students of varying socio-economic statuses are integrated, making it possible for rich and poor students to stay in the same classroom (with the opportunity to know one other), use the same resources and have the same quality teaching staff.

Schools follow a national curriculum and syllabus that dictate what the students must cover every year until the ninth grade. At the end of ninth grade, students decide whether to proceed to upper secondary school for 3 more years to continue academics or to attend vocational schools where they are trained for specific occupations and careers. Those who choose to pursue academics in upper secondary school may pick an area of study, such as mathematics, science, or the humanities based on interest rather than grades and test scores. The idea of education here is to produce students who can do more than score high in class tests and exams but go on to become entrepreneurs, creative leaders and nation builders as well as high order thinkers. Nevertheless, students take certain tests to ensure that they have basic knowledge and skills in all subjects.

Estonian schools still reserve the right to separate students into groups to promote better performance, as long as each group learns the same material. For instance, there could be high, average and low groups of students in a math class based on their performances. They are taught the same materials but at different paces and speed. Teachers try to plan and structure lessons that connect mathematics to real life. Estonia still runs more teacher-centred classrooms to drive the lesson content instead of putting more focus on students as individuals.

Shanghai

An illustriously affluent urban environment and the largest city in the Republic of China, Shanghai has experienced a dramatic improvement in education over the past two decades, causing it to excel above all other nations, occupying the highest PISA ranking in 2010 and again in 2013. Shanghai was one of the first regions in China to achieve almost a universal secondary school attendance. In 1985, Shanghai began a process of educational reform, creating exams that test the application of real-life skills to the extent that educators do not use "multiple choice" questions in exams. The reform included an attempt to step away from the high-pressure exam system but increase the quality of education. The main idea is to encourage student learning rather than simple accumulation of knowledge.

What is the secret to this giant leap in Shanghai's academic progress? Investigations reveal that the city government, administrators and education policymakers adopted an "open door policy" whereby they encouraged educators, scholars and even students to visit other nations around the world, learn from their school systems and bring back their best educational practices. The willingness to study what works elsewhere and adopt it where appropriate has helped boost educational reforms in China as a whole. Even though Shanghai should not be considered representative of the academic experience of most of China's approximately 250 million students, the average Shanghai parent culturally considers the education of their children as a more vital investment than any other.

As is the case throughout China, Shanghai's system of education consists of 3 to 4 years of early childhood education (ages 3-6), 6 years of primary schools (ages 6-12), 3 years of lower secondary school (ages 12-15) and 3 years of upper secondary school (ages 15-18). The first 9 years of school are compulsory for all students. Students take a locally administered senior secondary school entrance examination for upper secondary school. During their 3 years of upper secondary schooling, students take courses in core and elective subjects in preparation for university entrance exams. Vocational schools offer coursework for 2 to 4 years in several occupational areas, including skills for managerial and technical personnel or in agriculture. Across China today, about 95% of students choose to continue their studies after compulsory education ends. This accounts for a significant increase in enrolment from 2005 when only about 40% of lower secondary graduates went to upper secondary schools. Of those who enrol in upper secondary school, about 55% choose academic secondary education and 45%, vocational secondary education (NCEE, 2018).

In China, city schools are believed to have stronger educational resources; students' futures seem to be determined based on whether they were born in the urban areas. Often, students from rural areas have great potential but lag behind in academic performance because they receive lower-quality instruction than is offered in urban areas. In rural areas, especially in the southwestern province of China, students are academic elites if they remain in school long enough to take the PISA exam at the age of 15. Even though research conducted by the Rural Education Action Project at Stanford University estimated that fewer than 30% of the Chinese students in rural areas will make it to high school and only 5 students in 100 will get the opportunity to attend college, other evidence shows that these students can excel academically. Some Chinese organisations are recruiting top American and Chinese college graduates to teach in the country's most disadvantaged schools. Classes are introduced from curricula filled with open-ended problems to stretch critical thinking skills and hands-on experiments that bring the subjects to life.

Nevertheless, when the economy becomes impoverished and manual labour employments dwindle, rural students face uncertain futures. A strong education seems to be their only hope to overcome this pair of events. If China fails to equip these hundreds of millions of its young people with the skills they need to thrive in a global economy, the consequences will stretch far beyond China's borders. Learning from the Chinese experience, one can rightfully declare that Nigeria has far more to gain from collaborating to solve its common problems than competing for higher rankings in education. This is particularly true for China and the U.S., which grapple with huge student populations and a shortage of qualified teachers in the places that need them most.

What seems to make Shanghai great in its education system is not just the emphasis on the quality of teaching but the rigor with which teacher quality is tested both in hiring and professional development. Part of teachers' training is that they must now complete 240 hours of continuing professional development in 5 years. Unlike Finland, Shanghai does not require a prospect to hold a master's degree for teaching qualification, but it does demand a degree in the subject area that a teacher will be committed to, even at the primary school level. Particularly, one would need a science degree to teach science in a primary school. The same applies to mathematics and English language, among others. Shanghai also maintains a rigorous programme of observing teachers in the classroom setting. This type of observation could take place 20 to 30 times a year. Additionally, there is a practice of school partnership to narrow the gap between the best-and worst-performing schools. Under this arrangement, a top-performing school will send a team of teachers and a principal to lead a poor-performing school to improve it. It is also noteworthy that familial and societal pressure to do well academically is embedded in China's long tradition of respect for education.

Nigeria can no longer ignore the lessons from high-performing nations if it aspires to become and remain competitive in the world's education marketplace. Nigeria's status in Africa and the world is being continuously threatened by societies above and below us on every imaginable scale; political, economic, social, educational, or cultural. On the educational scale, countries with high-performing schools, colleges and universities consolidate their advantages, work hard and build on their strengths to improve. Some have made gains that are highly impressive to catch up from low levels of performance. This progress implies that, if things remain as they are now, nations that used to lag behind us in education, will one day outcompete and overtake us. Nigeria must learn from its external educational competitors and muster the resolve to make necessary policy changes to avoid falling further behind.

Commentary and Recommendations

The preceding discussions reveal that various countries' models have their own possibilities and limitations with transferability or exportability. Most of these high-scoring nations are internationally successful because of their abilities to forgo the irrelevant in their education policies and programmes in order to retain the substance of their education curricula, teaching and learning. They are conscious of what is relevant to their needs and goals and what is irrelevant. Based on the above findings, each nation is destined to have an education system that is the product of its unique set of historical, institutional and cultural influences. Each nation also requires an education system that suits its environment and the needs of its own people for national development, even though it may not be transferable to other countries.

According to Okeke (2014), social scientists, politicians and policymakers the world over have been preoccupied with the concept of national development. He further stated that, today, nations draw up development plans to serve as guide in reaching the Eldorado. Nigeria is no exception. In like manner, Nigeria needs to retain or develop a general education structure with curricula and instructional methods that are powerful, unique, need-based and above all, pragmatic. Additionally, the nation's education curriculum should not gloss over local attributes and distinct features of Nigeria as a society.

An in-depth analysis of educational development in both Hong Kong and Macau could show that these Chinese regions have much in common. They are both colonies of European nations but populated mostly by the Chinese. Both have great dependency on trade and commerce. Also, both territories became reintegrated with the People's Republic of China (PRC) by the end of the 20th century. Despite all that both cities have in common, their patterns of education display notable differences. Aside from differences in culture, economic structure, political circumstances, population, territorial sizes and geographical areas, the contrasting colonial histories of both cities have been implicated. While Hong Kong was colonised by the British, Macau was colonised by the Portuguese. How have these major differences impacted their systems and patterns of education especially with curriculum? Can Nigeria learn something strategic from both territories? Overall, what can Nigeria learn from other nations whose education systems were briefly analysed in this section?

Nigeria once had some of the Africa's best educational institutions that produced literature giants, seasoned educationists, celebrated academics, industrialists, illustrious scientists, renowned clergymen, politicians and professionals. Until the early 1980s, the nation had a core curriculum in which the style of teaching remains traditional with a highly scripted type of instruction, as obtainable in Singapore. This curriculum basically retained a certain level of academic rigor and structure, with an elementary school pupil able to recite mathematical, metrics and times tables, punctuate sentences correctly, list major capitals and cities in the world, plus name major rivers, mountains and wonders of the world, among other things. The same curriculum tolerated but did not encourage rote learning without understanding. Instead, it strongly encouraged memorisation but with understanding. In those days and even far back, emphasis was laid on diligence and Nigeria could even be lauded as among the best education systems in the world. It is noteworthy that great Nigerian academics and most renowned public and international figures passed through the mentioned curriculum. This curriculum looked like what can be currently found in Hong Kong. Salvaging and sticking to a similar curriculum at both the primary and secondary school levels would at least and first keep the foundation and framework of the nation's "traditional" education system stable. The foundation of Nigeria's education, teaching and learning, has to remain "old fashioned".

Second, for the sake of order and discipline, people believe that a quiet classroom is a good classroom. This is part of the classroom etiquette that the colonial masters left us. This also applies to countries like Hong Kong, Taiwan, Shanghai, Singapore and South Korea. Nevertheless, Nigeria could do something different that suits collectivist cultures more. For instance, besides encouraging pupils and students to ask questions in class, as has been the Nigerian education system's tradition, primary school pupils and secondary school students (at all levels) could be encouraged to discuss and debate educational issues in class, with the teacher playing the role of moderator and facilitator. Students could also be motivated to discuss academic and educational issues in groups outside classrooms but within the school premises, bringing feedback to the teacher on areas that they find problematic. This could be done as often as possible, preferably either shortly before recreation or before daily school dismissals. This strategy would mimic what happens in the Japanese classrooms over interactive learning or anticipate the same positive outcome and result of good education in Finland.

A new practice today in some of the Nigerian public primary school classrooms is the National Home Growth School Feeding Programme (NHGSFP), which the federal government introduced in 2015. This scheme is one of the four major components of the National Social Investment Programme (NSIP). School children, local farmers and cooks, at least, across 24 states of the federation have benefitted from this programme. It portrays further a desirable expression of Nigeria's communalistic culture in the school setting. It also typifies what is obtainable in the Japanese classroom as discussed earlier. Meanwhile, it is not yet clear what the programme's impact on students' learning, as well as in attracting and retaining them in school might be. Perhaps, the impact is yet to be scientifically studied. About N49bn was reportedly spent on feeding pupils in public primary school in the country (Agbakwuru, 2018).

Third, since the Nigerian educational approach, culture and history have always upheld necessary overlaps between curricula and examinations as well as classroom tests, Nigeria's education curriculum is strongly defined by what is examined or tested. This methodology reflects an effective connection, interplay and overlap between exam questions and the school curriculum, which is mostly exam-driven. Therefore, this type of curriculum often requires extra hard work on the part of the teachers, pupils and students as well as parental support. Sometimes, it takes the usual competition among peers as well as family and parental pressures because of the longstanding belief that a student's future survival and overall social status strongly depend on examination outcomes and academic certificates. Besides this approach, Nigeria could design a basic academic curriculum that encourages effort, student learning and personal achievement rather than mere accumulation of academic knowledge and certificates. This plan would be a type of localised curricular model that interweaves the past, present and future to produce an education system that is more flexible and diverse. It would encourage collaboration instead of competition. Indeed, elements of this prospective, unique and distinct curriculum and integrative education methodology for Nigeria are visible in Japan's, Singapore's, Shanghai's, Finland's and Macau's education systems.

Nevertheless, Nigeria needs to identify the type of curriculum and instructional framework it plans to work towards and give it a name and structure. What is such a framework telling lecturers, teachers and students to do in the classroom and outside of the classroom? Would it improve the quality of teaching practice, instruction and learning? How does one implement such a workable framework? The diverse but unique cultural configurations of Nigeria, the citizens' historical experiences and "essential" unity could produce an exceptionally effective, solid and successful education system that is sustainable over time. Because of the nature of its uniqueness, it may not be quite portable in the sense of being exported to other countries, but it could become durable, recognisable and globally acceptable in the long term.

Chapter Five
Integrating Technology into Curriculum

An Overview

Technology has transformed various human endeavours and organisations. It has changed the ways students are taught and tested in various nations around the world. Digital devices have become commonplace in the academic and education world, with a clamour for educators and teachers to learn to integrate technology into the classroom. The expectation is that technology tools can provide immensely for teaching and learning in the classroom setting, with computers forming the means to attain the goals of instruction.

Computers and digital technologies are here to stay, but how does one judiciously enlist the assistance of their related assets and components? Some of these devices are used in schools, colleges and universities that have computer accessibility and rich connectivity to the internet as in the United States, China, Japan, Britain, Germany, France, Switzerland and South Korea. However, even in those developed nations where the use of these devices is in vogue, limited capacity to transmit data with high speed internet inside schools and institutions of learning surprisingly remains a hurdle. When these nations jump this hurdle and achieve explosions of internet traffic, they still have difficulty sustaining the current traffic in those schools and institutions with internet accessibility.

It is true that gaining access to reliable internet connections can help students and teachers learn and discover new knowledge, skills and ideas beyond the classroom. Nevertheless, in some cases, a sudden, non-traditional, non-foundational and unregulated giant stride in learning approach based solely on technology could eclipse or obscure a people's basic academic heritage in building and laying the foundation of knowledge. In a sense, this leap would mean a major shift from the traditional method of teaching and learning, a familiar process that is now under unexpected pressure.

This monograph is not advocating a re-assemblage of Nigeria's education system with a view to returning to its pre-colonial and crude form. Nonetheless, while the nation does not need to perfectly preserve its core cultural academic system, it does need to reproduce and nurture its essential nature. Much emphasis is on its cultural heritage being largely communitarian; that is, requiring some form of basic human cooperation and interaction in both teaching and learning. Emphasis is also placed on effecting a balance between the use of technology and traditional methods of education in the nation's classrooms. In sum, Nigeria's method of education especially at its basic and foundational stages could become complemented, enhanced, or facilitated by computers without being controlled by them.

In his pastoral letter, *Catholic Education and National Development*, Most Rev. Dr. Valerian M. Okeke observes that technology can be helpful but not in itself. He further affirms that it is the human being who employs it and decides whether the good purpose it is meant for is achieved (Okeke, 2014). This observation is about applying discretion and moderation in the use of modern technologies. People can take personal precautions to avoid overindulging their cravings for computer and digital technologies that their use for teaching and learning does not result in accidentally or potentially grooming children and the young in "mental slavery and laziness".

Though quite innovative and helpful, using computer technologies judiciously, sparingly, or infrequently is the caveat. For instance, the computer could be used sparingly (both for teaching and learning) from the primary level of formal education to the junior secondary school level.

Implications of Digital Education

Education, as an endeavour, presumes some form of action as well as contact that is basically and totally human. In short, it is predicated on activity but a collaborative type of human activity. The nature and level of education acquired by a person is almost always determined by the nature and level of activity performed and the degree of collaborations channelled in that direction. Every human person is gifted with a mind and body destined for activity, yet modern life often seems to push humanity in the opposite direction. To help us reflect better on the implications of this discourse, one can liken education, in the form of teaching and learning, to eating. If Nigeria's traditional education system is comparable to cooking at home, the use of modern digital learning technologies in education would be like eating in a restaurant. To survive, everyone must eat, which is a goal that can be achieved either by cooking at home or ordering food at a restaurant. Both avenues are good, but which one suits us better? Most people eat at restaurants only to supplement cooking at home and only as the need calls for it. Meanwhile, this imperfect analogy should be able to elicit more elaborate analyses from other thinkers.

Unfortunately, most of what we hear about the modern technological education policy reforms sound more like ordering food from restaurants on a regular basis. People need to think deeper. It has been abundantly theorised that contemporary interactive digital learning on laptops and desktops will soon replace traditional teaching and textbooks as well as pen and pencil techniques in learning. For decades now, and in many instances, students have taken tests that are computer-based, while teachers gain online access to educational materials that were previously difficult to come by. To attract many students, boost steady enrolment and better compete with rivals, many educational institutions in Nigeria have introduced the use of computers and digital devices in small formats and some others in larger formats. Some schools, however, have ignored the trend but moved cautiously; perhaps, either because they could not afford the devices or because they were uncertain if Nigeria was ready for a successful initiation of sustainable digital technologies in its education system.

In recent years, some tertiary institutions have haphazardly brought in a few technologically skilled expatriates and "outsiders" to help them kick-start or jumpstart their struggling online computer operations. Schools have sacrificed their textbook funds to heavy expenses on digital learning. But has there been any unambiguous empirical evidence to prove that with digital aids academic performance or levels of learning have been on the rise? Note that the emphasis is on "unambiguous" and implicitly on "basic".

In 2006, Nicholas Negroponte, founder of the MIT media lab, launched the One Laptop per Child (OLPC) initiative to put computers in the hands of the world's poor children, saying: "We will literally take tablets and drop them out of helicopters". Even when cheap laptops were delivered by road to poor-country schools, they did not improve learning levels. In Uruguay, for instance, one million were distributed, but they had no impact on test scores (Technology and Schools, 2018).

The key idea about teaching and learning boils down to basic human educational development and the natural generation of knowledge. People need to exercise caution not to micromanage, circumscribe, or short-circuit what is supposed to be the natural process of knowledge generation.

In 2015, *The Guardian*, a United Kingdom newspaper, reported that many parents working in Silicon Valley were sending their children to a school where there is not a computer in sight. Silicon Valley has in its vicinity the Waldorf School of the Peninsula where Google, Apple and Yahoo employees send their children. However, despite being the digital capital of the world, there is not an iPad, smart phone, or technology screen to be found in its school. In this school, teachers prefer instead to take a more hands-on, experiential approach to learning that contrasts sharply with the rush to fill classrooms with the latest electronic devices. The teaching method emphasises the role of the imagination in learning and takes a holistic approach that integrates the intellectual, practical and creative development of pupils through more traditional methods, which do not incorporate the use of technology. Also, Beverly Amico, a leader of outreach and development at the Association of Waldorf Schools of North America, 136 explains that their approach uses "time-tested truths about how children can learn best". Teachers encourage students to learn curriculum subjects by expressing themselves through artistic activities, such as painting and drawing rather than consuming information downloaded onto a tablet (Jenkin, 2015a).

According to the Organisation for Economic Cooperation and Development (OECD), education systems that have invested heavily in computers have seen "no noticeable improvement" in their results for reading, maths and science in the Programme for International Student Assessment (PISA) tests. Also, the Director of Education (at OECD) Andreas Schieicher had this to say, "If you look at the best-performing education systems, such as those in East Asia, they've been very cautious about using technology in their classroom. Those students who use tablets and computers very often tend to do worse than those who use them moderately" (Jenkin, 2015b).

The cautionary word remains *moderation*, that is, not to overexpose school children and youth to all the obvious marvels of technology. It also recommends the need for the students to actively, creatively and naturally think, operate and independently find information for themselves without necessarily seeking instant information or completely indulging "artificial intelligence" in the form of computer and digital technologies.

In sum, using computers and digital devices in teaching and learning should not be likened to using sewing machines to either sew pieces of clothing or make dresses and garments. It is about the impacts they can have on their users and beneficiaries. In any case, evidence abounds that the Global Positioning Satellite (GPS) technologies and compass devices help drivers, pilots and sailors to get travel directions and reach their destinations. However, do such devices essentially improve one's knowledge of geography or the ability to drive, pilot and sail? Even though technology can enhance and improve teaching and student performance, does it improve, not necessarily, learning per se but the "basis of learning" in school? If so, how reliable will it be in the long term? Additionally, predicting the sustainability of the use of digital devices in a quest to promote education in Nigeria further begs the question on the reliability of the energy and power sector.

Barriers to Technology Integration
Poverty of Power Supply

It should not be overlooked that the ability to operate computers and digital devices greatly depends on having a reliable power supply. For decades now, Nigeria's education system has arguably been as stagnant and epileptic as the nation's power supply. Shortage of power supply in Nigeria in the recent past has almost paralysed the nation's ability to achieve systemic development in various sectors. It will, therefore, not be an overstatement or a digression to suggest that a reliable power source might also go a long way towards exerting positive and substantial influence on any developing nation's education system, especially in this age of the internet and globalisation. Revelations from this tiny piece of analysis constitute merely a tip of the iceberg when compared to the effect a reliable power supply would have on the economic growth and on the entire development of the nation.

Power outages that last up to 10 hours or more per day in the cities and about 14 hours or more per day in rural areas, relatively cripple economic progress and add some level of misery to people's general well-being and quality of life. Finding a lasting solution is a major unresolved problem that faces the Nigerian government. Both the private and public education systems in Nigeria and the country's total progress will automatically be supported as long as the federal government does not shelve its plans to implement a durable and more reliable energy system in the country. Any deviation, in this connection, might spell a major setback even after the government has spent billions, and almost 20 years, in its effort to build a solid energy sector. It would also leave the progress of other sectors with a darker outlook. Any nation with a strong investment in infrastructure, such as electricity, road networks and communications can thrive in any other sectors with relative ease.

Insufficient Computer and Technology Training

One would wonder how much the federal, state and local governments, in liaison with private corporations, NGOs and voluntary agencies are investing in the training of skilled computer technicians, engineers and technologists with a view to supporting this aspect of educational and developmental programmes in Nigeria. How cost-effective and expedient would it be for schools and universities to train teachers and faculties in digital proficiency? What would it cost to place students in internships for computer science, programming and engineering without indulging foreign assistance?

Even though there are few aggressively confident and technologically savvy youths spread across the country, Nigeria, to a greater level, seems to be currently lacking the professional and personal teacher-expertise and training skills needed for computer and digital technologies. Many who have received some training hover around either a low or mediocre level of skilfulness that would be insufficient and, in some cases, unsuitable.

Funding and Financial Challenges

The provision and maintenance of good computers and reliable internet systems to support classroom learning may constitute a huge financial challenge for many Nigerian schools. Nigeria as a country is struggling economically and might find it difficult to adequately fund the procurements and management of efficient computer technologies for both teaching and learning in its public-school system. Can the nation, with its fragile economy, suitably fund and sustain the development of skill with evolving technologies? The same applies to access to the hardware, software, necessary networks and administrative support essential to technologies in the classroom.

Overall, Nigeria apparently lacks the fiscal resources and may not also be quite able to provide the necessary personal and professional technology training. This same insufficiency or lack applies to supporting the infrastructure of technology. Budgeting for all these essential resources could be difficult.

Finding a Balance

To some people, a fixatedly tradition-bound academic system may appear extremely conservative or even defective. Moreover, it may not necessarily seem to offer much hope for growth in a rather competitive international academic marketplace, especially in this pixilated age of the internet and globalisation. Without a doubt, globalisation underscores the changing and evolving needs of students, scholars and educational institutions in a new digital world. Given this situation, struggling to survive or spark growth could become a strong sign that a given institution of learning is likely to steer itself away from tradition as it arduously adjusts to new realities.

Nigeria needs to "slow down" but also steadily and strategically progress in its teaching and learning techniques. This plan might help us to recapture the importance of the nation's academic and educational heritage. Ultimately, achieving success does not necessarily depend on how fast one runs but on how well.

Can we offer advanced curriculum with strong technology integration? Yes, but the Nigerian educational institutions that are not au fait with the integration of technology could gradually introduce it in a smaller format until a reasonable balance is struck without destroying a longstanding, traditional academic system. The following questions need to be asked: Can writing skills, critical thinking, fine arts/drawing, science and mathematical techniques be exclusively or properly learned with only digital technologies? Are students not expected to continue acquiring some of these mentioned skills and techniques through secondary and even into tertiary institutions?

Even though Nigeria's academic system does not have to remain rigidly tradition-bound, it still needs to be tradition-relevant, that is, retaining some basic elements of its heritage in the overall student learning process and teaching techniques: virtue lies in the middle (*virtus in medio stat*). A reasonable blend of the nation's traditional education system and technology will certainly give us an edge over economies that may have totally jettisoned their traditional and inherited education system to embrace an exclusively digitised model. Expansion and consolidation of this type of blended learning could give educational investors a more grounded power to push forward. To cite an example, a uniquely electronic learning or an online education system that is devoid of classroom human contact could be detrimental to Nigeria's psycho-cultural and socio-cultural heritage that is fundamentally both communitarian and communalistic. It could gradually decimate its interactive education culture; thus, it would be almost tantamount to building castles in the air.

The natural and unlimited superiority of interpersonal relationships in the classroom setting would remain. This contention does not signify or suggest a non-workability of the digital system. It is also not an attempt to dissuade, resist, or kick against relevant innovations in a country's educational development. Digital technologies would certainly work in any culture in so far as infrastructure and techniques are in place to support such innovations. Besides, the digital age has a lot of advantages when it comes to research, investigations and verification of ideas, but individuals must exercise some degree of restraint, caution and regulation to preserve the traditional elements that might enrich their lives, their children's lives and those of the future generations. The major caveat here is moderation.

Psycho-Cultural Appropriateness

A further major concern has to do with digital education's psycho-cultural appropriateness, suitability and sustainability in the long term. Every nation's education system ought to be fundamentally culture-friendly. Society will always clamour for the acute need to consolidate the basic elements of its educational foundation and tradition. An exclusively digital learning, if desirable, would probably be more psycho-culturally appropriate to individualist and regimented cultures. The time will come when overindulgence in the modern digital technologies might leave us with primary schools, secondary schools and universities without walls and fields where students can exercise and ones without libraries and science laboratories. Do people really need a future where a careful and curious rummage through students' school bags and lockers would find them without pens, pencils, exercise books and workbooks? The country still desires to run schools and institutions where the students will be able to study the history of Africa in general and Nigeria in particular, basic physics, chemistry, biology and mathematics in the traditional way. Nigerians need schools where children and young people will be able to join dramas, debates, language and other literary societies in schools, run cross country and cohabit in hostels and dormitories with other students. Students need an environment that will keep them at home with the culture, traditions and social lifestyles and where their classmates are drawn from various ethnic, cultural, tribal and religious backgrounds.

Understandably, the core idea of embracing the digital age is partly to switch over to what some education pundits consider more convenient and supplementary. Additionally, some believe that integrating technologies into the classroom can transform education positively and increase student achievement. This move involves a change from teacher-centred to learner-centred education, from absorption through the teacher to navigation by the student; from instruction to discovery, from learning as rigorous to learning as easy and exciting; from the teacher as transmitter to the teacher as a facilitator. Nonetheless, the teacher's role remains essential. At the very least, it takes one to dictate, transmit and teach the knowledge of computer operations to student learners.

Without doubt, education digital technologies can help overcome the challenges of poorly-educated teachers and basic teacher ignorance. For instance, teachers and students can deploy some modern digital systems with their letter-sound tools to help improve their English pronunciations with some degree of accuracy. When judiciously and properly used, they can mitigate the problems of poor learning among the students. However, even though technologies exist that can solve mathematical problems correctly, spell words, compose grammatical sentences in English and even offer a wide range of information through videos, basic reading instructions and drills in grammar and constructions need to be primarily carried out by human teachers. Also, granted that digital technologies can be used by teachers to manage a wide range of classroom abilities, they are still not substitutes or even alternatives for dedicated, motivated and well-qualified teachers.

From a psycho-cultural perspective, any adoption of the educational digital equipment would not be considered substitutionary to the traditional methods of learning but only complementary or supplementary. Education is not necessarily a stereotypically systematic, methodical and static process. It is essentially democratic, objectively elastic and culturally dynamic. Nevertheless, it is indeed a process. Students, therefore, need to get a good and balanced taste of the traditional primary and secondary school experience to be able to live and learn across villages, towns, cities and states in the entire nation. Ideally, Nigerian students would spend enough time in traditional classroom settings while also taking online lectures or completing other digital coursework in schools and at home. No courses should be purely and exclusively computer- based or online.

It is expedient to mention that this author is not advocating a "cultural revolution" or any cultural reformation that can retard an education system, devalue intellectual pursuits, or shrivel up academics. This argument is simply about rebuilding the nation's education system, cognisant of its precious cultural background and traditional educational heritage.

Commentary and Recommendations

No doubt, the components of the digital age are fascinating to many students, young persons, skilled teachers and indeed all those who are now harnessing the great power of the video technology, online animations and the internet to enhance classroom instruction and learning. Building technology infrastructure as well as providing cutting-edge internet connectivity to student learning is significant. It is indeed both innovative and exciting. Being exciting and given the Millennium Development Goals (MDG), digital technologies can be positively deployed to attract many out-of-school children and youth to school. Also, with adequate knowledge, skill and understanding of technology among students, the problem of future unemployment in the digital age would be mitigated, as digital skills remain highly in demand across nations.

Today, there are on-hand and portable devices to help teachers and student learners explore real-world data. Items, information, topics, subject matter and ideas that were previously too complex to relay in the classroom setting are now less tedious and more accessible online. The use of the internet could also help students find informative connections to ideas, topics and issues of relevance. Employing computer and digital technologies in education could become a stimulating, convenient and easy way to bring families, teachers and students together. It could also be an active and inspirational addition to teaching and learning in the classroom.

Certainly, computer technologies and digital devices will shift the way we think about teaching and learning in the classroom. Nevertheless, they should not change the true understanding of teaching and learning in general. Administrators, policymakers, teachers and educators are increasingly transitioning to the digital world. However, a complete and definitive switch to digital devices for teaching and learning in the classroom setting, no matter how promising, may have been ill-advised. No doubt, these devices are the products of a breakthrough innovation. Nonetheless, innovations also bring with them promise and peril, elation and sadness, delight and distress as well as blessings and woes. While computer technologies, in many cases, make teaching and learning easier, people can still make use of digital devices in education without living entirely digital lives.

It is commonplace that overdependence on the Global Positioning Satellite (GPS) devices has deprived many motorists of their natural sense of geography and directions. Also, we have seen people who have enlisted the use of typewriters and computer word processors for over a decade but seem no longer able to write as well as they should with pen and paper or maintain their proper hand-written signatures. The probability that excessive use of digital technologies could deprive a student learner and even teachers of individual learning techniques, strategies and creativity plus intellectual independence is not far-fetched. This type of "fast development", if uncontrolled, might have some untoward effect in the long term, especially on natural reasoning and critical thinking skills, among other defects.

It is not unusual to receive comments on how schools engage the most expensive, newest and fastest technologies in their classroom teaching and learning. But let us not be derailed in considering the students' needs. Policymakers, superintendents, administrators, educators, principals and teachers may have realised that they do not have to throw away the old system completely to embrace the new one; rather, they need to repurpose the old system to accommodate the new one and form its structural basis. For instance, schools can be connected to the internet without losing their teaching staff. Computers can be installed in the classrooms for typing and word processing without discouraging a more consistent use of the pen, pencil and paper in traditional hand writing. This combination is also applicable to the chalk and blackboard method of teaching and instructions. The long-term positive impacts and advantages of this simple, basic and traditional way of teaching and learning cannot be overemphasised. Children and even adolescents need to draw and write. These are learning imperatives. Writing with a pen on a sheet of paper, or on the blackboard with chalk, is quite different from typing script on the computer. The educational, practical, experimental, natural and kinaesthetic difference between the two methods cannot be any clearer.

Chapter Six
Children and Youth Education

One of the most effective ways to influence the mindset or the systems of thought of any nation's populace is to educate its children and youth in schools. The early missionaries and British colonialists utilised this tool effectively. It worked for them and it is still at work today.

Children and young people constitute a huge proportion of Nigeria's population, and are the most precious resource of every culture and society. Every society or culture believes in early childhood and youth education. Fafunwa (1971) suggests that education holds the key to human development. This type of education, for us, begins from kindergarten, which is expected to be content-rich and forward-thinking, a programme that is not only creative, practical and experiential but also cultural and developmentally appropriate.

What does "cultural and developmental appropriateness" of a child's educational life is appropriate. This comes in the form of playing, singing and dancing. Familiarising students with their mean? It means that the country's education system should be directed towards the overall development of every Nigerian child and young person that it structurally engages the minds of the younger generation in a familiar environment. The nation still needs a down- home approach to the education of its children and youth. Beginning with emotional, psychological and social skills training at the earliest stage environments and socio-cultural settings might be quite appropriate to foster analytical and abstract thinking. Children need a developmentally appropriate environment and conditions as they grow to build a solid foundation and progress in the core areas of literacy, mathematics, science, social studies, fine arts and physical education. This growth will also prepare them for a life of independence, responsibility and leadership.

Quickly jumping into academics at the earliest stage of a child's educational life can be patently inappropriate, inadvisable and inherently unreasonable. Ignoring the pen and paper method of learning at the early stage of a child's education in favour of the use of a computer for typing and tiny research engagements might be detrimental to a child's educational upbringing, learning and developmental process. Psychologically, it would be highly inadvisable since there are times and stages for most learning. How would such a child sufficiently develop literacy in the form of reading, writing and mathematical skills without a human coach, at least for a start? Could it be done by early initiation into the use of computers, video games and other modern electronic gadgets for learning? Certainly, it would be undesirable to produce huge swaths of next-generation Nigerian students who cannot read a bound book, write with pen or pencil, or calculate simple mathematical numbers coupled with having too low expectations in their own lives amidst an avalanche of digital educational gadgets.

Research conducted on students in the early stages of their academic adjustment, following migration from their countries of birth to a different country of sojourn, has demonstrated that certain psycho-cultural factors, essentially, influenced their school progress, especially in math and reading (Quatroche, 2000). This study found that with increased interest in preventing reading problems among school children, certain psycho-cultural variables, such as ethnic differences, early age reading, language literacy, home environment and mathematics achievement have been noted in an expanding literature that often points to the role of these factors influencing their adaptation to school (Anemelu, 2012, p.34).

People seem to have globally misconstrued mental and intellectual growth of children and youth, especially in the education and learning sector. Some people have argued that restricting children or leaving them unexposed to the use of computers and modern education gadgets will leave them almost developmentally disabled by the time they reach kindergarten, thereby making it impossible for them to compete with their counterparts overseas. How would one analyse this suggestion based on one's own opinion and experience? People often nurture some intellectual misconceptions and even unfounded fears when it comes to educating children and young people in general, forgetting that "the young shall grow". With these mindsets, they sometimes abdicate their relevant educational responsibilities or fail to confront and address problems in the right way. What are those fears associated with educating children? What are the common misconceptions about the human learning process? What are people particularly concerned about? Some parents and guardians entertain the fear that children and young people, who do not experience very early exposure to computer-aided forms of learning and education or any modern gadget-assisted learning, rarely match the academic performance of their peers. Can educators help children and the youth to learn according to their own unique natural patterns, capabilities, mental paces and healthy-intellectual dispositions? How do teachers better strengthen each child and adolescent's learning process?

Unquestionably, a wonderful child or young person who could be considered close to a genius in the Nigerian school setting, for instance, might be surprisingly and even wrongfully suspected to have learning disabilities in some foreign countries, especially when placed under certain learning assessment standards. Theoretically, such an apparent inaccuracy in judgement may result from basic psycho-cultural or socio-cultural differences that are either difficult to perceive or simply misunderstood by those foreign educators. Realistically, the perceived deficit could be a result of his/her customised level of social skills, emotional-psychological disposition and word-pronunciation adaptation or difficulty. Also, his/her limited participation in class overseas, a slow but natural pace in learning and perhaps the need for extra time on standardised tests, essentially, could have added to the unwelcome discovery. Such a child or youth could even be teaching other children in Nigeria how to solve mathematical problems and read literature, although without a computer and other modern learning gadgets that would allow him/her to be better understood by the teacher or peers in a foreign land and who probably frown at his/her learning methodology as vexatious. Alternatively, this questionable and deficient type of judgement from foreign educators might consider such a child to be mired in the 18th century method of education and learning.

Of course, there are differing learning methods and needs among students. There are also special strengths, dispositions, aptitudes, abilities and talents that need to be naturally nurtured, not artificially powered. The assessment of learning tools at various institutions seems often structured and organised under the presumption that a huge majority of students, irrespective of their backgrounds, are at widely similar developmental stages and learning methodologies. In detail, the learning needs of people from developing nations, for instance, could be generally inferred from the background and group to which they belong, with other factors put into consideration, gender, age, environment and nationality, among others. However, it must be acknowledged that even "geniuses" can have learning disabilities, depending on the yardstick that is employed to measure their performance. Most of the time, such assessments identify the learning needs of a child and after the assessments, the parents are contacted to develop a plan that, based on their own standards, might include provisions and accommodations to help the child do better. One would expect that such children and indeed everyone, could be better assessed by asking them to do some assignments and then evaluating the result based on its value, productivity, usefulness and helpfulness to both the student (child, youth, or adult) and the organisation or society writ large. Education should not be simply about a student's learning pace or performance in tests and examinations. It is more about preparing for life careers and good life choices. How many people clearly remember the statistics and scientific methods that they learnt in school many years back?

Education is about learning needs and the ability to use those materials, time, treasures and talents later in life for the common good. Expectations should not be about imposing artificial ceilings on students' learning without giving them the chance to achieve their true potential in the process. What basic education (both at home and in school) will make the children and young people realise their potential and flourish? True education and learning methods are meant to naturally challenge and stretch each student mentally and intellectually.

Quality assessment is ardently required, not necessarily quantity assessment, especially these days when schools and institutions are increasingly accountable in delivering results. It is not about achieving 5-year level expectations in 1 year with both artificial and minimal human efforts. Education and learning for everyone, at least, ought to be built on a solid and natural foundation.

A psychotherapist in the United States, given her experiences and years of practice, though with some peculiar cultural underpinnings, made the following observations:

What was missing… and apparently from parents' awareness, is that regular eye contacts and talking to and listening to others talk is part of how a child's brain develops. We develop in relation to other humans, not electronics. Playing blocks, water, sand and dolls develop gross and fine motor skills. Playing games, even without toys (such as hide and seek as well as pretend play), involves movement that develops our kinaesthetic skills, our sense of our bodies in physical space. Pretend play allows children to fantasise about and act out, interpersonal relations. Hoping to win at games and tolerating suspense and loss develop emotional regulation and a sense of mastery. Playing is a child's job and it is essential for development (Edelman, 2013).

What is Nigeria's priority in the overall education of its children and adolescents? Would a lightning-speed education style for children help them much later in life, going by the nation's cultural ethos? Does this have any empirical support? Even if it has, is early exposure of children to computers, digital gizmos and high- speed internet one of the best long-term provisions people can make to help them and the country? It is this author's contention that administrative tendencies and willingness to carry on with models that have a track record of success as well as expand workable traditional practices should be strongly encouraged in the country's entire education system. Schools and tertiary institutions should feel comfortable building on previous successes, whether colonial, pre-colonial or post-colonial. It is simply about pulling together the best practices without diminishing Nigeria's traditional education heritage. Retaining basic local customs on teaching and learning as far as possible and giving the same a certain degree of discretional digital enhancement would be appropriate, as whoever attempts to climb to the highest places rises by steps and degrees, not by leaps and flights.

The nation's children and youth need basic and appropriate human support, practical guidance and direction as they grow up. In teaching and learning, there are always practical, social, cultural, emotional, developmental and psychological benefits from having personal interactions and experiences with other students and teachers in the classroom setting. It is imperative that literate parents devote more time to teaching their children and preparing them for future life, career and the world as they grow. In teaching and learning, children and young people in general need some first-hand and applied experience to grow in knowledge, an experience to motivate and stimulate their interest for further education and encourage its application to the real world. They need hands-on learning and activities in and out of school that will impact their interactive and observational skills as well as improve their personal and social development.

School Climate and Culture

An assessment of schools and students may surprisingly reveal that some, if not many students, could be under enormous psychological stress within the school premises and in the classrooms. How do people know this? What is the percentage of those students? Often, students in some parts of the country or even in general do not reveal these difficulties for fear of imagined reprisals or repercussions. However, they might be willing to reveal such difficulties when strictly anonymous surveys are conducted, using them as participants.

Apparently, there is that continuous pressure among students to succeed and establish good relationships with administrators, educators, teachers, staff and fellow students. The same applies to their aspirations to get good marks (scores or grades) coupled with casual discussions about taking exams and possible comments regarding unfavourable, threatening and unhealthy school climates. For some students, these issues could be difficult and unsettling, and such could prove toxic to their psychological well-being. Of course, pupils and students need to be better prepared, but Nigeria can also achieve high academic standards in its schools and tertiary institutions without tremendous stress and anxiety.

In school and college environments, levels of stress, anxiety and depression tend to increase if not properly and quickly addressed. What is the goal of education, if not for the well-being of everyone involved, especially the students? In fact, it can be considered an unmitigated educational tragedy if any school or institution of learning is not able to make a total commitment to the entire well-being of its pupils and students. Education, care and compassion are integral to the pupils and students' learning process. The principles of psychology, social work and social care uphold that basic human care with compassion does not stop at home. Irrespective of their families of origin, cultural backgrounds, religious affiliations, ages, or genders, all students deserve emotional and social support in the process of education and learning. Being cared for, both at home and in school, even when it is difficult to do so, is key to unlocking each student's potential.

No doubt, institutional or campus climate is crucial to students' engagement in schools and universities. An unfavourable school climate can make school lessons and subjects uninteresting to certain groups of students. Thus, Nigerians should not necessarily bask in the long duration of classes or school hours for students' engagement and success; rather, they should think about how welcoming, relevant and less difficult a school can become for the students daily. Well-meaning schools and institutions of learning want their students to be disciplined and well-behaved but also to feel comfortable and happy during their stay in school and ultimately able to become successful in life. Schools can play a better role by getting the students to buy into the learning process. It is crucial to conduct experiments and consult opinions to find out what the children's lives, needs and feelings in schools are like and try to respond appropriately. Schools should also be equipped to cater for students who are in unusual situations, such as those with minor health or mental problems, especially those who would otherwise miss classes for treatments at home or in the close-to-home dispensaries.

Building a successful educational institution requires a collaborative effort by all parties. The entire school or college community needs to offer its support. Given the nation's cultural background, it may seem outlandish or even preposterous to some if this project recommends that Nigerian schools consider employing trained security agents, doctors, nurses, disciplinarians, psychologists, counsellors and social workers. More importantly, this strategy might reduce the need to deploy teachers for non-teaching tasks in primary, secondary schools and even in tertiary institutions. It could also boost students' enrolments in schools and other institutions of learning.

Arguably, schools and even tertiary institutions are not primarily designed to deal with certain socio-cultural, psycho-social and psycho-cultural issues among students. The help of experts, culturally oriented volunteers and trained professionals, nevertheless, needs to be enlisted in reaching out to pupils and students. There should be no confusion about conflicts or differences here, especially in this generation, where so much has changed in the global environment. Taking these steps would even boost employment in Nigeria's entire education system, as expanding services could lead to employing more workers in an educational institution or starting novel programmes. These measures will carry some costs but should be considered worthwhile, nonetheless.

People naturally get involved when they discover that a policy or programme works. Therefore, every government, ministry, school district, politician, educator and teacher should constantly be looking for the best ways to help pupils and students. This effort is basically about creating a supportive and caring school environment. Many pupils and students need help to maintain mental stability, healthcare and environmental security to thrive academically.

Dropouts, Absenteeism and Truancy

There is a wide range of reasons why children and the youth are either out of school or remain formally uneducated. Those reasons include cultural difficulties, academic challenges, social factors, poverty, economic hardships, financial constraints, child labour, early marriages, social misconducts and disabilities. Others include, but are not limited to poor infrastructure, dilapidated buildings and lack of facilities, or lack of water, light, toilet facilities and study desks in schools.

On poor toilet facilities, for instance: Could you imagine what the situation might be in a school where the only "restroom" is one toilet for as many as 300 children? Why would you not expect dropouts among those children, either for health reasons or simply at the bidding of their parents? A few more reasons include the brutal presence of untrained and unfriendly administrators and teachers and, in some cases, early marriage for girls. Data show that two-thirds of children in the poorest households in Nigeria are not in school and almost 90% of them will probably never enrol. In contrast, only 5% of the richest children are out of school and most of those are expected to attend in the future (Global Education Magazine, 2017). In most of these instances, there have not been any official inquiries or interventions either from the Ministries of Education, district superintendents, schools, or even parents. Moreover, the federal and state governments do not appear to have any organised systems, programmes or financial resources to follow up on the children and youth who drop out of school.

Absenteeism and truancy constitute two distinct patterns among children and youths, signalling that they may be starting to pull away from school if left unchecked. Research at Johns Hopkins University in the United States has shown that the chronic absence of students in schools is a strong predictor of who will eventually drop out of school, since this pattern begins early. The United Nations International Children's Emergency Fund (UNICEF Reports, 2011) stated in a report that even though more children then entered school, there had been little progress in reducing dropout rates. About 137 million children began primary school in 2011, but at least 34 million were likely to drop out before reaching the last grade; this translates into an early school leaving rate of 25%, the same level as in the year 2000. According to the same agency's report, in 2014, despite major progress over the past decade, sub-Saharan Africa was still home to more than half of all the out-of-school children of primary school age in the world. Moreover, millions who are in school are learning little.

On the Day of the African Child, June 16, 2014, UNICEF and the UNESCO Institute for Statistics released reports saying that over 30 million children of primary school age in sub-Saharan Africa remained out of school, with more than two-thirds of them in West and Central Africa (UNESCO and UNICEF Reports, 2014).

Another study in Nigeria, partly supported by the preceding UNESCO report, estimates that, on average, approximately one out of every five Nigerian children is out of school or perennially absent from class. Additionally, about 4 out of 23 of the nation's secondary school students were continually absent in class. Expectedly, dropout rates should differ across states in Nigeria. However, nationwide, both recognised and unrecognised absenteeism and truancy of pupils and students constitute a problem to the education system's development. This unfavourable situation, which has almost always been overlooked or insufficiently addressed, is more applicable to class attendance and school retention. Absenteeism, truancy and school dropouts should not be misconstrued as primary or secondary school non-attendance.

A survey was conducted in 2003 among young people aged 16 and 17 years old in sub-Saharan Africa (SSA), with the assumption that by this age bracket children should have completed primary education. Nigeria was among the nations that had a large proportion of children who never attended primary schools. This research accounted for 21.84% of the surveyed population, while the proportion of average children still in primary school accounted for 13.15%. The good news is that those who dropped out without primary school accounted for only 3.19% and as high as 83.66% achieved completion. Remarkably, the difference in the dropout rates across gender and socio-economic status (SES) was statistically significant: (Gender: Boys, 1.6%; Girls, 5.0% Wealth/SES: Richest, 0.7%; Poorest, 6.4%). Nonetheless, difference in locale (rural or urban) was not found to be statistically significant. Those in urban areas accounted for 3.2% of school dropouts, while those in rural areas accounted for 3.1% (Sabates et. al., 2010).

Undoubtedly, the early absences that lead to dropouts could leave the children and young people lagging behind in basic classwork, such as English language, mathematics, physics, chemistry, biology and social studies. Even though experts might caution against reading too much into absenteeism and truancy, research analyses have found a strong correlation between higher test scores and students' school attendance and punctuality (Enamiroro, 2010; Cassell, 2007). This class of delinquent students and children, if not properly and speedily managed or counselled, might wind up as juvenile social miscreants. Schools and other institutions of learning should, therefore, be encouraged to periodically conduct surveys to figure out the reasons for students' truancy in schools and how best to address this problem in time to change student patterns of attendance.

Monitoring and Boosting Attendance

Strong policies, mechanisms and strategies could be put in place to improve school retention as well as diminish the rate of dropouts. In being designed and implemented, these should receive sufficient attention from the Ministry of Education.

Principals and teachers need to look at their attendance data on a regular basis to determine who is not coming to school and why.

Evidently, some students absent themselves from school because of an unfriendly school climate. Some are reportedly kept home from school because of health problems. Some students keep away from school because of "abusive" or illiterate parents who use that as a disciplinary measure. Some stay away because of learning difficulties. Some keep away from school because of psychological or physical abuses from bullying teachers and students. Some keep away for fear of being punished (corporal punishment) when they arrive late. Understandably, to help improve personal development and discipline in schools, the use of corporal punishment is traditionally encouraged in Nigeria, though with restrictions. Moreover, in some rural areas, it is possible that students stay home because they are afraid to travel on a particularly dreadful road or street to avoid being kidnapped for ransom or ritual. In these instances, the school community or the government can help such students or correct what hazards urgently need correction.

Notably, one of the issues missing from this discourse is parenting. Lack of responsible parenting could make it nearly impossible for the teachers to teach. Schools cannot succeed if parents are failing. Children need support, sleep, nutrition, guidance, discipline and direction. If these components are missing at home, then schools will continue to wage an uphill battle. If children are not loved, nurtured, well-treated and nourished, encouraged to go to school and taught to treat others with respect, the teachers will continue to be faced with a difficult and daunting task.

The failure of the education system is a broad, societal one and it starts at home and in schools. Owing to illiteracy, poverty and, of recent, insecurity, among other causes, many Nigerian parents are not able to provide the direction, guidance, stability, role modelling and resources that used to be obtainable in a standard and functional family. Societal opinions and culture today for Nigeria's children and youth are partly driven by unethical values that emanate from poor family upbringing, over-pampering, low self-esteem and some inappropriate modern social media exposures. This complex scenario has become a great disservice to children and the society at large. Thinking about the children who must be brought up this way is cause for wailing. It is time society made poor parental care an unacceptable practice.

To increase attendance successfully, schools need to engage school administrators, their communities, parents and the students themselves. Particularly, a quiet, powerful and relevant campaign in a city or rural area by school liaison officers (or teachers) could engage an entire village, communities and voluntary agencies like the churches or mosques and other relevant faith-based groups. Schools could design programmes that deploy early warning sign sessions (either weekly or bi-weekly) to discuss an entire school's absenteeism-prevention efforts. These programmes would target chronically absentee students and develop fine-tuned support from parents, teachers and school administrators. High-performing independent and private schools and affluent communities could organise social services and employ counsellors to perform this type of task that is often overlooked. At this juncture, it can be opined that students who have strong family support and good counsellors or mentors are more likely to remain in school than those who do not.

Incentives and Rewards

Gifts and rewards could also be publicly given to those students who never absent themselves from school. The same applies to their families. School attendance could easily be improved by curbing absenteeism, especially when schools and communities see it as a shared responsibility. Things can be easily turned around by simply looking at the class-attendance data and promoting a culture that celebrates coming to school and being in class.

Students must develop a strong sense of belonging and they also need an exciting and non-stressful learning environment free from any physical, verbal, or psychological molestation, bullying, victimisation, or teasing for them to transform individually and progress in their studies. Finally, helping families to send their children to school would be tremendously beneficial. Incentive rewards are also recommended and could be given annually to encourage families that send their children to school, especially in those areas of the country where there are huge populations of out-of- school children. These rewards may or may not be monetary depending on the needs of the beneficiary families and their immediate environments.

Excursions and Field Trips

Schools and homes are not the only places where children and young people learn. They could easily find staying at home or being in school for studies all the time to be boring. Giving some time to out-of-campus experiences could be quite rewarding to pupils and students educationally. Therefore, excursions and field trips should not be viewed as mere extracurricular activities to be either side-tracked or cut out. Like every one of us, children and young persons like to learn about things new and perhaps different from their present environment. Extramural and exceptional learning tends to fire up children and young people to learn even more in the classroom setting. Because learning is an interactive and lifelong process of questions and answers, discussions, discoveries and finding meaning, students are excited to learn beyond the school walls. How is a genius formed outside the integration of knowledge, experience and skills? Elements that are usually found in excursions are illustrated in the figure below:

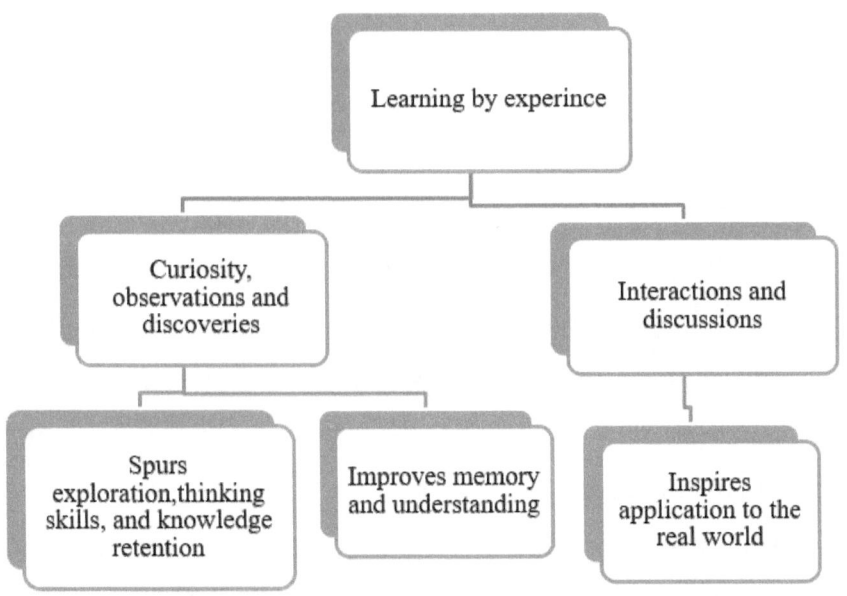

Figure 3. Elements and Benefits of excursions for students

Occasionally, children and young people like to get away from their schoolbags, notebooks, blackboards, pens, pencils and crayons to learn in a different environment. Indeed, educators can rebrand excursions and field trips as "classrooms without walls" in this context. When children and young people travel away from their homes and schools, they learn more about the world, other cultural ideas, special events, different people and new things, like how food or fabrics are prepared and tools or digital items are produced and used. These tours, field trips and experiences can broaden their intellectual horizons plus sharpen their memories and knowledge of nature, social diversity, real-world problems, cultures, customs and traditions as they resume their studies in geography, history and social studies. Such travels and field trips spur curiosity, explorations and discussions as well as help improve their critical thinking skills and knowledge retention and open doors to new and exciting lessons.

Excursions, incursions and minor pilgrimages can be introduced to the children and young students in Nigeria, if these outings are not already in practice. When carefully planned, excursions and field trips can motivate students towards active learning experiences. They can become a part of a school's or an institution's yearly educational programme to expand and enrich its curriculum. The sites of these excursions can be either local or beyond local, as long as they are out of school or off-campus.

Children and youths should be encouraged to pay visits to special places like museums, radio and television stations, police quarters, army barracks and cantonments, airports, zoos, hospitals, bakeries, soccer tournaments, engineering and mechanical facilities and fire control departments, as they grow intellectually. Many experienced teachers and educators have indicated that excursions are key components of classroom teaching because they widen students' educational experiences and make subjects more relevant. For instance, taking children and young people to a bakery where they can see bread being baked could illustrate practical applications of mathematics, statistics and even food and nutrition in general. In some cases, students get a sense of industry and even commerce for their futures in business. Taking students to a soccer tournament could help them to improve their soccer skills as well as teaching them the importance of teamwork in any successful organisation or enterprise, including group studies. Taking them to museums and cultural and historical sites might also remind them of history and even help them greatly in future leadership. Pilgrimages to holy sites when possible, appropriate and permissible and other minor pilgrimages could help students learn more about their faith, religion and ancestry in the concept of history and religion. It will also help them to learn more about their own and other religious and spiritual concepts. Visiting radio and TV stations and airports might ignite their curiosity about science, engineering and technology. It might even go a long way in getting them easily plugged into thinking about the modern world of science and technology and positively impact their future studies in tertiary institutions. Taking pupils and young students to universities and campuses where good graduate students act as their tour guides might initiate them into dreaming about higher education and becoming architects, medical doctors, engineers, lawyers, scientists, among other professions. When taken to the airport, students might begin to think about becoming pilots and even aeronautical and civil engineers in their future careers.

Overall, besides educating children and young people in the classroom settings, educators should also endeavour to see excursions and field trips as teaching and learning by experiences. During excursions and field trips, students feel, sense, smell, see, hear, taste, and even touch the real world around them. This type of learning is active, applied and engaging. Everyone knows that pupils and young students are capable of reciting and remembering things, but they do not always make connections or create links between learning materials and real life unless they have first-hand experience of them. In learning, there is always the need to connect dots to make understanding and knowledge more "real" and retention easier. In choosing excursions and field trips, visiting areas related to the content and subject areas of the students' studies is always highly recommended.

Chapter Seven
Infrastructural Investments and Education

Besides the quality of any nation's education system, order, stability and good learning environments can have positive impacts on its general progress. This observation means that a deep investment in the quality of Nigeria's public-school facilities and investment could boost teaching and learning and even students' academic achievement. Naturally, human beings need order, stability; safe and supportive environments in their lives. Also, students need comfortable classrooms and libraries to study well. Schools, universities and other institutions of learning would thrive better with well-designed buildings, decently equipped classrooms, libraries, laboratories and extracurricular equipment. Several studies have indicated that investments in quality educational infrastructure have huge positive impacts on student attendance, achievement, retention and learning outcomes as well as on teachers' motivation. Those studies found correlations between school infrastructure and improved educational performance across nations and schools in Asia, Latin America and the United States (Hanushek, 1995; Velez, Schefelbein & Venezuela, 1993). Coordinated and strategic decisions, therefore, must be made about education infrastructural investments to create a stimulating learning environment. These decisions should be taken seriously and given paramount importance.

Similarly, studies have found that wider access to clean water and school sanitation tends to increase student attendance rates, particularly for girls and children's ability to learn. In Bangladesh, for instance, the attendance rates for girls in school went up by 15% following improved access to clean water and sanitation. The sanitary and hygienic conditions of many schools in Nigeria today remain deplorable, with insufficient water supplies and poor hand-washing facilities. Such schools tend to have higher incidences of both children and young people's illnesses among the students' population. This type of situation could also increase student dropout rates.

There is no doubt that students who attend poorly equipped schools and tertiary institutions in marginalised and impoverished areas of Nigeria are doubly disadvantaged. What percentage of rural secondary schools in the country are missing science laboratories and indoor toilets or have dilapidated walls, leaky roofs, broken windows and overcrowded classroom spaces? Even some of the public education infrastructure that exist in urban areas are either poorly maintained or needs upgrading or full replacement. Even though infrastructure does not necessarily guarantee the quality of education, renovating or rebuilding dilapidated school structures is always beneficial and appreciated. It is critical that the government and education policymakers assess and prioritise education infrastructural investment across the 36 states in the federation.

Public Infrastructure

In a broader perspective, there is an overwhelming consensus among Nigerians that the government should be doing more to improve the well-being of the citizenry through the provision and maintenance of good infrastructure. Public infrastructural facilities are among the major prerequisites of constructive nation building as well as for the establishment of order and stability in peoples' lives. Basic investments in good road networks, security, electricity, communication and health centres are the responsibilities of every government. Good roads and security infrastructure constitute some of the most effective tools in alleviating poverty for any nation. Similarly, improved road connectivity programmes and security systems can have an immensely positive impact on both the economy and education. These two infrastructural elements will receive special attention in this section for deep-rooted cultural reasons. Arguably, their economic benefits, in the short term, may not be immediately verified or quantified, but the positive impact will be discernible and exponentially monumental overtime.

Nigeria needs to build more and consolidate public infrastructure quickly. The same is true for improving and maintaining the existing infrastructure. The highlight in this section is that investments in projects outside the education sector would, directly or indirectly, have tremendous impact on education in general and schooling decisions in particular. The country's aim should be to boost corporate key investments in roads, transportation, electricity, healthcare and security infrastructure.

Roads and Transportation

Previous research and a large body of evidence have shown that well-developed and safer road networks with better transportation systems, especially in rural areas, help to raise school attendance. As a case in point, in the Philippines, following the construction of rural roads, school enrolment and registrations went up by 10% and dropout rates fell by 55%. A similar road project in Morocco raised girls' enrolment from 28% to 68% in less than 10 years. Also, part of the reason for this growth was improved sanitation and clean water facilities. Since travel from rural to urban areas was made easier by better roads, the quality of education and learning also improved a great deal because of accessibility to schools and easy hiring and retention of teachers (Khandker, Lavy & Filmer, 1994). Good roads and transportation systems are indispensable because any country that is not on wheels seldom prospers in all aspects of its development.

According to an updated report from the India Brand Equity Foundation (IBEF), as at April 2018, there were 1,529 Public Private Partnership (PPP) projects in India, of which 740 were related to roads. At 5.4 million kilometres, India has the second largest road network across the world, a network that transports more than 60% of all goods in the country and 85% of its total passenger traffic. India's road transportation has gradually increased over the years with the improvement in linkages between cities, towns and villages (India Brand Equity Foundation, 2018).

Good roads have helped farmers not only in India but also in many other countries to convey their goods to markets, giving them better access to higher wage employment opportunities in the rural non-farming sectors and increased consumer's access to food markets. Investment in public infrastructure in general (roads, electricity and communications) have also reduced poverty by enhancing agricultural productivity growth, thus increasing farm incomes and expanding the non-agricultural sector. Improved infrastructure also decreased regional inequality. Villagers in India who lack access to durable road infrastructure are often characterised by greater poverty and lower educational attainment. Therefore, the Indian government's expenditure on road construction contributed more to poverty reduction than did its other investments.

A research effort by Ghosh (2017) that evaluated rural infrastructural facilities in 16 major states of India and their impacts on some income and non-income dimensions of rural development shows that varied types of rural public investments have a great deal of payoff: improved physical and social infrastructure and livelihood opportunities that boost agricultural productivity and output, improve literacy, quality of life and life expectancy, plus reducing poverty and infant mortality. Overall, the results show that the government should prioritise investments in electricity, roads, irrigation, housing and telecommunications to enhance national well-being (Ghosh, 2017).

A similar study examining the impact of a flagship rural road and transportation programme in India between 2001 and 2015 revealed large positive effects on adolescent school enrolment and performance. The same correlation applies to educational choices and accessibility. In the Prime Minister's Road Construction Programme (known in Hindi as the *Pradhan Mantri Gram Sadak Yojana*: PMGSY), the government built high-quality roads in over 115,000 villages across India, connecting over 30 million households to nearby towns. The period studied (2001-2015) was a time of substantial educational reform in India. Notably, a statistically significant estimate shows that the new roads led to a 7% increase in middle- school enrolment between 2003 and 2015 (Adukia et al., 2018). Roads played the most significant role in the non-agricultural economy's contribution to GDP growth and generated the second largest investment return for the rural Indian economy. This and similar trends in India might help illuminate what happens to any nation's education system when poverty is either reduced or eliminated through public investments in roads, transportation, healthcare, electricity and security.

A variety of other research also found that many of education issues are addressed with maximum impacts by the presence of good roads; poorer roads, by contrast, affect all areas of a country's development. In developing countries, education is identified as the dominant reason for non-economic travel purposes. Difficulty and distance in travelling to both primary and secondary schools have been implicated as impediments to school attendance. In Morocco, the presence of tarred roads in a rural community more than doubled the attendance rate of both girls (from 21% to 48%) and boys (from 58% to 76%). The absence of roads was considered responsible for low primary and secondary school enrolment in Ghana. In a similar note, research findings in Lesotho and Vietnam indicated growth in the secondary and tertiary school education enrolment where investment in road construction and transportation existed. The presence of paved or tarred roads raised the quality of life offered by areas with better access to healthcare and business services, improved the ability of teachers and students to get to schools, reduced travel times, resolved the problem of quality teacher recruitment, reduced teacher and student absenteeism and increased investment in school staffing (Lebo & Schelling, 2001; Van de Walle, 2002; Fuglestvedt et al, 2007; Schweikert, & Chinowsky, 2013).

Construction and maintenance of major road networks as well as those connecting rural to urban areas will enable the citizenry to function more effectively and increase commitments in their various areas of responsibility. Good road infrastructure can make new opportunities accessible. Additionally, adequate supervision and routine maintenance of solid roads in Nigeria should be able to save us from deficits in funding expensive improvements and emergency roadwork. Good road networks will increase access to any nation's existing education system and facilities, which can be very helpful to its general progress and well-being. As a result, productivity in education standards is increased and a better appreciation of a nation's education programmes is created.

Furthermore, with good road connections, more efficient and qualified education administrators, teachers and staff are attracted to work in both rural and urban areas. Good roads and transportation can make it possible for school districts and affiliated schools to share educational materials and resources with other districts. Given Nigeria's ever-struggling economy and often capricious education system, such an investment should make it easier for every school to own modern science laboratories and library materials. As a result, any governmentally mandated inter-school loaning and exchange of such materials for academic, scientific and technological advancement could be facilitated with the availability of good roads and a reliable transportation system. Mobile science and technology laboratories as well as library resources could be readily made available to institutions that need them.

Myriads of indicators measure the impact of good road construction schemes not only on economic recovery, security and health but also on the provision of improved education services. Villages linked by convenient roads, for instance, can enable otherwise illiterate and isolated villagers to have better access to educational institutions through private and public transportation. In a research conducted on the impact of Road Construction on rural labour force outcomes in the Republic of Palau, Akee (2006b) observes that well-designed, durable roads can greatly improve the conditions of rural populations. Households responded quickly to the new employment opportunities once the new roads were operational and experienced an increase in wage sector employment; there was also a decrease in the number of international emigrants from Palau. With a citation from the World Bank Document the author suggests that, in developing countries, infrastructure represents "if not the 'engine' then the 'wheels' of economic activity" (Akee, 2006b; World Bank, 1994, p.14).

During the colonial period, major road construction programmes were mostly focused on areas closely associated with the exportation of crops, local goods, oil and other natural resources. In 1977, many places in Nigeria that remained remote from paved roads saw the commencement of a massive all-season road construction programme focused on inter-urban connections. Between 1976 and 1982, there was an estimated doubling of the number of vehicles imported into the country. The two mutually reinforcing elements of road construction and rapidly increasing vehicle ownership contributed both to major urban expansion and rural organisation.

Today, even in the remote parts of Nigeria, the impact of improved access to both rural and suburban areas is almost always notable within days of the arrival, setup and completion of tarred roads by road construction companies. People, agencies and communities quickly build residential houses, schools, hospitals and stores and many relocate for business and education purposes. This type of road-infrastructure development leads to an increased connectivity with both the outside market and the outside world. It is not surprising that road construction is often seen as the harbinger of positive change in regional economies (Porter, 2012).

Students can travel from far places and cities for the sole purpose of education. The development of road transportation infrastructure and services should, therefore, be a major part of a long-term internal development of Nigeria across sectors, with education always given a very important place.

Security Infrastructure

Along with road infrastructure is a necessary investment in reliable security. Naturally and culturally, insecurity does not generate peace and prosperity in any form. Rather, it generates poverty, a poor economy and consequently a poor system of education. Internally, security in Nigeria has seemed more elusive from 2007 to the present-day. Previously, Nigeria as a country had fewer insecurity problems in the forms of armed robbery, isolated cases of kidnapping, rare communal skirmishers and ethnic and religious clashes. Recently, however, insecurity has taken different dimensions; the Boko Haram insurgency and terrorism in the north and kidnappings for ransom, ritual killings and militancy in the south have become rampant. The same increase applies to the incessant but avoidable killings across the country resulting primarily from clashes between armed herdsmen and local farmers and the herdsmen's killings of other helpless Nigerian citizens. Such a level of insecurity, if left unaddressed, could snowball into more serious a national crisis that will undoubtedly cripple education in Nigeria, among other sectors.

Investment in security infrastructure will help to provide order and stability in people's lives and have a strong impact on education.

Embroidered into the progressive education system of any known nation is an environment where the security of lives and property is assured to a decent degree. Nigerians (and Nigeria as a country) will excel in all aspects of nation building and general progress in an environment where security is up and running.

A thorough review of the non-viability of the present security situation in the country must be seriously considered, as the perceived and actual fragility of its symbols perennially stares people in the face. Any nation's education will plummet swiftly if its education policymakers, leaders and administrators are constantly exposed to peril. The same is applicable to educational facilities and the overall student population. The streets in the states, major cities and rural areas where people constantly feel insecure by night and day do not represent an environment that spells progress. According to Condoleezza Rice, the former United States Secretary of State, "the quality education of a nation is a direct function of a country's national security" (Ejirika, 2014). Where crime rates and violence have risen to historic highs with rampant and routinely ignored street crimes, any nation will have a feeble education system for various common-sense reasons. Such an insecure environment will always convey the message of a chronically challenged hope for a successful education system.

In addition to calls for a critical national dialogue, a huge investment in a fair, reasonable, organised and well-structured national security system could go a long way towards alleviating the current issue of insecurity in the country. In short, for the economy and education system in Nigeria to thrive and flourish, the nation needs a total and uncompromised security of its physical and social environment, including lives and property.

Power and Electricity

Unfortunately, nations do not have equal and reliable access to electricity and power generation. In fact, a country's access level to electricity is emblematic of its level of economic development. Reliable and simple access to electricity is used as a yardstick to measure the quality of life, comfort, healthcare and educational progress of the citizens of a given nation.

It is true that, in Nigeria, educators and teachers focus their attention more on class instructions and less on access to electricity since the non-availability of constant power and electricity in the country is not a new development. Electrification rate (s) is considered relatively poor at present and it remains a major economic and human development hurdle for Nigeria. Nevertheless, serious attention should be paid to electricity and power supply because it is also a huge component of the infrastructure required for national progress and poverty reduction. In some very rare cases, especially in countries and cultures where childhood labour and employment are highly encouraged, owing to extreme poverty rates, access to electricity can reduce educational attainment and possibly increase school dropout rates. This also applies to places where children and young people stay home to compensate for their parents' going out for daily work. Overall, availability of electricity in schools improves school attendance, retention and reduces dropout rates.

Minor researches have also found that the availability of electricity in a country and in schools helps to improve the learning process. Electricity and power systems not only enable students to study when it is dark, they also afford schools and other educational institutions the opportunity to use electronic equipment for teaching and learning. Access to lighting and information communications technologies (ICT) is crucial. Arguably, the use of computers may elevate the learning process by improving access to information, ideas and education resources online. Indeed, power and electricity can make a sizeable impact on schooling. In Nicaragua, 72% of children in the 1990s living in households with electricity were attending school, compared to 50% of those living in households without electricity (Saghir, 2005).

Energy poverty, owing to lack of adequate visibility and power sources, could reduce the amount of time students spend in primary and secondary schools and universities, thereby negatively impacting their educational attainment. It might limit the working hours in which students can study and complete assignments. Areas without access to electricity and power supply could repel or discourage well-trained, educated, dynamic and talented teachers from living and working in those communities that may be in most need of their professional services. Lack of electricity might also limit teaching resources and valuable instructional materials, resulting in lower quality education. The administrative sector is not left out, moreover, as electricity poverty would complicate work for the school staff and administration, especially in documentations and in keeping relevant school records.

For economic, educational, social and general progress, the issue of electricity and power supply in the country should be brought to the forefront of policy discussions in Nigeria. Electricity in the modern world can be considered the life blood of every nation on earth, since no project can be successfully started or sustained in the long-term without electricity and power generation. Power supply promotes economic growth, development and prosperity and has a great positive impact on all nations' incomes, expenditures and, above all, education.

Chapter Eight
The Importance of Competition

Among the universal concepts found in all human cultures and traditions are education and competition. They are found wherever human beings exist. People naturally compete for survival, inheritance and self-propagation. Even children impetuously seek competition with their peers and friends in the playgrounds and with their siblings at home. It is an intrinsic desire to compare themselves with others in every way, sometimes by forced wrestling (grappling) or running around. This tendency seems helpful and beneficial towards development, in its own way.

Ross (2016) opines that competitiveness is what it takes for societies, families and individuals to thrive. Like education, competition is directly or indirectly transmitted from one generation to another. The concept of competition, as an initiative in every field of life's endeavours, is to create a climate and opportunities where motivation, creativity, determination, perseverance, improvement and efficiency will thrive among people, communities, institutions and organisations. The demonstration, maintenance and protection of these constructive goals will usher in reliable and sustainable progress in the life of any society.

Encouraging competition in businesses, enterprises, sales and manufacturing, for instance, would usher in an environment where high-quality goods, products and services are provided at cost-efficient levels. This means that higher quality goods and services could be obtained at lower prices. The implication of competition especially when healthy, positive and vigorous is that every person, business, industry, institution, or organisation is striving to attract customers and clients for their products and services. The result of this atmosphere is not only a circumstantially compelled improvement in the quality of products and services but also a reduction in the costs and prices of those same goods and services. To illustrate, in an environment where only one organisation is providing goods and services, prices are likely to increase while the quality of the products and services diminishes. This trend is because such an organisation is not facing any known external challenges and therefore becomes less motivated to improve its products and services. It is not uncommon for a seller in the local market to fix and charge higher prices than expected without fearing the loss of his/her customers to any competitor.

Nevertheless, in an atmosphere of positive competition among individuals and businesses, efficiency is mostly guaranteed and consumers' purchasing power is protected. Also, employment will be created and increased, in some cases massively, especially when investment competitors come from other communities, states and nations. The ability to compete also creates opportunities for entrepreneurs and agencies to enter the marketplace and start new businesses. From competition, one acquires new skills from successful competitors and learns new ideas and strategies about improving one's products and services. Having competitors in business and services also affords people the opportunity to choose employers and workplaces that suit them best. Competition ought not to be restricted, but the processes of competition could be occasionally regulated with some need-based and truly democratic checks and balances to promote best practices.

Competition vs. Collaboration

Competition, although a universal concept and part of every culture transmitted from one generation to another, does not mean the absence of collaboration and teamwork, or the presence of aggression and greed. It is about the ability to use one's talents, resources and inventions to pursue excellence and best practices in relationship with others. Misapplication of competition in any form could invite government's intervention, which otherwise would not be needed. Checks and balances, regulations and fair government oversight would come in. For instance, individuals, businesses, schools, institutions and organisations could compete among themselves by displaying their own qualities and resources to achieve their own goals to make sales, get more customers and recruit more students. They could also collaborate, cooperate and form advocacy groups with one another to work for their common interests.

Competition must be put in context. To illustrate, school competitors could work together to get the government to provide portable water for their schools, build good and accessible roads and hospitals and provide electricity. A healthy competition does not kill the sense of community. This is where the common good, well-being, collaboration and team spirit are applicable. Such human traits and needs should not be constrained or sacrificed to unhealthy competitions. Competition can improve collaboration among individual competitors and within their organisations and institutions. Theme-based competitions would require administrators to work together. Their members and staffs could collaborate to out-compete another group of competitors. It is not uncommon that competitors work together to defeat a common challenge or challenger. This happens in politics, where competing parties coalesce or merge to defeat one common party whose policies have been consistently adversarial to the common good and well-being of citizens in a given nation. Liberalising competition in the private sector, in keeping with the principles of a free market economy, will certainly make it difficult for the government, which represents the public sector, to impose control, regulate, or interfere in businesses indiscriminately.

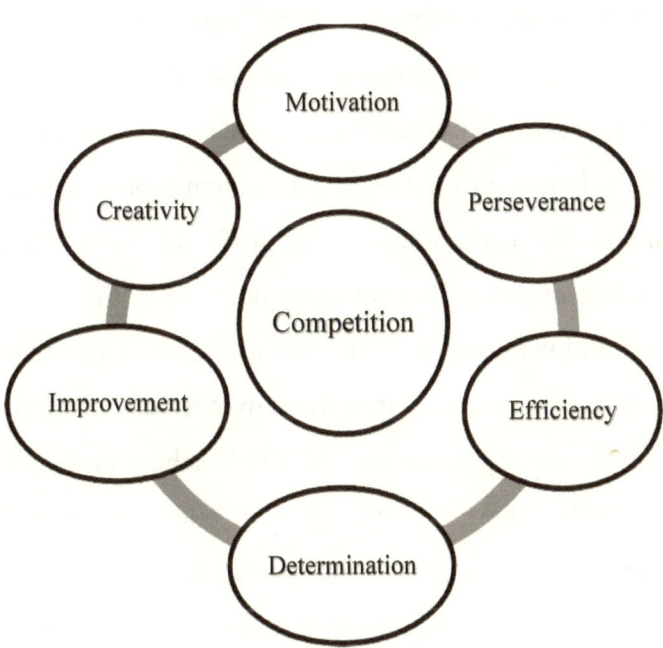

Figure 4. A framework of some elements of competition in education

Competition in Education

Formal education is not only an enterprise, it is also both an industry and a business. In this vein, competition, as an inevitable aspect of the business world, could be likewise and suitably applied to schools and tertiary institutions. Indeed, competition is an important part of the education economy and ecosystem. It can be an effective tool for growing and improving education in any society. Because of the idea and presence of competition in education, schools and tertiary institutions now strive to provide pupils, students and undergraduates with high-quality, efficient and affordable education. This is because students in general have the option to choose between competing schools (or tertiary institutions). If they happen to select one's institution, for instance, it is not because the institution is the only one in existence, but because it has something outstanding and unique that appeals to them. Perhaps they like one's academic programmes and services or notice that certain teachers or professors on the teaching staff have distinct qualities that set them apart from those in other schools and institutions. It could be that the administrators and staff are more helpful, friendly and caring than those in other schools. It may be that the academics are top-notch and the whole school atmosphere is inclusive. Certainly, there are things that one does that one's competitors do not do. It is usually the distinct qualities of a school, college, university, or any institution of higher learning that set it apart from others. This is where and why each school and institution of learning needs to be creative.

Competition is critical in the education system because it helps each institution to identify its specific and unique qualities that are appealing to prospective students. Identifying and harnessing those qualities will enable one to market one's schools, institutions, programmes and services more effectively; recruiting and possibly retaining new and more students. Something good and positive must set one apart from the rest. An institution's spectacular qualities will help students to easily identify and develop interest in it based on the level of trust and loyalty that has been built and this positive feedback will be transmitted by its former students and their families to their peers, friends and families, creating long-lasting and strong student-institution relationships. This type of bond will induce the future doctors, engineers, lawyers and architects to support, advocate for and broadly defend the programmes, services and the institution in general.

Competition and Curriculum

To help students learn at the various stages of their educational development, curricula are usually designed to help cover diverse subject areas. Essentially, curricula include the structure, process and course of studies that incorporate instructional resources, the syllabi (contents) and materials needed to achieve given educational outcomes. They prescribe processes or specify courses of study and requirements that students are expected to complete in order to pass a given level of education. One of curriculum's advantages is that it can be altered or expanded to suit either older or younger students. Increased pressure on schools and universities, because of competition from other schools or institutions of learning, could promote changes, diversity, creativity and even innovations in any school and institution's curriculum. Such a competition could result in a sound, productive, dynamic, pragmatic and expansive education curriculum for the beneficiary institution. New courses and syllabi, essentially, could be added to an existing curriculum, provided that they are aligned with what is already being taught. Every curriculum is loaded with information to help students improve their academic performance based on the content standards.

In the secondary school setting, academic standards based on a given curriculum system are essentially designed to prepare students for the universities, colleges of education and other tertiary institutions. Any curriculum is concerned with the expected performance, skills and knowledge required of students. As an aggregate of courses in any academic programme, a curriculum should also be designed with a view to preparing students for the workforce, life after secondary school and future careers. The standards are expected to be uniformly implemented across a country. There is no guarantee that any approved curriculum standards will succeed, nevertheless, they will reshape the vast majority of Nigeria's classrooms when fully implemented by the states.

Normally, going through curriculum standards to roll out a standard that school personnel will fully understand and be able to implement could take years. It is still doable in a shorter period, provided that attempts at any quick approval of irrelevant draft standards or other unnecessary bureaucracies are eschewed. By way of illustrating an instance, curriculum standards that advocate and include a more rigorous digital approach to English language, mathematics, physics, chemistry and biology over more common and traditional approaches should be thoroughly reviewed with careful deliberation. The first question in the review would be whether such standards have been successfully used in any classroom within Nigeria or in any country around the world. Also, any curriculum that puts greater emphasis on critical thinking and problem-solving skills should be upheld as an asset.

Education curriculum should be flexible and pragmatic in the sense that educators should be allowed to use ideas they consider better because clear evidence demonstrates they have worked in the past. However, there is often no clear prescription as to how these should be taught in terms of pedagogical standards. The establishment of a Nigerian Retired Teachers' Association (NRTA) is hereby being proposed when it comes to looking for avenues to procure and salvage past teaching curricula and practices that worked successfully in the classroom.

Any sound and valid academic standards should be tested in real classrooms and made familiar to educators for easy implementation. Literate parents and guardians should also be able to recognise an academic standard or related syllabus when their children and wards come home from school with workbooks and homework. Modifications could be made to an already approved curriculum standard, especially if parents, teachers and administrators determine that the assessments and examinations are too stressful for the students. With the growing national push to reform education in Nigeria, a coalition of educators, academic engineers and scientists can propose new approaches to studying English, science, math, technology and engineering. This type of proposal could be incorporated into the national education curriculum.

Curricula items are generally and ultimately formative by nature. They are thoughtfully and methodically designed to train every student as an important member of the society with certain desirable characteristics and qualities. In drafting the academic curriculum, efforts must be made to ensure that it invokes the Nigerian philosophy of citizenship, individuality and "limitless potential" instead of an approach that positions us all as insignificant members of the society. This could be permitted only when the education system of an independent nation is being brazenly and cliquishly politicised. Nigerian states need to uniformly sign onto and put standards into place to prepare students for life after secondary school as well as test their performance and proficiency. Therefore, an academic standard that is common to all the states in the federation should be specifically prescribed as the preferred option, if it is not already in existence.

Curriculum materials and resources can also reflect the mission of a city or community. That is precisely what it means for a curriculum to be expansively pragmatic. As is often found in some foreign nations, a community that has frequently experienced tragic suicidal incidents among students, for instance, may endeavour to prevent more teen suicides. Such incidents could push members of a given community to wonder if schools should do more. This has taken the shape of parents' recommendation that mental health courses be taught in classrooms and therefore included in the curriculum. This could also be applied to any community, country, or society where crime, insecurity, or terrorism is an issue.

In this modern age, Nigeria can begin to consider creating comprehensive institutions of learning and curricula, based on both tradition and technology, to provide high-quality education for every student irrespective of their social status. Also, all secondary school students should be encouraged to take at least one of the more rigorous academic curricula, such as physics, chemistry, biology, mathematics, music, or languages.

The Nigerian Situation

The current absence of decentralisation in the Nigerian system of education, which otherwise encourages competition, does not diminish the essential role of competition in the education marketplace. This process of decentralisation should transfer education decision making, policy powers and even financial control from the Federal Ministry of Education to the state, regional and local governments, communities and schools, that is, from the public sector to the private sector. The success of this type of reform would, however, require strong leadership and policy commitment.

Decentralisation or regionalisation could improve efficiency, accountability, transparency and responsiveness in the provision of programmes and services comparable to the centralised system that exists in Nigeria today. There is no gainsaying that competition and constructively competitive undertakings are necessary for the comprehensive growth of any society. With competition involved, a decentralised or regionalised education system would encourage improved curricula and teaching methods, programmes, services, efficiency and local participation plus increased access and enrolment. It would also improve the quality of education to reflect local needs and priorities. When decentralisation is properly enforced, poorly illiterate regions in the country might be circumstantially compelled to enrol and seek access to formal education; a prediction that is based on the natural human quest for survival, inheritance and self- propagation. These mentioned bases of competition would naturally make this anticipated progress happen out of the innate desire to compare oneself with others.

Decentralisation and a sense of independence from the central government could trigger such a reform and major change of mind-set. Competition can be healthy as well as breed progress in any nation's life with comparatively insignificant shortcomings. In this generation, events have shown that necessity borne out of competition is truly the mother of inventions, new discoveries and progress. Competition with the Soviet Union in the 1950s led the United States of America to initiate its space programme, which then vaulted to global status in remarkable scientific and technological innovations. It was competition that drove Taiwan to pursue Japan in electrical and electronics engineering, creating immeasurable progress along the way.

When it comes to formal education, it is no longer a secret that billions of people and hundreds of nations around the world are working incredibly hard every day to outcompete and consequently out-educate others. Corporate competitions can provide a useful toolkit in driving education costs down. Likewise, the importance of competition in the development and consolidation of the education system in Nigeria cannot be overemphasised.

Nevertheless, caution only must be strictly exercised to ensure that competition does not lead anyone into casting suspicious or envious eyes towards others' success rather than joining forces with them to develop a given community or society. People need to understand why the idea of competition in the nation's education system has apparently been neglected. Despite tolerable support from the central government, the Federal Ministry of Education, state education commissions and boards, good-government groups (GGGs), agencies and education advocates, it is necessary to investigate if competition was ever in existence or put into consideration in Nigeria's education system in the first place.

For any sector in any organisation (let alone a nation) to grow, there is the need for a healthy and constructive competition to usher in progress, best practices and excellence. The nation should not rest on its oars to make its education system competitive and effective at all levels. Finally, what would it take to establish a well-grounded education system in Nigeria? It would take proper educational engineering rooted in a sound, dynamic, pragmatic and expansive curriculum system and quality instruction. If Nigerians can carefully foster these initiatives, then they may succeed in creating great sparks of educational prosperity and innovation.

Chapter Nine
Education and the Nigerian Culture

The formal education that faith missionaries and colonialists left here in Nigeria should inspire one to constructively re-evaluate their legacy without trampling their phenomenal accomplishments. The same seems applicable to some enriching elements inherent in the nation's pre-colonial and informal system of education. Nigerians must highlight the strengths of those traditional and culturally crucial elements. Primarily, education represents a unique opportunity of transmitting cultural heritage from one generation to another. It also constitutes a process whereby a comparatively lasting transformation is introduced into general human behaviours. It bears emphasising that any community, society, or nation's future very much depends on the quality and level of its citizens' education.

Esu and Junaid (2010) observe that, in all human societies, education is meant to pass on to the new generation the existing knowledge of their physical environment, introduce individuals to the organisation of society, give them skills for performing their daily tasks and enjoying their leisure and inculcate sound morals within them for their own benefit and that of the society. In other words, education is a process by which society assists the younger generation to understand the heritage of its past, participate productively in the present and provide for the future. Based on this reasoning, formal education draws inspiration and nourishment from a society as well as adds to the growth, renewal and development of that society.

Culture and Education.

People's beliefs about the meaning and value of education are influenced by their cultures and worldviews. Cultures and values include belief systems, customs and religions as well as art, language and literature as forms of expression, among other elements. Indeed, education modifies, renews and preserves culture. It teaches people how to live in a society and provides them with a better understanding of their society in a formal setting, that is, the school or university.

It is important to note that education cannot be separated from the social system and environment that it is meant to serve. Education also helps to upgrade any society's level of culture and civilisation. A community's history and expectations can also have a significant impact on its form of education. To that end, enforcing upon the students one's personal cultural patterns or views that counter their own values, customs and traditions can cause enormous problems. It is important for teachers, principals and administrators to study and gain a strong comprehension of the influences and thought patterns of the students and their environments. What is good, edifying, moral and ethical in other cultural systems must be respected. Negative and harmful components of cultures should also be addressed but in a calm, objective dialogue, with politeness and positive mannerisms that demonstrate why those elements could be considered both adversarial to formal education and dangerous to the society, especially values that are detrimental to people's well-being: health, lives and property. Culture and education influence each other. They are mutually exclusive concepts with a symbiotic relationship. Therefore, to understand and appreciate any culture, people need education. The educational level, behaviours and moral values of members of a society are reflected in their culture. While culture teaches people how to live in a community, education, as the wider face and reflection of culture, teaches them how to live in a society at large. Education can help us learn as well as admonish us to live together in peace despite tribal, ethnic or religious differences. Through education, the features of a culture are transmitted from one generation to another. Practically speaking, education is the process of facilitating learning or the acquisition of knowledge, skills, habits, values, etiquette (s) and beliefs and is therefore a prerequisite for the development of cultural values in the world. It strengthens a culture and gives it identity as much as it aims to instil positive, broader and higher values in the learners' minds.

Every society's culture impacts the way students and even educators in general participate in education. Culture could be basically and primarily broken down into two major predominant orientations and contrasting components: individualism and collectivism. Individualism and collectivism are so deeply ingrained in a culture that they mould people's self-conceptions and identities (Anemelu, 2012; Conover, 2009; Toomey, 1999). Research has revealed important distinctions between the collectivist cultures found in Africa, Asia and Latin America and the individualist cultures more commonly found in North America and Europe (Anemelu, 2012; Heine et al., 2001; Hogg & Williams, 2000; Singelis, 2000).

Anemelu (2012) aptly notes that individualism values the virtues of independence, autonomy and self-reliance, while collectivism values the virtues of interdependence, cooperation and social harmony. In collectivist cultures, the person is first, a loyal member of a family, team, company, church and state. By contrast, under the banner of individualism, one's personal goals take priority over group allegiances (Anemelu, 2012, p.8-9). Because of this cultural contrast, foreign teachers and educators from individualist culture-oriented nations who lack knowledge about Nigeria as a collectivist culture-oriented nation might interpret the behaviour of a Nigerian student from their own cultural standpoints. This difference could cause such educators to inaccurately assess the behaviour of such a student either as too exuberant, or "hyperactively disordered" in some cases, or even autistic, among other assessment possibilities. A student may also possibly find himself penalised by a teacher even without knowing what he did wrongly. By way of illustration, in collectivist cultures, students are expected to keep quiet and be respectful in class to learn well and without necessarily making eye contacts with the teacher, whereas individualist cultures often encourage students to engage in discussions and debates in a bid to learn critical and creative thinking. Direct eye contact with teachers and peers is also a plus. Eye contact with teachers and peers among Europeans and Americans is often interpreted as a sign of respect, engagement, readiness to learn, active participation and even competence. Moreover, in individualist educational cultures, parental roles are crucial to a child's academic progress and active participation in school, while parents in collectivist educational cultures submit to the expertise of teachers to provide academic instructions and guidance to pupils and students.

As the figure below demonstrates, cultural values express themselves through freedom, democracy, diversity, dynamism, fraternity (friendship and unity) and resilience. These elements are interwoven in the sense that one leads to the others in all ramifications.

Figure 5. A framework of components and offshoots of human culture

A fair exploitation of these factors, as illustrated in the figure above, is what perhaps sustains Nigeria in its continued quest to maintain a common, united, stable and strong education system, although with some presenting challenges and conflicts in their application. This also applies to all its common national interests. Nigeria, as a large nation in Africa, has hundreds of different tribes, languages, customs, traditions and cultures within it. Invariably, the more homogenous a society is, the more stable its culture tends to be. With its heterogeneous but related cultural values, Nigeria has always striven to keep its unity and stability albeit with sporadic but continuing challenges of bigotry, intolerance and extremism.

However, in the same troubled unity, there still exists what appears like a reassuring diversity. People have not lost confidence in their ability within Nigeria's culture to seek unity in diversity, unity amidst diverse belief systems, customs, religions and languages. When people are among those with whom they share common experiences, strongly encourage, or allow such situations to exist, true freedom, democracy, growth and development, in all aspects of life, are bound to occur. Progress in education would also be unlimited in such a case.

Diversity and Fraternity

No society in Africa has more cultural potential for unity than Nigeria despite all its differences because the nation's inherently rich African culture encourages democracy and true freedom in the form of association, communion and communitarianism. This type of freedom brings about and nurtures diversity and fraternity. It is also the natural, cultural and societal sense of fraternity, unity, or togetherness that provokes the feeling of friendship and mutual support among citizens, students, educators, policymakers and education administrators in the thick of diversity. This observation is encapsulated in Nigeria's original National Anthem, excerpted as follows: "Though tribe and tongue may differ, in brotherhood we stand". This is indeed a collectivist cultural notion that spurs true success and progress through unity, collaboration and teamwork, not *per meipsum*: "for me alone".

Experience and evidence have shown that a healthy sense of diversity could be quite beneficial to communities and schools, thereby leading to positive and powerful outcomes not only in schools but also as part of life in general. From a positive perspective, it reassures and strengthens a society. It is in schools and other institutions of learning that the ground for fostering national unity and cohesion is prepared. Since the school climate and classroom culture directly impact students' success, it is critical for schools, colleges and universities to recognise, appreciate and embrace diversity in every way, constantly celebrating it both in schools and in extracurricular involvements. This recommendation calls for the recognition of the variety of social, cultural, ethnic and religious backgrounds of students. It also points out the need to treat them equally by offering them equal chances for admissions, success and equal access to the school and college curricula. The same applies to the issue of gender.

Education policymakers, administrators, educators and teachers must acknowledge and recognise the uniqueness and individuality of every student and treat each one fairly. Likewise, students and learners are expected to show the same recognition and respect to their teachers, educators and administrators. It is certainly in the best interest of Nigeria to focus on the richness of its diversity that cuts across all sectors. Depending on the educational situation and setting, diversity could be considered both in theory and practice when developing teaching and learning curricula, as diverse groups of students respond differently to the school curriculum. In this scenario, the encouragement and support of fraternity, unity, understanding and respect for each other among educational stakeholders will foster harmony in ensuring quality education for students in Nigeria's schools and tertiary institutions.

The country's coat of arms displays four relevant and reassuring words: *Unity* and *Faith, Peace* and *Progress*. Nigeria's unity in diversity is not yet perfect. The nation is still in the process of transformation and should therefore work towards finally making itself a positive melting pot of cultures, customs, religions, languages and values. The dictum "United we stand, divided we fall", which ought to inspire the principle of unity in diversity, needs to be upheld in this context. Since the collective interests and desire that bring Nigerians together (unity, peace and progress) are far more important than those things that divide them, people can harness diversity and use it for the common good.

With dialogue, Nigerians should be able to amicably address the drivers and purveyors of conflicts. In fact, culture and religion, in all their shining beauties, should be used to preach and spread unity, peace and true love among people. With growth in population and immigration around the globe, in this age of globalisation, today's young Nigerians need to be prepared to succeed in a more diverse and even more global workforce than ever before.

Dynamism and Resilience

One of the major characteristics and variables of culture is dynamism, since culture is not static but always in motion. The cultural mobility of every education system and the ability to change will always help it meet future challenges. This flux is where dynamism transforms into resilience. Positive and fair competition in the Nigerian education system, which requires a level playing ground, would give rise to high performance and dynamism. Dynamism and resilience are the two major qualities inherent in the Nigerian culture that any country would need to survive the pressures of the changing world. An interplay of the two features, dynamism and resilience, would make a great impact on the Nigerian education system.

Figure 5 indicates that dynamism leads to resilience. An admirably dynamic person or nation would likely survive difficult societal contexts and crises. Nigerians, as a people, have been able to survive and adapt to changing economic, social and political situations for decades. It is the dynamic aspect of a culture that enables its affiliates to invest in and appreciate formal education both in schools and universities as necessary for their future social security, independence and survival as a people. The goals of this investment are positive results and success, not failure. The nature and structure of any nation's education system could help to predict its impact in the lives of its people. The nation's education system is expected to equip people with the relevant knowledge and skills needed for survival in society. This dynamism of culture has left us with the clear mission and long-held vision that education is the right of every child: That high-quality education must be free, compulsory and accessible to every child irrespective of socioeconomic status or socio-cultural background.

The dynamic nature of the nation's culture will make it easier for it to make provisions, design state-by-state policies and scholarship schemes that could attract poor and underprivileged children to formal education. Federal and state governments, through their education ministries, could partner with health ministries, hospitals and health centres to render health services to locals and the underprivileged as a way of bringing them to school. In addition to these strategies, Nigeria's schools could organise culturally appealing workshops and outreach programmes aimed at attracting illiterate sections of the country to school for formal education. Both the public and private sectors could train personnel for this type of outreach. The training will be designed to sharpen the knowledge, cultural skills, capacity and dynamism of the trainees, so they are able to represent the school system, ministries and governments effectively in their relationships with the target groups. Also, this is an area in which the internet and social media can be very useful, especially in spreading and propagating the news of promising educational opportunities and outreach.

The government must act and, in some cases, continue to act to emphasise a type of cultural dynamism that prevents any child's or young person's formal educational rights from being violated. The latent dynamism of the Nigerian education system, when explored, would expose it as a driving force that could promote the sustainable development of the country in its entirety. When education is made widely accessible and literacy extended to poor corners of the country, it will become evident that education is not only for the rich but also for the poor. Illiteracy should not be a reason for poverty in Nigeria.

Democracy and Freedom

There is no freedom without a true democracy. Democracy, along with collectivism and individualism, is originally a socio-politico-cultural concept. In this context, however, it is considered a presumed offshoot of societal culture that resonates with people in general. By way of illustration, a system of government does not suddenly change into a democracy simply because it has popular support. Democracy in practice is not always determined or premised on popular votes or choices. It does not necessarily rest only on the entrenchment of the will of the majority, it also respects the will of the minority. Democracy seems to be much closer to collectivism than it is to individualism. This means that the African culture in general and the Nigerian culture, which are collectivist or communitarian, are even more democratic than most of the individualist European and Western cultures.

Arguably, the Nigerian education system has been growing at a snail's pace; for it to grow geometrically and have tremendous impact on the populace, by contrast, it must be rooted in and employ two major tools of culture: democracy and freedom. Experience has shown that democracy goes together with basic human freedom and fair treatment of everyone according to the generally accepted cultural norms or the laws of the land. By nature, democracy is supposed to be a system of government that protects people's liberty in contrast to tyranny, despotism and dictatorship. Democracy implies equity, justice and inclusiveness, which make provisions for comparisons and innovations along with the explorations of positive options and alternatives. The same democracy applies to its relationship with education. When an oppressed people, for instance, cry for democracy, the immediate implication or presumption is that they are crying for freedom, self-determination, survival and peaceful existence. The extended but presumed implication is that injustice, oppression, marginalisation and victimisation are the opposites of democracy.

Even though democracy does not essentially guarantee freedom and peace, it remains a path to freedom and peace. The same path is applicable to equity, justice and inclusiveness. By the way, freedom (positive freedom) "denotes the right of each human being to live his own life, develop his own distinctive capacities and beliefs and, in cooperation with his fellows, determine the laws and the institutions under which he is to live" (Butts, 1953). This type of freedom is sufficiently broad but not limitless, as it does not include either harmfully exploiting or violating the rights and lives of others. Democracy is more about the freedom of choice, equality under the law, transparency, justice and fairness. To illustrate, in an educationally democratic environment, parents have the right to choose the school or institution to which they will send their children. Likewise, students are free to make a choice of schools and universities for themselves. Also, it implies that each child or student has the right to a high-quality education regardless of whether the provider belongs to the public or private sector. Proprietors, private and voluntary agencies have the right to establish schools and tertiary institutions.

This value of democracy and freedom should not be abused. In this regard, Oluoma Udemezue, in an online educational review titled, "The Tyranny of Private Schools in Nigeria", makes this insightful remark:

A situation where some of these so-called private schools force students to take all manners of international exams with the aim of belittling the WAEC, SSCE, NECO and JAMB exams in Nigeria; such exams have certainly lost their value, to the extent that some of these exams are not taken in some private schools, therefore, it becomes a great loss to the country. What happens in future where no Nigerian child would want to attend any of the Nigerian universities because such children and their parents have been brainwashed to believe that the best universities can only be found abroad? (Udemezue, 2018).

Some of these private schools are international schools located in Nigeria's major cities. These schools often operate strictly on Western standards, following the British, American, or international Baccalaureate standards for higher education. Many of these schools equip their institutions with state-of-the-art facilities for lessons and extracurricular activities. They may follow the school year of three- semester schedule in their home countries. Nevertheless, besides charging inordinately high basic school fees, uniforms and study materials, admission processes could become very competitive and selective, typically favouring the affluent. In some cases, those admirable systems could defy the core Nigerian or African values and culture. In addition to opening Nigeria up to innovations, critical thinking and problem-solving skills, the education system is expected to transmit its core cultural and traditional heritage, which is rich in moral, ethical and spiritual values.

Democracy and freedom, as aspects of societal culture, guarantee the rights of individuals and the private sector to participate in formal education in Nigeria. In this way, the dynamism of education and people's survival, rooted in resilience, is assured. Private sectors' involvement in a country's education system can improve its effectiveness and competitiveness in a cost-effective manner, because a broader participation of the private sector in education brings about competition. This engagement can lower the cost of education, challenge and improve the quality and efficiency of public schools and develop skills and innovations. Citizens should not become oblivious of the fact that formal education in Nigeria began in the private sector with the work of the missionaries and voluntary agencies, extending later to the public sector during the colonial era.

Curriculum and Culture

Nigeria can operate a uniquely differentiated system of education whereby its secondary school courses and some of the college courses are modelled to match the exigencies of changing times and still remain relevant to the nation's cultural heritage. This model would mimic the inimitably democratic character, pragmatic nature and primordial strength of the pre-colonial traditional education system. It is high time educators reconsolidated traditional values with new ways of teaching writing skills, fine arts, social studies, civics and the sciences in the primary and secondary school system. Based on Nigeria's cultures and traditions, it should be able to work out a fine system that is suitable for its children and youth. Colleges and universities can design and model their practical curricula and courses of study in agriculture, healthcare system's development, local services, local or internal security, local constructions and engineering, home technology, meteorology, erosion control, political participation and industry.

The nation's curriculum needs to be not only coherent, culturally and environmentally relevant, it also needs to be diversified and made flexible if its aim is to cater for diverse students' abilities, needs and interests. Indeed, it must nurture the development of the whole person and his/her own lifetime learning capabilities. This same curriculum must be constantly implemented and reinforced in schools, colleges and universities because it fits better into Nigeria's needs and is more appropriate in preparing its young people for the nation's workforce. This proposed flexibility is similar to the way many mission colleges in South Africa modelled their practical courses in industry and agriculture, a curriculum known as 'differentiated education' or 'adapted education' on those of black schools in the United States such as the Booker T. Washington's Tuskegee Institute (Freedman, 2013). When the education curriculum is static, inflexible, or non-pragmatic, it could be considered sterile and dysfunctional because it is doomed to produce unemployable graduates to populate society.

For decades, Nigerian educators and allied agencies have attempted to make notable progress in the process of educating students by organising extramural classes and, in some cases, by opening long-vacation remedial schools for students preparing for the WASCE, SSCE or falling behind their peers. This practice is not only culturally appropriate but should also always be encouraged and expanded. Since such remedial and extramural education strategies have not always been offered freely. Such programmes could be structured to provide discounts to students who are economically and financially disadvantaged. The country's traditions and cultures also believe in and adopt policies that give people both the benefit of the doubt and second chances. Cognisant of this cultural element, schools and institutions of learning could also adopt remedial- programme policies that encourage students who are below-average academically to retake certain courses or examinations. An initiative of this nature could help them to improve their performances. It is assumed that institutions can always reasonably move in the right direction with a view to achieving significant outcomes.

Nigeria's school cultures should also be revisited with concerted efforts to make it clear to educators and administrators that all students can learn and be successful. This could be done through solid capacity-building, professional development, evaluation of learning processes and teaching assessments. Such professional trainings should convey the practical message that how well a student performs does not necessarily depend on how intelligent and clever (s)he is naturally, but rather on how hard (s)he works individually and in class.

Language of Instruction

Language is a major aspect of a people's culture and tradition with its importance appreciated as a means of human communication, spreading information, social interaction and preservation of values. Language gives identity to a people and it is also the most powerful tool for teaching and learning. A person will learn very little of even basic ideas and facts if (s)he has not mastered the language of instruction. All scientific and technological breakthroughs in history are attributable to the existence of language. Nigeria itself is a multi-cultural and multi-lingual nation with over 250 languages and dialects.

Ojetunde (2012) observes that scholars like Fafunwa (1989), Emenanjo (1990) and Bamgbose (1991) advocate the need for the mother-tongue to be used as the medium of instruction in the formative years (up to age 12) and possibly later. They argue that this offers children the opportunity to explore their natural environments, interact in their natural languages; develop curiosity, reasoning abilities and self-confidence, as are obtainable in India, China, Malaysia, Hong Kong, Japan Kenya and Tanzania, among others.

Even though the preceding advocacy for the use of mother tongue as a medium of instruction sounds appropriate and reasonable, especially for children in the primary stage of their education, the use of English language, which has remained the nation's *lingua franca* (national, literary, or standard language) for over a century and with an unbroken history should be retained, especially at the secondary and higher levels of education. For various social, multicultural and global reasons, English should be maintained and sustained as the language of instruction in the classroom from the primary to the tertiary levels of education. Nevertheless, Nigerians can still strongly promote and boost the local languages through dramas, literature and poetry.

The federal government has advocated that every child should learn the language of their immediate environment (the mother tongue) as well as, in the interest of national unity, one of the three major Nigerian languages: Hausa, Igbo and Yoruba (Federal Republic of Nigeria, 2004). Interest in and policy statements on teaching indigenous languages at various levels of the Nigerian education system began with the federal government's National Policy on Education initiative in 1977. It was revised in 1981, 1998 and 2004. Nonetheless, English has remained the language of instruction despite divergent policy pronouncements.

Although beneficial, in some ways, English as a foreign language was superimposed on Nigeria by the colonial masters. It has continued to occupy a priority of place in the nation's education system for over a century now. English language is used today in business, church, government, literature, mass media, trade and commerce. It is not only a unifying language, an indispensable requirement, it also determines an individual's successful travel and social mobility across the country and beyond. Moreover, it is a language of compromise among three major languages (Hausa, Igbo and Yoruba) and many other minor languages and dialects vying for attention. It is a unitary language because the adoption of any of the major competing indigenous languages would have meant an alienation and even marginalisation of the others. Understandably, it would be hard to handle a class in some of the states in Nigeria that have many ethnic groups as indigenes with multiple local languages and dialects. A situation like this can be found in Lagos state, Rivers state and the FCT Abuja, among others.

The only ensuing problem is that many people have found it fashionable to consciously or unconsciously jettison their native languages and mother tongues in preference for English, thereby giving a foreign language a superior status in preference to their traditional and cultural languages. This choice is because a lot of Nigerian nationals feel that English language commands more prestige and status globally. It has also acquired a wider geographical spread both nationally and internationally in comparison with indigenous languages.

Efforts must be exerted to preserve and encourage Nigeria's major local language courses, such as Hausa, Igbo and Yoruba, in primary schools, secondary schools and even up to the tertiary institutions. Difficult scientific and technological terms can be comfortably explained to students in vernacular at any time, to bring the knowledge down to earth for them when the need arises and to help enlarge their scientific language vocabulary.

Chapter Ten
Education and Quality of Instructions

The quality of education and instruction in any nation's schools and institutions of learning is dependent on their development of knowledge and skills. This chapter explores the positive qualities of education, instruction and student learning as well as their implications for Nigeria. This topic should be of interest to the nation's proprietors, schools and institutions as they consider investing in teaching and learning.

First, adequate provision should be made to produce qualified and dynamic teachers and make them relevant within their areas of specialty. Nigeria, therefore, must spell out in clear and unambiguous terms the philosophical basis of its committed investment in education that includes quality teaching and learning outcomes. Few items have captured the attention of education ministries, stakeholders, policymakers and administrators as much as the link between teacher quality and student learning outcomes.

Even though policymakers and stakeholders often hold varied opinions and views regarding the meaning of high-quality education, most people judge the quality of education in their environment, society and nation in terms of the goals they set for their communities and themselves. Goals such as social promotion, survival and employment must be clearly defined. The same applies to institutional visions and the resultant outcomes of student learning, often in the retention and graduation rates. This observation suggests that the quality of teaching and instructions matters a great deal to students' educational and academic achievements.

Indeed, what helps an institution of learning earn high-quality status is not only its healthy combination of family, community and culture in a given environment, it also has much to do with its strength, visionary leadership and teamwork plus broad student access and rewarding opportunities. All these elements apply to promote quality teaching and learning. Therefore, to improve the education and learning that children receive in the classrooms, the nation needs to maintain veteran teachers and sustain support for the preparation of new ones — hence, the need for solid teacher training. To ensure the quality of instruction in schools, Nigeria must prioritise intensive training of teachers.

Teacher Training and Classroom Instruction

The qualities of good teachers are reflected in their students. So, the essence of teacher training programmes is to ensure the preparation of educators who are willing and ready to succeed in the classroom setting. This is indispensable because some teachers are eager to make positive impacts in the lives of students but at the same time not ready to do so. In short, they are unprepared for the realities of the classroom. Teachers need to know not only how to teach well but also how to manage classrooms and redirect undesirable behaviours in class. This is where teacher-student interactions and relationships can make a big difference. Extensive research reveals an emerging and convincing consensus in this regard.

According to Okafor (2008), teacher education is a form of education that is systematically designed for the cultivation of those who teach or will teach, particularly but not exclusively in the primary or post primary schools. Nakpodia and Urien (2011) observed that it is the process which nurtures prospective teachers and updates qualified teachers' knowledge and skills in the form of continuous professional development. It revolves around the policies and procedures designed to equip prospective teachers with the knowledge, attitude, behaviour and skills required to perform their duties in the classroom.

Teacher training in Nigeria can be traced back to the introduction of formal education by the early missionaries who enlisted the service of zealous literate converts as catechists and interpreters. They interpreted Sunday sermons and gave catechism lessons and religious instructions to children and adults. Nevertheless, their training was not formal. Similarly, those who graduated from standard four were recruited as primary school teachers. In this way, strategic collaborations between the missionaries and the colonial government produced primary teachers in some parts of the country. However, Nigeria's education in that period faced a lot of challenges. In 1896, the first teacher training college was established as St. Andrew's College, Oyo, in the western part of Nigeria. The college increased the quality of teachers who were until then standard six-level graduates. The Ashby Commission's report in 1960 gave birth to massive expansion and upgrading of the existing teaching force both at the primary and secondary school levels in the country. Besides the strong existence of Teacher Training Colleges (TTCs) across the country, Nigeria began to see an emergence of Advanced Teachers' Colleges that offered Nigerian Certificates of Education (NCE). With a surge in new programmes at the existing and emerging tertiary institutions, other graduates also became teaching professionals by earning Post Graduate Diplomas in Education (PGDEs). Teachers at this time were not only enthusiastic in their duties; they also had a sense of pride, achievement and fulfilment in their profession.

Teacher Training Colleges (TTCs) were up and running in Nigeria until 1998, when the Nigerian Certificate in Education (NCE) obtained from Advanced Teachers' Colleges, at present known as Colleges of Education (COEs) — became the minimum certificate requirement for teaching both at the primary and junior secondary school levels. The original idea of the NCE programmes was to strengthen the teaching force in both primary and secondary schools. Unquestionably, teaching must be seen and appreciated as a noble profession in Nigeria; therefore, the need to restore and revitalise the TTCs in such a way that they will become attractive once again to prospective student teachers is urgent.

How would people assess the teacher training system in the Nigeria of today? Is it an enterprise that constantly rolls out flagbearers of mediocrity? Can anyone confidently assert that 50% of about 500 trained teachers in Nigeria are of high quality? Perhaps some of them have low or even no academic standards for entrance in the first place. What are the prerequisites for their admissions? Are Nigerians drawn to the teaching profession by money or by natural interest, personal inclination, or instructional aptitude? According to Adeniran (1991), the teacher's professional ability is crucial in the educational development of the student. Good teaching is incontestably the best examination preparation available for students everywhere.

A revitalised teacher education programme in the 21st century should begin with a strong and far-sighted national decision that encourages the training and preparation of qualitative, efficient and innovative classroom teachers. This type of initiative should meet up with the manpower needs of the present-day Nigeria and if possible, with an extension into the universities, even though their instructions are often relatively less challenging and non-rigorous. Nonetheless, this type of situation in universities will largely depend on the level, degree and classroom teaching coverage and practice that are required to be filled. Generally, when teaching is professionalised and given the high value it deserves, then the nation will have succeeded in making teaching one of the most popular and exciting occupations for its people.

Quality of Teaching and Instructions

Improving the Nigerian education system would certainly begin and end with good teachers who are talented and skilled. Countries across the globe that seem to have established better teaching credibility than others have been shown to have more rigorous and selective teacher-training systems. Does this mean that Nigeria would copy everything other countries do? Of course not. In teaching, however, such nations lay more emphasis on quality than quantity or volume. What appears striking is how those nations fund their schools and institutions of learning. Teachers are transferred from cities to rural areas and vice versa. Comparatively stronger urban schools are paired with rural schools in a bid to improve teaching practices, methods and techniques. As often as circumstances demand, strong schools can take over the administration of weak ones. Nigerian educators and school administrators can export the teaching and management styles employed in stronger schools to weaker ones. State governments and state education commissions can establish and incentivise agencies that audit and measure if teachers use skills and techniques that keep students focused on the nation's shared educational goals and objectives.

In teaching, especially from the secondary to tertiary level, care must be taken not to emphasise teaching more and learning less over teaching less and learning more. The former would likely make most learners passive and even lazy, while the latter would make most of the learners active, committed and dutiful. Moreover, it is not advisable to change any instructional method, teaching technique, or practice that has been tested and proven, a type that is found workable and well-entrenched. Such an approach might not be sustained in the long run and the outcome can be challenging if not disappointing. Teachers should rather be encouraged to develop, share and introduce any new methods of teaching that have proved beneficial to students' learning despite how unconventional they might be.

Pivotal Subjects and Teaching

Mathematics, for instance, seems to be the natural heritage of every human culture, since all the activities of humans on earth are almost always mathematically engineered and executed. The utmost importance of mathematics can never be underestimated. It is a *sine qua non* for the development of any human and, above all, any student and prospective scholar. The knowledge of mathematics helps to build some sense of judgement. Successes in everyday life hardly come without some form of calculations. Also, the natural sciences essentially involve subjects, such as physics, chemistry and biology, as they seek to investigate and have "knowledge of things through their causes" (*cognitio rei per causas*) as stated by the Greek philosopher Aristotle. Science is a part of the corporeal and tactile contacts with the environment.

The educational development of any nation, community, or society, with that of Nigeria firmly included, is based on the knowledge of mathematics and relevant sciences. Additionally, some people believe life on earth would be boring without mathematics, the sciences and their affiliates.

Since these sciences are neither culture-specific nor enjoy any cultural restrictions, a language of preference would certainly be needed to study them. That language, in this case, happens to be English. For students to do well in language and linguistics, they will certainly need some basic knowledge of mathematics and the sciences. Ultimately, students need good teachers in studying these subjects to apply them for their future development. Giving every single one of the students a solid foundation in mathematics and in other relevant sciences as listed above, especially early in their academic lives, should put Nigeria in a super-exalted position in educational development among other nations in the future.

Division of Labour

From years of teaching, policymaking and education administration, experts have revealed that one of the things that kill teaching in the Nigerian system of education and consequently impact student performance upon graduation into secondary schools is lack of division of labour or specialisation. Division of labour in teaching not only entails dissecting teaching methods and processes, but also breaking down academic curricula in such a way that each teacher handles his/her own area of specialty instead of teaching all courses, disciplines, or subjects.

Even in pre-colonial times, elders and masters took turns in teaching the student inductees their (elders' and masters') own areas of specialty like in crafting and weaving, among others. The same was applicable to extracurricular activities. No elder or master enjoyed monopoly of work over the other elders regarding instruction. Arguably, having one teacher for all subjects in the primary schools, for instance, might help to keep classroom members constant and stable with a view to cultivating a sense of responsibility for the entire class; in the sense that the students will gain familiarity and develop rapport more easily with one teacher instead of more than one for different subjects. Nevertheless, even for various academic, social, psychological and disciplinary reasons, it is inadvisable for students to have one teacher for all their subjects or courses in schools and institutions of higher learning. For example, it may be difficult for a teacher or professor who has not impressed some students in civics or social studies to impress them in mathematics or English language. For psychological reasons, it might even be worse if that teacher happens to be a well-known (but unpopular) disciplinarian in school. Variety is always the spice of life, even in the world of teaching and learning.

Although "one teacher teaches all" (or one-size-fits-all) strategy has endured and gained relative success in the nation's primary education system over the decades, circumstances of student underperformance in a given school or institution of learning will sometimes require school administrators to enlist supplementary or remedial teaching assistance and intervention from experts in the fields, courses, or subjects where students have been determined to consistently lag behind.

Recruitment of Teachers

Nigeria should readopt a catch-them-young strategy in the recruitment of teachers and classroom instructors. This scheme should aim at recruiting teachers primarily from among diploma and degree holders and secondarily from the top quarter of the graduating senior secondary school students. This type of initiative must come with noticeably solid demonstrations that teaching in Nigeria has a prestige that is perhaps lacking in other countries around us. One could predict the level and quality of teachers that the nation might get if about 7, 650 graduating secondary school applicants in each state of the federation competed for 860 available primary school teacher preparation slots in the 10 prospective Nigerian colleges and universities that educate and train teachers. If possible, let caution be exercised when it comes to admitting students into the teacher training programmes. Nigeria must exercise flexibility without being overly selective. Finland is much more selective in this exercise whereas the United States is often not very selective. Nigeria could create centrality or maintain a middle ground when it comes to teacher training admissions, given the nature of the nation's complex education culture that might be helpful even during the screening exercise. Is it not possible, for instance, when conducting proper screening, to find a senior secondary school graduate who can teach primary level mathematics or any other subject better than a candidate with a master's degree?

Insufficient recruitment and employment of teachers can impede the educational development of any school or institution of learning and possibly cripple its future progress. Regarding the recruitment of teachers in Nigerian schools, valuable insights into the core academic developmental challenges of a given institution should be seriously and primarily considered as applications for teaching employment roll in. In the context of schools' core academic development and curricular requirements, administrators and policymakers should give mathematics, English language, physics, chemistry and biology priority of place. The abilities to reason, conduct logical analysis, think critically and problem-solve are almost always traceable to an in-depth knowledge of the abovementioned courses. All other courses are essentially based on them. The pivotal importance of mathematics and the sciences, for instance, cannot be underestimated.

Think about daily activities, such as business transactions, analyses, innovations, inventions, travel, agriculture, weather forecasting, daily food purchases and consumptions. Even in the agricultural and farming industry, workers need to count days, weeks and months to estimate what seasons will be favourable for cultivation and harvests. A professional chef or simple cook also needs to add, subtract, divide, raise, or reduce whatever amount of ingredients are needed to make delicious meals. The same process applies when the intention is to give the food a unique flavour. Education heralds in pre-colonial Nigeria did all of these to become useful in their life careers. In sum, people's general life activities are intricately connected with mathematics and the sciences. It has been variously established by research that the previously mentioned academic subjects, beginning with mathematics, are certainly courses that can influence a student's entire life and career.

Remuneration and Rewards

Any society that is passionate about seeing its education system improve and making it a top priority would ensure that teachers are highly paid. Unquestionably, Nigeria, as a nation, has the right to require high and stronger academic credentials for its primary and secondary school teachers. The nation is also bound by justice to reward them with decent salaries following recruitment. The same is applicable to university lecturers and professors. The ability to comprehend the financial and sundry challenges that teachers, lecturers and professors generally face should facilitate appropriate decisions and actions in remuneration. That teachers constitute a group of professionals that do not always get the recognition they rightfully deserve in Nigeria remains incontestable.

In many countries around the world, with the rare exception of Nigeria, it remains inconceivable even to learn that teachers would not be paid their monthly salaries as and when due. Sometimes this non-payment of teachers, especially in public or government-owned primary and secondary schools, extends to months and even up to a year or more. The Nigerian Union of Teachers (NUT) has on occasion threatened to embark on strike if defaulting states fail or failed to clear salary arrears of its members (Agency Report, 2018). Such occurrences always constitute a national embarrassment, even when the issue occurs only in a few states.

Nigerian teachers should be encouraged to flourish and blossom in their profession. In fact, there are many brilliant, effective and wonderful teachers in the country that should be both appreciated and celebrated. In 2017, two Nigerian teachers were among the world's top 50 nominees for the prestigious 2018 Varkey Foundation Global Teacher Award slated for Dubai, United Arab Emirates. This nomination was reported to be the first of its kind since the annual US $1 million award introduced 4 years earlier (Oyowele, 2017). Compensation serves as a legal incentive and motivating factor towards productivity. Paying teachers enough should help to attract more people into the profession as well as strengthen the teaching force. Also, teachers should be rewarded or compensated in kind by public esteem in Nigeria, that is, publicly acknowledging teachers who distinguish themselves in the profession plus applauding teachers in general.

These measures can help to attract the brightest into the profession. Brilliant young men and women in Nigeria should not become teachers in the primary and secondary schools simply because greener pastures are not open to them in other professions. Such a mentality and trend, if accommodated, would not benefit the children and youth academically. Having dedicated teachers who are decently paid, on the other hand, could be enough to eliminate academic underperformance among the children and youth. Nations like South Korea, Singapore and Finland, where teachers are hugely respected and valued, get their teachers "intoxicated" with excitement upon learning that they have been employed into the teaching profession because salaries are generous and benefits enticing. In such nations, teachers earn even more than engineers and lawyers. Furthermore, school teachers and university academic staff members are not remunerated based on their students' grade or scores in exams, nor are schools and universities penalised on the same basis.

It is justifiable enough to assert that if governments nibble away at pensions and reduce institutional funding, then they must pay enough in wages to stay even. Cutting corners in the budgetary allocations to boost teachers' salaries makes sense in any nation that is interested in education. However, any strategy aimed at improving an education system without the necessary investment is bound to fail.

Teacher Evaluation

Rolling out aggressive teacher evaluation programmes designed to improve the academic performance of students who consistently rank below average in educational metrics would yield fruitful results towards achieving quality instructions. These evaluations could also benefit an entire nation's education system. Such a scheme, no doubt, might still spell controversies or draw deep resentments among school superintendents, principals and teachers along with their associates in target cities, districts and states. Notwithstanding potential hindrances, introducing workable teacher evaluation systems to increase teacher accountability is the surest way to help Nigeria's struggling schools improve teacher performance.

Teacher evaluation, though often contentious, has been trumpeted as a way of identifying ineffective teachers and sharing best practices. Nigeria's traditional teacher evaluation techniques such as filling out questionnaires and surveys coupled with occasional classroom teaching observations by visiting supervisors, which leave some teachers anxious and nervous, could be considered bearable and fair enough. Nonetheless, schools can adopt a strategy where the students themselves are asked to evaluate their teachers at the end of each term or semester prior to an independent supervisor's visit to measure teacher effectiveness. It is advisable that the supervisor's visit remains confirmatory in its function. The same method could be utilised in the university system, as can be found in many foreign nations that are politically and educationally democratic.

Since the Nigerian culture is basically democratic, communitarian and non-autocratic, teachers could be asked to recommend more suitable and valid ways in which they would wish to be assessed or evaluated without disregarding or negatively influencing students' vital contributions to the process. Students are co-participants in the democratically education process, besides being the immediate beneficiaries of school, college and university instruction. Therefore, this approach should not be considered disrespectful to those working and teaching in the nation's classrooms.

Essentially, in a democratic arrangement, students and even their parents or guardians, where applicable, should have strong say on how their teachers and lecturers are assessed. Nigeria certainly needs a school system where parents are real and genuine partners in progress. Also, decisions about teacher evaluation programmes should never be left solely to people who are out of touch with what goes on in the classroom. This type of precaution could reduce miscommunications, misunderstandings, frustrations and preventable aggressions. More importantly, teachers' recommendations should be able to discuss anything that is happening in the classrooms or schools that is preventing them from effectively communicating the learning materials to the students.

In Nigeria, too much heft seems to have also been given to a supervisor's classroom observation of a teacher to measure teaching effectiveness. A counterargument against this method can be that the actual beneficiaries or recipients of teaching practices and methods are the students, not the visiting supervisors. Besides, in the evaluation of teacher effectiveness, students can be more trusted not only to share their understanding of the items of instruction but also to assess their interactions with a teacher or professor. Supervisors visit only occasionally or periodically, while the students interact with and learn from teachers on a regular basis. Students could fill out structured questionnaires designed to evaluate each teacher in that teacher's absence. This strategy might enable administrators to forestall possible bias and unwanted influence over students' evaluation of a given teacher and instructor.

Instructors could be reassessed as often as policymakers, administrators and superintendents consider fit, especially if the students show no significant progress in their academic and educational performance following previous evaluations. The results of evaluations could be subsequently communicated to the said teachers early, with tips on how to improve and with assistance proffered when and where it is desirable. Incidentally, some of the schools interfere with teaching in many ways, from not retraining or reassigning (or dismissing) poor teachers to not supporting good ones. Teachers' concerns should also not be disregarded or ignored, as long as they are helpful, and that students' educational success retains priority of attention in any such negotiations. These measures should be adopted to stunt any opposing criticisms, which suggest that rigorous teacher evaluations do not necessarily improve students' educational achievements and other contrary recommendations.

Retired Teachers

In the field of teaching, people look for remarkable versatility and creativity, heightened by excellence. These qualities could attract the attention of education stakeholders, policymakers, administrators and leaders towards recruiting talented teachers. People should begin to look at the teaching profession as an investment and an industry in Nigeria. Establishing a practical teaching forum under the canopy of Retired Teachers Association (RTA) may be a good idea, as it might enable us to bolster teaching marketing campaigns. In this forum, retired school teachers with extensive teaching experience will get the opportunity to discuss and demonstrate their experiences of best practices, skills, styles, techniques and strategies in teaching and their plans for future generations with younger teachers. Not only will this organisation draw attention to best practices that have yielded positive results in the past, it will also help the nation to groom a new generation of innovative teachers who will still be well-grounded in the traditional teaching methods and skills. In liaison with the younger generation of teachers, veteran teachers can evaluate and predict how the integration of traditional methods of teaching and modern teaching technologies might impact the education system in the long term.

The idea is that the Retired Teachers Association (RTA) can be a forum where retired and older teachers will be free to express themselves with deep commitment, engagement and seriousness of purpose. Under the aegis of the same association, workshops, symposia and conferences could be organised to which parents, all teachers and students across the country would be invited. At these conferences and sessions, among other programmes, experienced administrators, teachers and veteran educators with vast experiences in curriculum development and teacher evaluation should be able to school young administrators and educators and help them develop knowledge of the pivotal roles that teachers play in the nation's education system. Consequently, thoughtful and insightful feedback from participants should be solicited to make the entire engagement fruitful, meaningful and productive.

Commentary and Evaluations

Even though the evaluation of teachers by the students might have some good impacts as well as highly recommended, the reliability index of those assessments should not be solely depended upon, since biases could often arise. There could be a student-teacher evaluation bias just as there could be a teacher-student evaluation bias especially at the higher levels of students' education. These biases or potential prejudices could be exclusively non-academic in many cases. In some cases, their bases could be personality or gender-related, ethnic, religious, tribal, or cultural, among others. Indeed, any education administration should take the responsibility of appraising how a class works. Therefore, there is the need to always educate both teachers and students on the sacrosanctity of such evaluations.

Understandably, the results of baseless and negatively biased ratings of teachers by their students could be quite humiliating to dedicated, hardworking and unsuspecting teachers. Assessing the standard and quality of students' education, offering teachers permanent employment, raising their salaries, or granting them promotions should not be completely based on the students' evaluations of the applicable teachers. Students might have the tendency to consistently give favourable evaluations only to those teachers who are either friendly with them or score them more generously even without understanding the implications of their actions. On one hand, this type of scenario might cause supposedly uncommitted teachers to habitually exploit this type of student behaviour to their own unmerited advantage. On the other hand, students could also exploit such acts of misapplied generosity from such teachers, thereby, resulting in potentially poor student academic engagements and learning outcomes.

Students should not be treated as business customers, partners, or clients that ought to be pleased or kept happy at all cost. Therefore, every effort should be made to encourage the students to be thorough, objective and honest in their assessment. Also, care must be taken not to create the impression that the total responsibility for students' progress or success in education rests on their teachers. Teachers are paid to give students good education, at the same time the students are expected to give their best in personal commitment to their studies regardless of the teacher's presence and directives.

Chapter Eleven
Endemic Challenges and Investments

This chapter highlights certain problems in the nation's education system that one knows to exist even though one might not recognise them at present. These are the problems of corruption and fraud. Indeed, corruption and fraud are stories that should sound uncomfortably familiar. Nigerians are quite familiar with such problems, knowing that they will probably always exist because they have always existed, often because of human acts of indiscipline and inherent greed. Such challenges commonly assume dimensions and nuances that are either predictable or anticipated; therefore, people should always anticipate and be prepared for them. Also, they often involve trade-offs that cause us to believe them to be irresolvable or simply to feign ignorance of their existence.

The problem of corruption in Nigeria is never truly surprising, as no country in the world is totally free from its grip. It seems to be present everywhere in Nigeria and to be implicated as one of the major causes of poverty in the country, however. In the Corruption-Perceptions Index of 2016, Transparency International placed Nigeria in the 136th position out of 176 countries. In 2017, Nigeria was placed in the 148th position out of 180 countries (Transparency International Surveys, 2018). This means that Nigeria further diminished in transparency by dropping 12 places from the previous year.

Many people who grew up in Nigeria seem to have accepted corruption as an unavoidable political, economic and social component of the country, that is, "a normal part of everyday life". If not aggressively and judiciously checked, corruption can dismember an entire nation. The past experiences and honest evaluations of various sectors in the country could show what corruption can do. Nevertheless, an in-depth look into this lingering problem will reveal that there is a much more complex story to tell.

The Nature and Causes of Corruption

Every so often, corruption and fraud seem to show up in perhaps new and unsettling ways. The possibility that funds released by the federal government in previous years to various sectors in the country might end up in some private pockets and bank accounts could never be ruled out. Such tendencies, if existent in any sector, public or private, need to be nipped in the bud. In such cases, it sometimes seems difficult to either name or point an accusing finger at an individual or group of individuals.

The root causes of corruption in every sector appeared to be either created or nurtured by latent bureaucratic indecencies, indiscipline, greed and disorderliness. They are either deliberate or inadvertent in rare exceptions. Corruption is also associated with certain socio-political conflicts, slow growth and low levels of economic development. Above all, it is rooted in human selfishness, greed and indiscipline.

Corruption in Education

The popularity of any nation's formal education system will always plummet if it wrestles with latent corruption, let alone public corruption scandals. Corruption in the Nigerian education system, which is not a part of the African traditional and cultural heritage, is still not believed to have become an old story. Nestled among the difficulties and troubling issues that allegedly misshape the direction of Nigeria's education system are the grievous allegations of corrupt practices. Obasanjo, in Yomere (2010), as cited by Asiyai, (2015), observed that corruption kills innovation and creativity, compromises public morality, contaminates individual and collective dignity and distorts the dignity of labour (Asiyai, 2015).

Corruption in the Nigerian education system appears to be an evergreen concern with no perfect solution. To cite an example, people still subsidise or complement their income on campus by hook or by crook under the excuse that they are not decently paid. How does one define a situation where some teachers will demand or accept bribes to either admit or promote an academically poor student to a higher level in school? Describing corruption in the Nigerian education system, *Sun Newspaper* observed:

> It has become a deep-rooted norm in every sector, occurring in different forms; giving the so-called "egunje", a local parlance for bribes; being favoured at the expense of a more qualified and experienced colleague; nepotism or giving favours in exchange for gratifications; and in some schools, a student cannot pass examinations without bribing the teachers. How about parents buying examination papers for their children in advance? Children learn societal norms and behaviours through their schooling. We often hear of students paying bribes, in all its different forms, for good grades or to purchase questions in advance of structured examinations (Durojaiye, 2017).

These corrupt practices seem to have pervaded all three levels of Nigeria's formal institutions of learning.

Reports from several newspapers have indicated that corrupt practices in the nation's education system are found especially in the universities. Also, research has revealed that the types of corruption prevalent in Nigerian universities is related to examinations, admissions, finance, accreditation and sexual solicitations. The causes of corrupt practices are attributed to greed, moral decadence, poor management, lack of the fear of God, the desire to get rich quick and students' academic laziness. Each has different manifestations. Sometimes, corruption shows up in the form of using personal connections to gain unmerited favours and higher places in schools. It can also indirectly take the form of donor appreciation and support, which unfortunately sometimes infiltrates and even compromises areas of student academic and admission processes.

Corruption in university education distorts the efficiency and quality output of the system (Asiyai, 2015). Schools and higher education authorities should be able to establish the required ethical and moral boundaries in this regard. Concerned about the rising incidents of corruption in Nigerian universities, Okojie (2012) urged the management of Nigerian universities to respect the sanctity of the education system by ensuring that their institutional environments are free of corruption. He further lamented that corruption had reached such a deplorable level in Nigeria that universities, as an integral part of the nation, could not even be shielded from the scourge. This admonition is appropriate because Nigerian universities are supposed to be centres of education, learning, scholarship, community service, moral values, innovation, research, teaching excellence and professionalism. Overall, schools should play the role of active agents that set a course for moral and social transformation.

Unfortunately, it is evident but still hard to accept that while the rest of scholars teach, lecture in classes and conduct useful scientific research in all honesty, a supposedly negligible number of policymakers, administrators and academic staff seem to be figuring out how best to subvert everything that is honourable for their selfish interest. Is it not high time Nigeria ranked high in the world for things that matter, like transparency and its affiliated concepts? According to *The Guardian Newspaper* (2013), Nigeria was ranked the 33rd most corrupt country in the world by the German-based organisation Transparency International. In the group's Corruption Perception Index of 2013, Nigeria ranked 144th, out of 177 nations in the world, scoring 25 points out of a possible 100 (Kalu, 2013). While Nigerians do not have to hold onto this report and assessment as an article of faith so as not to dampen their aspirations, they still need to seriously sit up and consider matters of transparency.

Negative Impacts

If, for instance, an academic staff or a group of academic staff members is responsible for corruption in a given educational institution, it could be difficult to imagine what those same academic staff members might be teaching their students, as future Nigerian leaders, relative to the supposed crimes, corruption and public misdemeanours in the nation. It is expected that the youths are well-trained in schools and tertiary institutions to be able to take up their proper place and play crucial leadership roles in the future of Nigeria's political landscape. It is noteworthy that the dictum, "action (or behaviour) speaks louder than words" also applies to the education sector. Furthermore, a crumbling education is a national security risk, as education and national security are closely linked. A poorly educated workforce might be the greatest long-term threat to national security that Nigeria could face as a nation. When the youth is morally and intellectually enfeebled, it will not be able to promote stability and growth or defend the nation indirectly from future external aggression.

A Positive Foundation

Young people everywhere have the constitutional right to be educated in an intellectually stimulating and morally nurturing environment. Nigeria's young people need to be exposed to a strong and positive educational foundation to enable them to outsmart others in creativity, innovativeness, morality, discipline and positive thinking. This foundation will also afford them the ability to out-compete others in global contests. In today's global competitions, there is a presumption that all students are properly educated and ready to compete. The nation's youths need support systems and relationships that extend outside of the school to reinforce what happens in the school system, instil positive values and the lifelong desire to learn to take on challenges and succeed. Students are unlikely to succeed in school in matters of discipline and morals if they do not have those positive values driven into them at schools and universities as well as cultivated and proclaimed at home.

Solutions and Recommendations

Which is the way forward? Allegations of fraud, bribery or corruption in any education system should not be covered up or glossed over. Ignoring such a trend might make education administrators and policymakers appear complicit. It could seriously weaken the entire system ethically and morally.

Predictably, veteran and experienced Nigerian professors, educators and a few erstwhile Ministers of Education of trusted and distinguished repute would consider any attempts at reforming education in Nigeria without fundamentally addressing the issue of corruption and fraud to be profoundly misguided. It also leaves us wondering what must be done to achieve a meaningful, reliable and corruption-free academic system in the country.

To fight and curb corruption effectively, transparency, accountability and responsibility are the key words that must be put into action. Nonetheless, in Nigeria, where cronyism and conflicts of interest seem rampant, it may be difficult for stakeholders to come up with appropriate and definitive solutions. What remains a problem in the fight against corruption is that people are sometimes unable to factually specify or describe a corruption-related issue with exactitude. In most cases, corruption is a covert activity and thereby difficult to either measure or detect. This does not negate its credibility and existence. It certainly does exist and can be detected when seriously and honestly probed. Usually, the impact of some of the malpractice and fraud in academia remains largely invisible until a moment of broader educational crisis in a district, state, or nation. This could certainly be prevented in Nigeria if the government, education regulators, legislators and policymakers would forge ahead with a refreshingly frank and properly guided attempt to enforce responsibility, accountability and transparency in the entire education system.

The federal government must lead the way and set the pace. It is mindboggling to note that people often treat anticipated problems such as corruption as if they were never anticipated. But how would eradicating this problem help to address actual but unanticipated challenges in the education system? Removing, dismissing, or prosecuting the patrons of frauds and recipients of corruption proceeds, essentially, may not necessarily address the issue of corruption, but it could serve as a serious starting point. Nonetheless, it would still look like alleviating the symptoms of an illness without removing its cause or source.

Aside from penalising offenders, it seems that being proactive might be an additional and even better way of addressing the issue of corruption in Nigerian education. Specifically, an across- the-board emphasis on ethics, moral education, spirituality and good character formation might be instructive in conjunction with a reorientation to the nation's traditional values. Because of the political, economic and social harm that corruption has caused in Nigeria, a mandatory introduction of ethical values, character and morals into the primary and secondary education curricula should be seriously considered. This target curriculum content should be able to criminalise and discourage all types of corruption and fraud in the education sector, among others.

Moreover, occasional and unannounced visits to schools and tertiary institutions by reputable superintendents, supervisors and education ministries can be established, if not already in practice.

External and independent auditors are also recommended for schools and tertiary institutions across the country. Moreover, the idea of establishing centres, units, or departments within the school and tertiary institution premises to monitor and effectively check corruption is highly encouraged. These measures could be taken to hold educators and their affiliates to uncompromising standards of accountability. Overall, concerted efforts need to be made, with the help of the students and their families, to address the root cause of corruption in the education sector in Nigeria.

The solutions to these challenges will be complex. Nevertheless, tolerating or attempting to softly manage such endemic problems might give an undesirable impression that they are unspoken and acceptable behavioural norms. This type of nonresponse could also become an unintended enabler that might breed poor and corrupt graduates, citizens and consequently leaders, thereby worsening the level of corruption in the country and furthering its inherently cyclic pattern.

Additional Comments

To solve the problem of corruption and fraud in Nigeria as a whole, bureaucracies must be overhauled from top to bottom and not the other way around. It begins with the nation's constitution (laws, regulations and orders) and the enforcement of its laws, regulations and orders.

The likeliest solution is to eradicate the causes of corruption through focused education and conscientious programmes that will effect a change in people's thinking by teaching helpful social norms and instituting the right values in addition to investigating and penalising more serious cases. When someone succeeds in changing other people's mindsets through education to the extent that they become intolerant of corruption in a given environment, the natural result is that corruption will gradually disappear from the same environment.

In the education system, some problems are considered major, while others could be judged as minor. For instance, that some students engage in counterproductive behaviours, refuse to follow directions, disrupt teaching in the classroom, or fail to do their class assignments are minor endemic problems and should be addressed specifically and systematically. However, when ministers, commissioners, stakeholders, policymakers, administrators, teachers and educators embezzle education funds or systematically steal, or tamper with education resources and school properties, these are major endemic problems that ought to be addressed both specifically and proportionately.

Ideally, the training for education administrators and teachers would address some undeniably endemic problems and prepare them to respond. Endemic problems often wrongfully enjoy the patronage of receptive, supportive and like-minded promoters. Certainly, specific approaches will always help to address predictable or endemic problems and perhaps isolate unanticipated ones. Of course, the result would always reflect the approach used. Also, applying specific solutions would certainly help to narrow down areas that need improvement.

Investigations and Transparency

It might sound ironically far-fetched to suggest that Nigeria puts less emphasis on the issue of corruption in its education system and instead embarks aggressively on a new system of education that would groom modern academia for posterity. Nonetheless, this recommendation, if at all tenable to positive reception and influence, does not also suggest a total disregard of what has previously gone wrong in the Nigerian education system. No, corruption and graft practices can still be fought or probed with a view to gleaning clues for a better future progress of the nation's overall education system and practice.

Any clear case of bribery, corruption or fraud in the education sector could be promptly and thoroughly investigated, with reports of the investigation publicised with transparency. Monitoring and investigating all incident reports of corruption in a timely, thorough and manner might help prevent future reoccurrences. As a forewarning, these processes of investigation could be clearly described and added to the notes of undertaking that every employee of any educational institution must agree to sign prior to employment. Indeed, every institution or organisation needs some checks and balances to enable its sustainable growth and progress. Fighting corruption systemically is an aspect of such checks and balances. This implies that investigations against corrupt and sharp practices can still be considered and properly prosecuted. Investigations are always necessary to douse the flames of ignorance. Investigation and prosecution will also help to establish certainty regarding what may have factually gone wrong in the system and aid the government in determining where to put appropriate restraints.

Transparency and honesty in investigations have always been cherished by the Nigerian culture. Arguably, fundamental misunderstandings and conflicts may sometimes generate accusations and counter-accusations of corrupt practices within the education system. Nevertheless, these belong only to the realm of possibilities and probabilities. Independent and objective investigations would help allay people's fears, restore trust and confidence in the system and clarify inaccurate analyses, misguided reports, wrongful accusations and possible misconceptions. In this type of situation, governments, their representatives, organisations, agencies, individuals, or groups of individuals must not attempt to influence panels of investigators, either directly or by proxy. Otherwise, such a constituted panel would suffer from a disturbing lack of transparency and flawed process instead of being operationally reliable. Legislators should endeavour to address these problems at the federal, state and district levels to help citizens resist the urge to interfere in any credible investigative process.

On the progressive side, investigations could also, surprisingly, reveal positive elements of educational stability, strength and prosperity that could even be widely applied to bolster best practices in education.

Economy and Education Funding

The endemic issue of corruption or fraud in any country's education system, though a hindrance, should not prevent it from funding education as well as encouraging investments in education to enable growth and lasting progress in the nation's economy. Education funding and investments should be heavily encouraged and supported. Meagre or poor funding of education programmes over the years has made it difficult for us to embark on any serious reforms and innovations in the education sector. Critics of the Nigerian education sector have severally blamed its failures on either poor or lack of funding on the part of the government. In this century, why would 80 pupils and a teacher still sit under trees outside school buildings for lack of classrooms in some states across Nigeria? Pundits believe that insufficient funding of the education system in Nigeria might lead to an increase in adult illiteracy, social ills, conflicts, violence, diminished public health, extremism, general insecurity and even a lower national GDP index. Giving education priority of place would certainly encourage general economic prosperity. There should be no contrary debate over this priority.

Can these suggestions help Nigeria to consider re-prioritising education in a profoundly strategic manner? With Nigerian schools, colleges and universities imperilled by a struggling economy and verifiable allegations of corrupt practices in the country's education system, the persistently high costs of running institutions and declining government funding should not come as a surprise. ASUU, ASUP and COEASU often embark on strikes and industrial actions to make their own cases or press for improved education funding. On one hand, there seems to be an almost unanimous agreement that the education system in Nigeria is poorly funded. On the other hand, claims that the education system is poorly funded have been debunked by some government officials as untrue, unrealistic, or simply exaggerated. The same response has been given to claims about low teacher salaries in the country.

For any nation's education system to address the needs of each student, the education sector must be sufficiently funded. While the vision of the Nigerian education system since 1977 has promised to provide education to millions of young and growing citizens, this expanded initiative always comes with a cost. It is perhaps the case that no amount would be considered sufficient to fund education in Nigeria, just as no amount of money would be considered more than enough. However, the impact of underfunding education programmes and services in Nigeria could be enormous. Among other advantages, funding would enable any institution of learning to provide its students with quality and effective education, solve the problems of dilapidated structures and facilities, acquire equipment for teaching and learning and promote the general welfare of the staff and students.

Additionally, every progressively inclined and forward-looking academic institution requires some academic building booms. Classrooms, laboratories, libraries, study halls and other activity centres need periodic renovations. The same is true of dilapidated infrastructure. These programmes cost millions and in some cases billions of naira. Chronic underfunding of the education sector in any nation naturally results in chronic understaffing, besides cutbacks in educational programmes and services across the nation. Therefore, any call to different government institutions and agencies to inject sizeable funds into the Nigerian education sector for the nation to achieve its goals is always helpful.

The benefits of literacy would require us to reduce some less useful entitlements and drive value for funds through the governments, so the nation can channel enough public spending to areas that are more likely to boost its educational productivity. It must be particularly noted that some insist that debt and deficit reductions in funding are incongruous with national educational development. That is an incorrect premise. As Nigeria pursues long-term economic plans, such efforts also must be extended to the education sector until there is a clear evidence that a well-monitored strategy is workable and sustainable.

Funding from the government is indispensable, since public schools and tertiary institutions in Nigeria must periodically embark on construction and renovation programmes to give the learning environment both a facelift and a new shape. Some public universities could also wish to make their campuses into technology and applied science research hubs, building large facilities that focus specifically on advanced scientific research. In such remarkable instances, they would need funding from both the state and federal governments or joint public-private partnerships or investments. As a case in point, the University of Abuja has long planned to expand its campus by building hostels for its teeming students and a staff housing estate using a public-private partnership (PPP) education project development model. In 2014, it spent two billion naira (N2bn) of a Federal Government's Intervention Fund on some costly projects, including physics and chemistry laboratories and a 500- capacity lecture hall for the Faculty of Science (*Premium Times*, 2014).

In this technology-driven era, some Nigerian universities are scrambling to build computer centres to promote technical and vocational education through information and computer technologies. Many of the universities are also grading and paving the campus premises and installing external electrification, drainages, boreholes and overhead tanks and so on. Some of these programmes and projects are large and complex enough to require many years for their completion. In some cases, instead of awaiting response from the government through their federal and state ministries, the universities are simply availing themselves of the PPP arrangement.

Education Budgets

Nigeria should jealously protect key budgets that do not exclude the education sector. Within this sector, people can easily think about schools, colleges, universities, salaries, emoluments, science and technology and increased planned infrastructural spending to invest in the nation's long-term educational success. Because of the scourge of corruption in some schools, colleges and universities, some constructive public critics of the Nigerian education system have argued that any continued or improved funding of such institutions by the government would be tantamount to incentivising unethical and counterproductive behaviours. Others might consider it to be showering expenses unnecessarily and lowering accountability, which, in fact, should require school administrators and educators to render transparent accounts of their stewardship. Nevertheless, starving educational institutions of necessary funding under the guise of reducing deficits or curbing corruption would leave lingering damage that can drag down the nation's academic and, by extension, corporate growth.

Implementing free education policies in the Nigerian primary and secondary schools and nixing unscrupulous practices such as the underground charging of fees in schools by administrators will require a reasonable though prorated allocation of funds to the education sector in the annual budget. Enough funds should always be made available by both the state and federal governments for the continued, supervised and well-channelled transformation of the education sector.

Based on innumerable historical evidence, the post-colonial reintroduction of the Universal Free Primary Education (UFPE) in Nigeria in 1976 was considered a progressive and laudable innovation in Nigerian educational development. Following this trend, the nation witnessed an exponential increase in pupil enrolment and in the expansion of primary education. Indeed, there was unprecedented growth at all levels of education plus an increased financial involvement of all stakeholders and the three tiers of government as a result.

No one is advocating that Nigeria decreases funding, but economic progress cannot be solely relied upon to solve a structural budget deficit. Unfortunately, governments will continue to make difficult decisions by reducing less-valuable entitlements and increasing public sector pay. For this reason, schools and institutions should strive to strengthen their reputations with the government and their communities. They can accomplish this feat by judiciously using fund allocations from the government. Understandably, the idea is not only for the government to control general spending but also to run a surplus and pay down debts. This approach is like fixing the roof of a house in anticipation of the rainy season. Even though governments ought to live within their means without piling up debts and deficits to burden future generations at the same time, considering the education sector among the areas that deserve priority of attention in the overall budgetary allocations is crucial.

A cursory review of Nigeria's government spending from 1999 to 2016 shows that the education sector budget allocation is far below UNESCO's benchmark of 26%. This percentage is required of any nation's annual budget to fund education. Nigeria's annual budgetary allocations for education, by contrast, recorded an average of 8.4%, far below what would normally be expected for the development of education in Nigeria. In 2012, the World Bank Report showed the average percentage in the education sector budgets among a few African countries: Ghana spent 31.0% of its total budget on education, Cote D' Ivoire, 30.0%; Uganda, 27.0%; Morocco, 26.4%; South Africa, 25.8%; Swaziland, 24.6%; Kenya, 23.0%; Botswana, 10.0% and Nigeria, 8.4% (World Bank, 2012).

Based on Table 9 in the next page, Nigeria's budget allocation for the education sector increased slightly from 2013 to 2015 but plummeted significantly in 2016. Particularly, in 2012, N468.39 billion (9.86%) was allocated to the sector out N4.7 trillion, an increase from the previous year's 9.32%. The sector got N509.4 billion (10.21%) out of N4.10 trillion in the 2013 national budget, a marginal increase from the previous year's 9.86%.

In 2014, the sector received N495.28 billion (10.67%) out of N4.6 trillion. In 2015, it was granted N483.7 billion (10.75%) out of N4.5 trillion. While in 2016, however, the same Nigerian education sector got N483.7 (7.98%) billion out of N 6.1 trillion, a downward plunge from the previous year's 10.75%. Based on these statistics, there is an acute need for the federal government to seriously review and steadily increase its budgetary provisions for Nigeria's education.

Table 9. *Total Budget vs. Educational Sector Budgets and percentage Equivalents from 1999-2016*

Year	Total Budget Allocation	Education Budget	Percent of Allocation
1999	60,549,835,647	2,700,000,000	4.46
2000	470,009,971,781	40,940,663,330	8.71
2001	894,214,805,186	63,783,776,990	7.13
2002	1,064,801,253,520	73,435,499,300	6.90
2003	976,254,543,375	75,707,827,520	7.75
2004	1,790,848,344,588	93,767,886,839	5.24
2005	1,799,938,242,138	147,835,527,799	8.21
2006	1,876,302,363,351	195,693,672,666	10.43
2007	2,226,394,423,477	221,071,774,929	9.93
2008	2,492,076,718,937	250,144,818,579	10.04
2009	2,870,510,042,679	252,204,813,495	8.79
2010	4,608,616,278,213	339,634,791,000	7.37
2011	4,226,191,559,259	393,810,171,775	9.32
2012	4,749,100,821,170	468,385,490,528	9.86
2013	4,987,220,425,601	509,039,713,761	10.21
2014	4,642,960,000,000	495,283,130,268	10.67
2015	4,493,363,957,158	483,183,784,654	10.75
2016	6,060,677,358,227	483,666,376,895	7.98
	50,290,030,944,307	4,590,289,720,328	8.54

Source: Bello et al., 2017. *Asian Journal of Multidisciplinary Studies*, 5(6).

Corporate Investment

Education in Nigeria and its funding should not be an exclusive responsibility of the three tiers of government. Because of the growing population of the nation, it could be overwhelming or simply burdensome for the government to handle it alone. The country must therefore resolve and be content to diversify the provision of education, its management and funding. New education policies are often created out of necessity and demand. There is a growing need to involve corporations and non-governmental organisations (both indigenous and expatriates) and voluntary agencies in the business of funding education across the country. As the need for education increases, funding education in Nigeria should be considered a matter of joint and collective responsibility by all stakeholders.

Funding remains key to bolstering educational advancement. Unquestionably, it is the basic duty of the government to provide a favourable environment for investment in education and a type of coordination to promote educational growth and development. Nevertheless, the private sector, communities, corporations, alumni associations and even well-placed families and persons in the society can make their own provisions to augment government funding efforts. This could also be done through the provision of grants, loans, scholarships and endowment funds. There is a provision — section II, sub-section 109 — in the National Policy on Education (NPE) that permits the private sectors' involvement in the development and funding of education in Nigeria. Hence, the public- private partnerships (PPPs) would always be tremendously beneficial in providing, developing and funding education in Nigeria. Such models would improve the education system and, therefore, the future of Nigeria in general.

Prudent and resourceful policymakers, stakeholders, education managers and leaders could adopt strategies with committed government backing. These strategies could be applied by initiating safe and endogenous financial sectors, endowments and fundraising machineries for their institutions. To be specific, the National Open University of Nigeria (NOUN) sought to establish a N150 million multi-functional centre for the university community within the campus at Jabil, Abuja utilising a PPP arrangement. The proposal finally met the approval of the Infrastructure Concession Regulatory Commission (ICRC) with the procurement of an Outline Business Certificate (OBC) from the commission as a licence to look for private investors (Ishaya, 2017). The idea is to produce a complex that would include supermarkets, restaurants, banks, bookstores and retail shops.

Others might encourage or introduce corporate investment partnerships that provide opportunities to facilitate financial growth for an educational institution with government support. These investments should be socio-culturally relevant to Nigeria, given its large population. The partnerships could afford schools and tertiary institutions the ability to grow financially, provided the aimed investments are properly monitored, supervised and periodically audited by the government or other appropriate authorities. Some degree of concessions, exceptions and privileges could be given to independent educational institutions in this connection. Also, negotiations to obtain approval from the federal, state and local governments when required for corporate investments could be tough, therefore relevant provisions might be made, if necessary, to ensure that the country's education system does not fail the next generation because of inadequate support from the government. Schools and educational institutions can often be subsidised with initiatives and industry.

Chapter Twelve
Reconfiguring Nigerian Education

To properly reconfigure the Nigerian education system, Nigerians should always bear in mind this thoughtful maxim from Albert Einstein: "Education is what remains after one has forgotten what one has learnt in school".

Lessons from Colonialism

Granted that the British colonialists did not necessarily exceed both the primary and secondary levels in the initial education system they brought to Nigeria, nevertheless, people should not become retrograde or stagnant in their mindsets. Should one continue to play the blame game or rather brainstorm on how best to solve educational and national problems? Brainstorming is a better alternative because Nigerians did not stay where the colonialists dropped them off. Rather, they forged ahead positively.

Even though "indicting the colonialists" is not the title or purpose of this work, it could still be justifiably argued that the British colonialists' social, economic, political and education policies in Nigeria and Africa were, in some instances, exploitative and unfair. Self-interest and nationalist aspiration, which manifested in their exploitation of both natural and human resources in the country, would not be ruled out.

Historical evidence of resistance and protests from the citizens against unfair economic and social policies of the colonialists could be found in the Aba Women's Riots of 1929, the Tax Protest of 1938, the

Owerri and Calabar Oil Mill Protest of 1940s and the Onitsha Aba Tax Revolt of 1956. In the education sector, even as the colonialists modified the programme that was being provided by the European missionaries with the 1882, 1887 and 1916 education ordinances, they still wound up tailoring the policies towards their own imperialist goals and objectives. In fact, education policies were colonially controlled. When the colonialists stepped up educational developments and economic programmes during the latter part of the 19th century and into the early 20th century, they seemed to have done so indirectly for their own benefit, which led to both systematic and systemic exploitations. However, people should be able to overcome their colonial mentality, their perceptions about the progress of the nation's education system. It is time to seek a long-lasting solution.

Scholars have argued that the colonialists' policy intervention in the Nigerian education sector was conditioned by both their own needs for revenue generation and those of Great Britain to boost their home economy, hence the need for African raw materials for their own industries, creating markets in the colonies for their manufactured goods and preparing African natives for Western education and, above all, an orientation towards their imperialist commitment. This situation created imperialist expansion, with the European powers scrambling to partition the African continent from 1870 to around 1914 (Robinson, Gallagher & Denry, 1995; Shillington, 2005).

Besides what would yield profits for the colonialists, it is unlikely that Britain planned to invest financially in the Nigerian education system or in any substantial and helpfully human intellectual development during the colonial days. They probably thought that too much knowledge or higher education for native Africans would undermine their objectives and pose a threat for them as colonialists whom the natives had often considered imperialists and "taskmasters". Moreover, if huge developments were made in the colonies, they would have no choice but to be compelled to maintain and sustain them with local revenues. While the missionaries came on a humanitarian mission to evangelise, introduce civilisation, fight the slave trade, combat savagery and introduce the positive rudiments of Western education, it is difficult to suggest that the British colonialists likewise necessarily and exclusively came for charity or on a philanthropic mission. It is also difficult to declare that their mission was neither mercantilist nor profiteering. On the other hand, to the advantage of the colonies, which the colonialists perhaps did not directly intend, a lot of fruitful human elements and variables were inadvertently engendered. These elements came in the forms of future true independence, progressive curiosity, enlightened inquisitiveness, inventiveness, resourcefulness and industriousness.

But what is the best way to prepare a person or a people for independence? What would all the listed variables mean for the exploited colonies and the Nigerian citizens? Objectively, answers vary as to what it means to practically prepare a person, a people, or a country for independence. What type of independence: mental, physical, social, intellectual, emotional, cultural, economic, or political independence? And is the answer "to do everything for them?" Would that not actually prepare them for future dependence by rendering them passive, lazy and unproductive? A teacher, for instance, guides a student on how to solve problems but does not solve the problems for him during exams. The same is applicable in many aspects of life. Is it not possible that the colonialists generally but unknowingly adopted Maimonides' influential medieval (12th century) philosophy of life and policy teaching as described in the maxim: "Give a man a fish and you feed him for a day. Teach a man to fish and you feed him for a lifetime?" Is it not possible that they gave Nigeria a fish and Nigerians lament that they did not give them a goat, a ram, or even a cow? People seem to imply that the colonialists should have given them a "cow" (university level of education) to enable them to learn how to get an "elephant" (do scientific research, manufacture cars and airplanes, invent computers, build industries and manufacture medications). Maybe people are right or wrong in this type of sweeping judgement and these overblown expectations of the colonial masters. At that time, however, there had not been much global advancement in science and technology as such. Almost no computers were in existence when Nigeria gained independence. How many common drugs and medications for major or deadly diseases, for instance, had been invented around the world by then? Not too many.

Later Progress in Education and Scholarship

Advancement in education is always a gradual process, irrespective of the time or duration. Education brought an early wave of Nigerian immigrants especially to both the United Kingdom and the United States in the 1970s and 1980s. After the Nigerian-Biafra civil war (1967-1970), the federal government sponsored scholarships for Nigerian students to pursue education abroad. Many of these students were in the American universities. These scholarships were funded to enable the students to acquire relevant education with skills and come back to build their own nation and infrastructure.

As at 2015, the Nigerian-American population stood at 376,000, making up about one percent of the black population in the United States, according to the Rockefeller Foundation-Aspen Institute. Many of these immigrants are highly educated, hardworking, high-achieving and professionally successful. An approximation based on previous statistics suggests that some 61 percent of Nigerian Americans hold a bachelor's degree, while about 32 percent of those older than 25 years hold a master's degree, doctorate or advanced professional degree, out of which about 19 percent specifically hold a master's degree. In 2016, an American Community Survey found that among Nigerian-American professionals, 45 percent work in education services and many are professors at top universities (Fosco, 2018; Jayawardane, 2018). Nigerians enter the medical, engineering, science and technology fields in the U.S. at an increased rate, leaving their home country to work in American hospitals, agencies, industries and organisations, where they can earn more and work in better facilities. A growing number of Nigerian-Americans are becoming entrepreneurs and CEOs, building technology companies in the U.S. Some are making their marks in the field of entertainment, sports and culinary arts.

Today, Nigeria as a nation has many potentially gifted and talented young people who have in the past and recent years "invented" or manufactured cars, motorcycles, helicopters and airplanes that have been on display in both print and visual media. Among all these talented persons, how many of them have (or had) a university education? Even if they do (or did), would one argue that they were influenced only by the level of education they received?

Without second-guessing the intentions of the colonial masters or defending their potential prejudices, marginalisation or discriminations, one can hold the opinion that Nigerians may have generally misconstrued some of their intentions. Excepting some areas where the colonialists obviously exploited the nation, a thorough analysis of the entire situation, back then, might not necessarily or evidently indict them completely. After all, most of the Nigerian founding fathers and early public leaders in the church, politics, education, industry and commerce owe their education (s) either in part or entirely to the enterprise of the colonialists and European missionaries, at least their rudimentary formation.

The Colonial Time's Educational Status in Europe

Experience and records show that many European citizens and Americans during the colonial times did not (and even in this present day do not) have college or higher degrees. Today, many of them still end up with only high school or secondary school diplomas and certificates. Even though intellectual research is very important to them, education, economy and national development are more about utilitarianism, efficiency, productivity and pragmatism.

According to *The Guardian*, almost half of all young people went to university in 2011/12. Nevertheless, in 2012, only 34.4% of the working age population of Great Britain (aged 16 to 64), achieved the National Vocational Qualifications (NVQ4+) — a degree-level or equivalent qualification or above. What happened to other 65.6%? Related data reveal that 40.2% of those employed have a degree or its equivalent. What of the other 59.8%? What level of education did they attain? The Office for National Statistics (ONS) also reported in

December 2012 that 27.2% of the population ages 16 to 74 had a degree or equivalent or higher, that is, about 12 million people. This proportion is believed to be lower than the proportion for 16 to 64-year-olds because of the much smaller participation rates for the 64-74 age group covered by the census (Ball, 2013). The NVQs, earlier mentioned, were obtainable in England, Wales and Northern Ireland. They were work-based awards or certificates given to candidates who, through assessment and training, were able to display their skill, competence and ability to carry out their job to the required standard in their career path. The NVQs range from level 1, which has to do with basic work activities to level 5 for senior management.

Furthermore, the United States Census Bureau published that in 1940, an average of only 4.6% of the country's adult population (25 years or older) out of a total population of 132.1 million had completed 4 years of college or more. Censuses from 1940 through 1980 showed even lower levels of education at the high school and bachelor's degree level. In 2006, only 28% of the adult population in the U.S., of a total population of 298.4 million, had reached that level of education. In 2010, less than 30% out of the adult population in the U.S. of a total population of 309.3 million had completed a bachelor's degree or higher. In 2016, this statistic was 33.4% of 323.1 million (Bauman, 2016). These snippets of progress in education in both the United Kingdom and the United States give us a clue into their situation regarding education when Britain came to Nigeria for colonisation far back in the late 18th and early 19th century. It is to be hoped that this summary might help us withhold any further harsh judgement.

The Way Forward for the Nigerian Education System

The European colonialists had come and gone, although some of the impacts of their actions, whether positive or negative, may remain. Nevertheless, those perceived negative effects should not hold sway in this 21st century, especially in the nation's education system. Nigeria has come of age as a nation and can always make good decisions and policies despite its complicated colonial inheritance.

The needed reconfiguration of the Nigerian education system's development, process and policy implementation schemes could become a huge success only when the nation must have established a solid educational structure with a curriculum that both modifies and supports culture and tradition, ability, aptitude, creativity, resourcefulness, capacity-building and development. This type of structure would serve as education's policy implementation framework, basis and standard. Despite the level and nature of intellectual trainings given to Nigerian pupils and students, educators should come to the recognition that individual students are not only unique human beings but also persons with great and diverse potentials, gifts and talents. These human elements and variables must be objectively and energetically explored, treasured and ultimately mobilised.

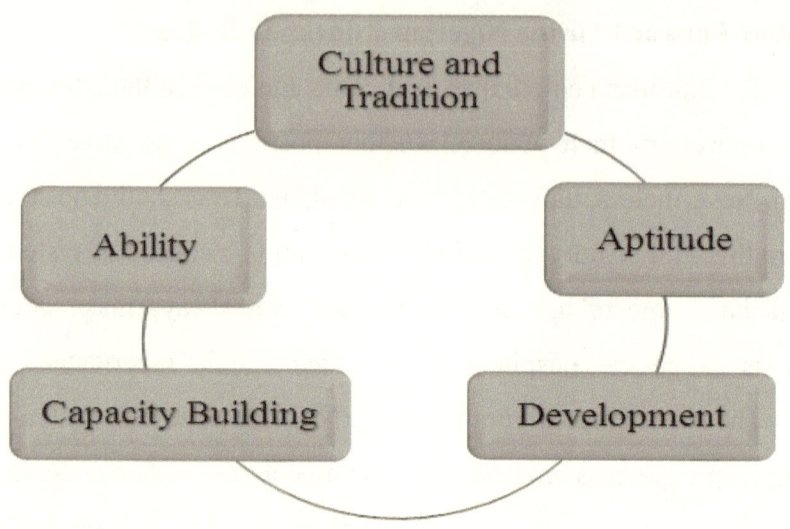

Figure 6. A conceptual framework for reconfiguring the Nigerian education system

Culture and Tradition

Following the examples of Asian, European and American countries that invest more than 26% of their annual budgets towards education curriculum reforms, Nigeria can restructure or reposition its non-functional curricula to make them more functional, need-based, self-reliant and pragmatic, but in a way that fundamentally suits its own culture and environment. No doubt, countries that have restructured their education system to suit their own cultures and environments are today reaping the benefits in the sense of creating employment and reducing crime rates.

Any well-structured education policy and curriculum in Nigeria should be anchored in the cultures and traditions of the people, which embed freedom, unity, democracy, fraternity, industry, dynamism and resilience as central values. These core cultural ideas should guide and direct the development and implementation of education policies, keeping them organised but qualitative and motivating the stakeholders to run programmes that are not severely deficient owing to lack of cultural relevance. Essentially, even though rightfully conservative, the dynamic aspect of Nigeria's culture is what constantly nudges its education system towards innovation, making it more relevant and globally competitive in this era. This dynamism should be reinvigorated and reengineered towards national educational goals. Because of the complex and systemic nature of education, furthermore, these basic dimensions of culture affect each other, with positive outcomes and linked to national goals, in ways that are sometimes unpredictable.

A culture-related curriculum is about equipping an individual with knowledge and skills to enable him to transform the world, beginning with his immediate environment. It is about preparing the students for a useful and purposeful life that leads to knowledge, skills, fulfilment and self-reliance. This idea should continuously influence education policymaking in Nigeria, as in some advanced countries of the world. To arrest the crises not only in the education system but also in the social, economic and political sectors today, the nation must enthrone the use of functional and need-based curricula in its schools and tertiary institutions. Specifically, if there is a prolonged problem of security in the country, why would policymakers, stakeholders and educators not consider developing a given education curriculum in response to this national need?

Ability and Aptitude

Tests and examination policies in Nigerian schools and universities are strictly meant to determine students' academic achievements, not necessarily their overall knowledge, skills and abilities. What do people know about students' abilities and aptitudes? Are they hereditary? Are they determined by tests and examinations alone? Indeed, what a pupil or student can learn is the product of his ability, aptitude, interest and effort. Often, Nigerian educators assume that any of these four mentioned elements alone can determine what a student can learn in school. This commonplace assumption seems to have been institutionalised, if not continuously reinforced by common practices. However, the four always work in concert. To illustrate, a student could have talent but lack interest in a subject, course, or programme. The nation's education process should be able to effectively and accurately determine who is genuinely inclined towards science or art. Arguably, schools and universities can make art courses a requirement for science, technology, engineering, electronics and math students, since they would need to gain broader perspectives of all human endeavours in order to practice and expand their work. These areas of human endeavour, among others, include philosophy, psychology, ethics, music, economics, political science, languages and anthropology. Nevertheless, this determination has to do with students who choose their career subjects, academic courses, majors or programs of specialty while they are in school or on campus.

There are students who are naturally science-inclined, but they end up in art classes or similar programmes in Nigerian schools and universities. Why are some pupils and students not interested in certain subjects at the primary and secondary stages of their educational growth and development? Educators must be able to make these determinations after thorough investigations to decide on the nature, level and method of teaching and learning intervention needed.

Nigerian educators should utilise mechanisms that will enable them to help students who are held to low expectations and perhaps not trying to break through that barrier. Undoubtedly, some students are more gifted and talented than others: they can learn faster in a given time and space. Nevertheless, in the field of teaching and learning, there does not seem to be any such thing as an inborn or hereditary educational ability, aptitude, interest and effort. Educational ingenuity or artistry is more about using various simple strategies to teach cognitive, logical, creative and critical thinking skills associated with knowledge and understanding. Indeed, intelligence can be acquired through practice. Knowledge is acquired but only in conjunction with the space and duration given to it. Of course, children who have not been taught relatively challenging or demanding subjects like English language and mathematics at the primary school level may find these subjects much more difficult at higher levels of their educational growth.

Since knowledge and thinking are closely related, the Nigerian education system must engage pupils and students in active reasoning, critical thinking and problem solving to lay a solid foundation for their overall educational development. Certainly, because of differences in the manners and methods of learning, some students might need extra time, space and even quality instruction to meet these expectations. The Nigerian education system can harness efforts to create ability, develop aptitude and interest and encourage effort and hard work to build a more educated future.

Creativity and Resourcefulness

The democratic and egalitarian nature of the Nigerian culture, though innately communitarian, fosters real social independence and individuality. This cultural and personal development in relation to the education system encourages creativity and resourcefulness. Creativity and resourcefulness are often infectious concepts that could set other aspects of a nation's educational growth in motion, getting it literally up and running. Administrators and educators who form, guide, lead, mould, or help students blossom in their (the students') own ways and at their own paces, lay emphasis on reasoning and discussions, without unnecessary restrictions or constraints. Good teachers help students draw upon their own inner resources and strengths to flourish in the world around them.

Resourcefulness is one of the most sought-after and precious ingredients for inventive economies across the globe. Students who are in schools and tertiary institutions should learn resourcefulness from their model administrators, principals, headmasters, teachers and educators. Arguably, highly resourceful students are more effective in making academic progress than non-resourceful ones. The same applies to navigating and surviving challenging situations. The role of resourcefulness in the educational development of any nation cannot be overemphasised and no nation can rise above the education and resourcefulness of its citizens. This notion is perhaps also applicable to Nigeria as a country that is full of bright and new opportunities.

With a difficult economy and recessions facing Nigeria at present, the citizens should learn to manage what they have in the education sector and still strive for great achievements because they can do so, relative to other surrounding African nations' public schools and universities. Success in this regard is not impossible. It is about the ability to survive difficult challenges, not about navigating through any kind of purposeful or deliberate deprivations. Resourcefulness might enable a school or an institution of learning in the country to manage their infrastructure facilities in a simple and cost-saving fashion, even when it is difficult to do so. This is where the conservative nature of the Nigerian culture meets resourcefulness. Where people can leverage their gifts, time, talents, treasure and resources as a people, they empower themselves to fulfil their goals despite challenges.

Few public schools and academic institutions in this country currently display this feature of resourcefulness, but it is the key that could open the floodgates of future accomplishments. In fact, resourcefulness, which makes use of alternative and desirable possibilities, empowers education as an instrument of invention, innovation and change. Creativity and resourcefulness imbue people with a type of spirit that enables them to transcend despondency and cease blaming the colonialists for Nigeria's educational woes by marching on confidently into a brighter future. It is about not standing still where the colonialists left us but rather celebrating the lessons they have left us.

Being open-minded is critical to putting resourcefulness into action with possibilities. Resourcefulness can generate a "yes, we can" attitude and resolve for educational growth and nation-building. To configure and reposition the nation's education system, stakeholders should adopt education policies and curricula that sharpen Nigerian students' imaginativeness, creativity, innovativeness and resourcefulness. To encourage the spread of creativity and resourcefulness in the Nigerian education sector, administrators, stakeholders, teachers and educators must ensure that the students' remarkable accomplishments are publicised, praised, recognised and rewarded.

Capacity-Building and Development

How people initiate change and manage real progress as a feature of the Nigerian education system will have a lasting impact on the students' overall educational achievement. When people compare the current Nigerian educational practices to the world's and the vision of the 21st century classroom and virtual education, it becomes clear that the nation needs to build up capacity and a positive change. This change will make room for effective teaching and learning around innovative skills and self- efficacy among all our stakeholders in schools and tertiary institutions. They are imperative for educational growth and development in this era.

Administrators, principals, teachers and students need self-efficacy in their abilities to complete tasks and reach set goals. Therefore, capacity-building is highly needed in every aspect of the nation's political, economic and social sectors and, above all, in its education sector. Capacity in the Nigerian education system will enable collaboration and teamwork, problem-solving and critical thinking skills. It will foster a deeper appreciation of literacy, diversity, creativity, leadership and accountability both in the Nigerian education sector and the entire nation.

The capacity-building of educationally systemic models would offer an enriched alternative to traditional approaches to educational reforms in Nigeria. Traditional methods of reform often recycle or replicate an already-developed method of reform which comes from the government, the Ministry of Education, or other governmental agencies. These entities only prescribe solutions for schools and educators. Nevertheless, the capacity-building model will focus on the organisational or institutional learning curriculum with a view to building an institution's or organisation's capacity, or ability, to solve its own problems. The real solution resides inside the school or district. This more local type of reform will enable the institution to adapt or use innovative methods to solve the problem of student low achievement in schools or universities. Reforms will be based on best practices and conditions that suit the students in their local environments. Districts, schools and educators do not prescribe solutions: They investigate problems and determine solutions together. Capacity-building in Nigerian schools and institutions of learning would lead to changes in teaching methods, leadership and institutional and organisational practices. It would show that the quality of teaching has a positive impact on the Nigerian education.

Creating a curriculum to focus on the manpower needs of the nation and promote capacity-building in both content and methodology is crucial. By contrast, Nigeria's education system seems to be currently producing graduates who are alienated from their home environment and are, instead, more attracted to foreign countries. Some of them roam the streets looking for employment that is non-existent. A part of what capacity-building does is to allow education to satisfy the needs and goals of the person being educated. The educated person needs basically to earn his living and survive in his environment, hence, the need to review the curriculum and restructure it in such a way that it will cater for the needs of people's immediate environment. The emphasis should be education for living, not education for certification only, with an inclination to vocational training, introduced right from primary education and practical training at the junior secondary school level.

The need to expand colleges of education (technical colleges) and increase polytechnics even without upgrading them to universities should also be stressed. To focus and promote this policy, employers should not grant employments based on certificates alone but also on proven ability. No doubt, other than population growth, structural changes in the nation's economy since independence have brought about various dimensions of manpower need. The same need applies to the continued expansion in the educational and other intellectual training institutions.

Managing Nigeria's Education System

Any proper restructure of the Nigerian education system's protocols should strictly promote continuity, uniformity and originality. This section will look at the ways in which these three factors can influence proper planning, effective management and control of education in Nigeria.

Continuity

For workable policies and programmes, pragmatism without pessimism is always key. One of the most striking qualities of every successful education system in the world today is continuity. A salient continuity pattern promoting education administration, leadership policies and policy strategies that have proved workable in the past should be encouraged in the Nigerian education system. The essence of any structural continuity is to sustain models that have track records of success and expand practices that have been previously workable, such as beneficial class hours and good teaching staffs. Through classroom observations, a school or institution of learning in Nigeria could decide to continue any student initiative or innovation in teaching activities and learning experiences that proved successful over time from one education level to another.

Any attempt to reform the Nigerian education system or, to review its implementation of policies, must first consider past performances of the Nigerian education sector under various administrations. Second, it must consider how the implementation of education policies during those administrations helped in advancing the goals and objectives of education in the country. Unfortunately, frequent changes of government and political instability have made the continuity of good education policies and best practices nearly impossible. The same lack of continuity in policy implementation can be attributed to previous governments' laissez faire attitude towards the education sector.

Continuity, as highlighted in this context, is not rigidity, nor does it discount flexibility or necessary school transitions. Despite the need for continuity, an institution of learning can still decide along the spectrum of total continuity to complete discontinuity in its education policymaking. Did an individual teaching approach and intervention help students to improve in certain challenging subjects? A decision can be made based on the outcome of this question. Compulsory age for schooling could be modified based on reliable assessments. For instance, repetitions in the curriculum that have not shown success in the past could be discontinued. This could vary from one institution to another.

Uniformity in Practice

Aside from continuity, one of the strengths of any nation's education system is uniformity in practice. Nigeria also must take several approaches to repair whatever disparity exists among strong and weak schools in various towns and cities across the nation. Apart from other criteria, the status of a given school should easily be determined by its overall infrastructure and educational quality. The idea of uniformity is not to create a "one size fits all" type of education structure. The central idea of uniformity is to make the education system in Nigeria more organised, understandable, approachable and properly channelled. This could be done by simply eliminating measures that have hindered the progress of the system overtime.

There is always the probability that states, regions, districts and cities might permit flexibility of policy implementation in some areas owing to lack of resources. To address this, some poor schools, namely those low in population, enrolment and completion rates or suffer from chronic teacher shortage, could be closed, reorganised, or merged with higher performing schools. Alternatively, governments could fund visibly poor schools in rural areas, construct new buildings and update their educational status. In support of uniformity, moving away from a status quo in which greater funding and resources are given only to politically favoured schools and colleges to a more egalitarian practice and distribution of resources should be encouraged. A formula could be adopted whereby funding inequalities are addressed, minimised, or simply eliminated. If government funding of education is being distributed based on each school or school district's size and needs, how are those criteria measured?

Uniformity will usher in an unbroken growth in the nation's education system and higher approval ratings by the citizens as they strive to flourish in the information age and globalisation. Uniformity will enable Nigeria to better regulate its education system and implement workable policies. By keeping the education system relevant based on uniformity and originality, Nigeria, as a nation and its educators, will have endeavoured to carry itself along to progress at its best. Flaws in the education system will also be exposed and demystified as their complexities unfold.

An example of uniformity in progress: If an area or region experiences massive expansion either in admissions or enrolments at any level of education, the admission and enrolment process could be recommended for replication in other regions across the country, especially those that share similar social values and culture. The same sharing of new techniques and strategies is applicable to the guiding method of education leadership, administration, management and policy. Overall, this type of policy implementation will help ensure that Nigeria's system of education remains balanced.

Originality of Structure

To establish originality of structure in the nation's education system, policymakers, administrators and educators should be ready to accommodate some complicated and disruptive controversies. Roller-coaster moments could be anticipated when undertaking a volatile adventure. When related issues are constructively handled, they would initiate and shape peoples' legacies and contributions, as academics and educationists work towards the progress of education in Nigeria. Beyond uniformly remaking the protocols of the education system, effort must be exerted to reintroduce a system that is based on originality, as it will endure only if it is rooted in the dynamic culture, psychology and sociology of the people. If Nigeria, for instance, settles for a system of education that is structurally hybrid or a macrocosm of pre-colonial, colonial, modern and contemporary elements as its basic and driving structure, it must be followed through as a reliable framework that guides the entire nation's educational practice. Therefore, all decisions to reform Nigeria's education system will be a logical crisscross and conceptual crossroad of the people's psychology, sociology and culture.

The need for continuity, uniformity and originality comes from the necessity to help the citizenry by establishing a system that will last. How can Nigeria do this? It is not by prioritising any specific culture but by exploiting the day-by-day rhythms of our common and popular culture, psychology and social systems. This prudent step will enable Nigeria to redefine and rebrand its education sector.

Summary, Evaluation and Conclusion

The Nigerian education system can still attain an enviable position in the world's competitive education arena. It can also morph into a magnet for the brightest and most motivated students. Leaving the system in perennial stagnation and long-term decline would make it impossible for today's educators to promise the next generation of Nigerians access to a better literacy than their own. People need schools with excellent curricula, academic programmes, teachers and facilities. Nigeria, as the largest country in Africa, has every powerful tool at its disposal: psycho-socio-cultural strength, the might of the central government and the nation's decades-old reverence for education and scholarship. Assuredly, the country's prominent education leaders and policymakers would affirm without qualification that Nigerians will be most unwilling to accept defeat in the global educational race or consequently resign themselves to decaying literacy standards. The best way to avoid this destiny is to acknowledge the present condition of Nigeria's education system as a reality and then take the necessary actions to surmount the nation's education problems.

For far too long, the nation seems to have lost sight of what is important and possible for its children and young people in its education system. It is time Nigeria put aside every obstacle in the way of its common progress in its educational enterprise as a nation. It can earn its way in the world by aspiring to produce or export goods and services of sufficient quantity and quality to capture the world's interest. Nigeria can also earn its own fortune by making itself attractive to foreign investors, with better training and education for its workforce and by providing a type of environment in which its education system will be able to thrive and flourish. Let it be an environment in which commitment to education is geared towards developing the whole child and the entire person, so (s)he can grow physically, emotionally, intellectually, morally, socially and spiritually. Let it also be an environment with a strong foundation where students will learn to become good citizens, filled with enriching experiences and great memories as well as receive education at an affordable tuition and reasonable cost.

Scepticism and challenging circumstances are bound to arise as academics of illustrious calibre and educational scientists grapple with determining the best education system for Nigeria. Does it need to be locally inspired and endowed, or does it need to be totally imported from abroad? Should it rather be a prudent and meticulous blend of both? This author honestly thinks that a meticulous blend of both indigenous and exogenous education traditions would always put Nigeria in good stead, with the indigenous consolidated as the cornerstone. Addressing this issue might appear like a nation searching for the best way to remake or overhaul its broken healthcare system or even its political system. In this case, the nation's education system appears to be in a more centrist mould. What will ultimately be implicated in the system being advocated is a hybrid curricular model of both Nigeria's traditional system of education and Western education traditions, with neither being predominant. However, it is always expedient to sift out whatever is essentially incongruous with the country's socio-cultural, psycho-social and psycho-cultural environment in the process.

Educators can posit that a hybrid model of education system will most likely put Nigeria in good stead in the long run. With anticipated mad rush and surge of nations into digital technologies and robotics, the possibility that many jobs will be displaced in future, causing huge unemployment crises and potentially sending many back to poverty is not doubtful. To be specific, while some nations might be elevated economically under this emerging globally digital and explosive robotic technologies, there is the likelihood that others will be challenged economically. Clearly put, even though some nations will be on the gaining side, such predicable explosions in digital and robotic revolutions might negatively impact beneficiary nations' business institutions and even their education systems.

Figure 7. A conceptual depiction of robotic revolutions (Picture adapted from Felix Decombat)

Already, nations like Japan, China and South Korea have not only created markets for robots, they have also created rooms for the substitution of some of their workforce and human capital with robots, especially in those jobs that do not require sufficient personal interactions, reasoning, knowledge of contexts, situational awareness, judgement and personalised skills.

Certainly, there is always a huge difference between artificial intelligence and human intelligence. But how would the future innovations and explosions of digital technologies and robotics, among other advancements, impact other countries as well as Nigeria? An economic crisis yields widespread economic suffering and that would naturally feed an appetite and desire for autocratic, despotic and, in some cases, extremist leaders. For various reasons, being conservative and content with a progressively hybrid model of education system in Nigeria will likely be beneficial in the long term. It might put the nation in good stead amidst crises that may arise from future overdependence on machines and robots and the predictably resultant situation of human unemployment.

Seldom are people able to ignore distractions to understand the pulse and heartbeat of their own existence. This exercise of thought could be employed in the education's developmental process with a view to understanding what is more important for the healthy development of Nigeria's education system. Although people cherish and relish the beautiful and luxurious trends in the urban and city lives, there is still that rural and precious aspect of people's lives that is waiting for them, if only they allow it to flourish. The same is true with the role technological advancements play in their educational lives, as they also need to permit their traditionally solid educational upbringing to endure. The Nigerian system of education should always be allowed to stand for itself when it comes to originality. Training students as robots who will ultimately find it difficult to readjust or reintegrate into a larger original and cultural society, let alone function effectively across the world, should be dreaded and discouraged.

The Nigerian system of education is certainly in need of drastic review and upgrade. Reconfiguring its structure effectively will also require strengthening and realigning its basic cultural foundations. If one cannot effectively adapt or adjust to the future without many tears, one therefore needs to resort to the old for a clue as well as rediscover one's footing. To improve, reconfigure, redefine, realign and refine the nation's system of education, Nigeria needs to take an in-depth look at its precious traditional education system for clues on how to advance plus consolidate an original, strong and reliable education model. A cross-pollination of experiences and ideas from Nigerian education experts, administrators and policymakers would put it in good stead in this regard. Indeed, what Nigeria's education system essentially needs is not necessarily rebranding but rebalancing.

Our educational resources should be refocused on traditional public schools. Providing more training to teachers and educators and giving parents more active roles in decision making will be crucial in making the nation's education system workable. It is also strongly recommended that the goals of its education system's approach do not consist of throwing out everything that works and starting afresh. The "one size fits all" mindset should also be discountenanced.

Sometimes, it seems much more difficult to take a pause and reflect on how the future citizens are formed. However, Nigeria needs to make its approach to education and schooling more functional, especially in today's knowledge-based economy. Nigeria's education system should help students become more self-driven and independent. This effort is about envisaging an education system and curriculum that impel students to become responsible both to themselves and to the society, a type that will enable them to eventually become gainfully employed or able to create employment. This type of system will inspire them to explore great opportunities within the country rather than aimlessly searching elsewhere. People should also envision the uniqueness of everyone's success and the ways in which each person's individual character will be valuable to the society at large. Ours should be a system where individualism is celebrated in the context of communitarianism with a view to engendering real success. With this idea in mind, the Nigerian education system should be geared towards helping individuals find their own paths with and among community pathfinders.

In the Nigerian education system's development, educators need to create a clear set of priorities by picking a few policy areas and setting concrete goals upon which they can measure their educational achievements. Concerning funding, some education advocates believe that the country's education system can be more effective if it is given requisite financial support by the government. Ultimately, it is crucial that people apply themselves with the optimistic mindset that Nigeria can merit and gain respect by working to improve its education system. In a generation where many people appear to be lacking relevant inspiration, students and young people need to be creative and mentally inspired with the freedom to explore their heartfelt passions. Nigeria cannot afford to allow the future of its children and the youth to wither.

Epilogue

Although successive governments in Nigeria have formulated and implemented policies for improving access to education in the country, statistical reports in this volume show that illiteracy is still rising and the number of out-of-school children growing. It is lamentable that large areas of the country have been badly hurt by illiteracy and lack of interest in education. Frustration about this situation is growing in the minds of the millions of Nigerians who were privileged to receive good education. In addition, the continually growing population of the country puts tremendous pressures on educators, complicating and overstretching efforts to remedy this decades-old problem. Nonetheless, high-quality education initiatives and the provision of needed services are highly encouraged. Finding parents who cannot afford to send their children to school in Nigeria today is not difficult and finding students sitting in ill-equipped, under-furnished, dilapidated, or overcrowded classrooms is not unusual.

In summary, the Nigerian education system has not satisfied the longings and needs of most of its citizenry, especially those of the millions of children in the country, and it seems obvious that reconfiguring the system does not depend only on ensuring massive enrolment or keeping statistics on out-of-school children. Indeed, there is no evidence that these measures have improved the quality of education in the country. The changes required are more expansive than might appear at first; but they depend more on the proper implementation of relevant education policies, especially ones that are psycho-socio-culturally appropriate to the Nigerian environment.

Nevertheless, any effort to transform the nation's education system depends on the government's ability to provide enabling environments for education to thrive. The same applies to improving education and schooling standards in the country.

Among the plausible solutions that have been proffered in this work for Nigeria's feeble education system, decentralising the education sector from the federal to the state, local and municipal governments is most likely to encourage reform, innovation, creativity and resourcefulness at all levels. These impacts of decentralisation will go a long way towards helping institutions of learning achieve greater success with students and improve their skills and ability to compete globally. Detailed case studies from Mexico, Indonesia and Kenya have found that decentralisation policies can enhance the quality and functionality of education and increase accountability in the system (Channa, 2014).

Alternatively, privatising the education system by securing collaborations between the public and private sectors could invaluably strengthen education in the country. A public private partnership (PPP) initiative, for instance, could ensure that the nation's education system is producing the skills needed both in the present and for the future. Closing the skill gap by supplying skills to meet critical needs seems to spell the future of the Nigerian economy. The coming together of the public and private sectors could ensure that the nation's education system, from its traditional structure to technical, vocational and innovative forms will produce the skills to meet Nigeria's present and future needs. The PPP initiative could also be applied to the management of the nation's higher education to make the education market more collaborative, competitive and flexible than other arrangements in the public sector. PPPs would enable the government to increase access to high-quality education and reduce inequalities by using private-sector efficiency to reduce the cost of running public schools.

In planning educational reforms and ensuring that all Nigerian children enjoy good education, especially those from poor, disadvantaged and low-income families, a good idea for policymakers and stakeholders would be to take a cue from charter schools and school voucher programmes that are used in several countries around the world. These arrangements let parents use public funding allocated for their children's education, in the form of subsidised vouchers, to pay tuition at other public and private schools of their choice. One effect of the voucher programmes is that they encourage competition in the education marketplace and can push public schools to improve their education curriculum and infrastructure. Also, charter schools, which are independently run public schools, are still owned by the government but have their daily operations contracted to private sector management. Underperforming schools can be converted into charter schools for better teaching and learning as well as better student outcome. In this context, reconfiguring and revitalising the Nigerian education system will primarily involve reviewing education policies to ensure that they are culturally appropriate and provide for the needs of the immediate environment along with national development. Failures in the education sector would amount to failure in other sectors including the economy, healthcare, technology and telecommunications and politics (Aremu, 2017).

The nature of Nigeria's education system will certainly determine the nature, level and pace of its development as a nation.

Invariably, the determination of the level of its national development has a certain dependence on the improvement of the status of women whose empowerment is also directly linked to education. Since the issue of gender disparity continues to evolve in the country, women's level of educational development and their economic, political and social empowerment could be used as a reference point in evaluating the effectiveness of education policies in Nigeria. While Nigeria neither occupies the first nor the last position among countries that do not empower women, we still need to pay heed to the admonitions of Alec Ross who is one of America's leading experts on innovation and competitiveness. Unified excerpts from various pages of his book, *The Industries of the Future* run as follows:

> And there is no greater indicator of an innovative culture than the empowerment of women. Fully integrating and empowering women economically and politically is the most important step that a country or company can take to strengthen its competitiveness. Societies that do not overcome their negative cultural legacies regarding the treatment of women will founder in the next wave of innovation. Innovation doesn't happen in closed environments and innovative companies will continue to steer clear of countries with regressive policies on gender. The states and societies that do the most for women are those that will be best positioned to compete and succeed in the industries of the future. Treating women well is not just the right thing to do; it makes economic sense. Women are half of every nation's workforce – or potential workforce. If a country is cutting off half of its potential workforce, it is taking itself out of the game. Countries that are closing the gender gap are

competitive; they are the nations of the future, educating boys and girls and ensuring that their entire citizenry is skilled and ready for the global economy. Put simply, nations that empower women reap the benefits. In the developing world, women can tip the scales between economic success and failure (Ross, 2016).

Any sound education policies should, as a matter of necessity, seek to exclude unhealthy gender rules and cultural norms that diminish the education and social empowerment of women.

Additionally, but on a different note, any curriculum or system rooted in the acquisition of technical and vocational skills is culturally appropriate for Nigeria, considering its pre-colonial education system that resonated well with the indigenes and locals because of its functional, practical and pragmatic features. Practical knowledge is to be greatly desired in the nation's education system. At this juncture, the following question bears repeating: Is the Nigerian education system a far cry from what it should be? Is there anything fundamentally wrong with the system? Has it fallen short of expectations? Does it produce low-quality and unemployable graduates? Why? Any attempt to answer these questions will depend on one's knowledge and review of the country's education history, since history is crucial for any aspect of national growth and development. To understand where the country's education system is going to, one needs to first understand where it is coming from. Obviously, a review of Nigeria's history will reveal a wide gap to bridge and a big hole to fill in its education system. Thus, installing the right curriculum, system and structure is a good place to start. Efforts must be made to implement a curriculum system that links classroom knowledge with the real world. The system must be also open to the introduction of courses and programmes that speak to current issues in the country: security, infrastructure, economy and healthcare. The education curriculum structure and content need to be tailored to address Nigeria's societal needs. Indeed, the ideal education system is a type that leaves no child behind, one in which every child counts and a type that can mould the youth into responsible members of society. This system can enable students to put their knowledge into practice and thrive in today's world.

Curriculum-based qualitative professional training, for instance, can help drive students to the peak of their future careers. Educating and training students to a level of excellence will be based on their individual inclinations, abilities and aptitudes. Education can open doors to many human abilities, potentials and individual developments. Therefore, we need an education system, curriculum or learning approach in which students who study from primary through senior secondary school can keep their environments clean; teach various sports, art works and photography; provide security support and other services, such as repairing watches, cell phones and computers; providing IT support services; shoemaking, tailoring, book binding, barbering and hairdressing and doing various electrical, technical, engineering and mechanical work. Likewise, we need training for workers in plumbing, physical therapy, legal, clerical, pharmaceutical and medical assistance; substitute teaching, working in hospitals, industries, businesses, banks and post offices and leadership seminar participation. Nigeria needs a curriculum that allows civil and structural engineering students, for instance, to do minor building and road projects. It also needs educational environments that allow business graduates to start businesses and offer employment to others.

How would one explain a situation in which Nigerians bring in shoemakers, watch repairers, tailors, hairdressers and artisans from nearby countries to offer their services or build houses for them? Why should they import bricklayers, glaziers, carpenters, welders, plumbers, electricians and tilers to build their houses? Why should Nigeria export jobs that belong to millions of their youths to other nations? These needs can be solved or minimised with local, vocational and technical skills. In short, Nigeria needs to arm its students with the knowledge and skills they need to work in the banking, agricultural, engineering and manufacturing sectors as well as in the petroleum industries to drive economic growth in the nation.

In 2016, the UN Human Development Index ranked Nigeria 152nd in educational achievement, out of 188 countries (Alake, 2018). A situation in which only about 3 percent of employment applicants are considered qualified based on application reviews and job interviews is unacceptable. Improved vocational and technical training can meet Nigeria's labour force needs. Overall, private schools in Nigeria seem to do a better job than public schools at equipping students for the workforce. Fully integrating the technical and vocational aspects of education curriculum will help the nation solve the problem of unemployment in the long term. This type of education programme empowers its recipients for future survival and responsibility in society.

For many decades now, investments in the education, formation and development of human capital have fallen below expectations in Nigeria. And so, there is an urgent need for massive investments that are amenable to vocational and technical training. In response to the country's alarming unemployment rate and the need for reforms in its education system, the federal government approved the establishment of the Vocational Enterprise Institutions (VEIs) and Innovative Enterprise Institutions (IEIs) in 2015. These are secondary and post-secondary school level programmes that award National Vocational Certificates and National Innovation Certificates, respectively. This strategy is commendable but needs upgrading. With appropriate funding of public institutions and more cooperative investments, technical and vocational curricula can be introduced into more schools and tertiary institutions, public and private alike. Among the strongest reasons for encouraging collaborative funding and corporate investments in the nation's education system is to support vocational and technical training and retain the best brains instead of losing them to other countries. With increase in the number of new universities across the country over the past decade, the population of students gaining admission into specialised and competitive degree programmes have also grown both steadily and proportionately.

For some better and nobler reasons and desirable production of indigenous power and control, the founding fathers of Nigeria substituted the inherited colonial curriculum for their once-precious indigenous system. It is hoped that Nigeria will not allow their dream, expectation and hope to be dashed. To address failures in the nation's education system, the Nigerian government at all levels should be expected to make amends for some of its past failures. It should make serious investments in infrastructure and in the overall funding and implementation of good policies. Taking these steps will help to make the nation's education system more progressive and propel it to thrive past all known limitations.

References

Abdulkareem, A. Y. (1992). *Issues in Nigeria education.* Ilorin, Nigeria: Kewulere Press.

Abdulrahman, A. (2013, June 11). Shocking: Nigeria holds world record in number of children out of school. *Premium Times.* Retrieved from https://www.premiumtimesng.com/news/138442-shocking-nigeria-holds-world-record-in-number-of-children-out-of-school.html

Adamu, A. U. (1994). Reform and adaptation in Nigerian university curricula, 1960-1992: Living on a credit line. *African Studies Series, 33.* Lewinston, New York: The Edwin Mellen Press.

Adavbiele, J.A. (2015). Implications of incessant strike actions on the implementation of technical education programme in Nigeria. *Journal of Education and Practice, 6*(8).

Adedigba, A. (2017, July 17). WAEC releases May/June 2017 results: Records high pass rate. *Premium Times.* Retrieved from https://www.premiumtimesng.com/news/headlines/237202-waec-releases-mayjune-2017-results-records-high-pass-rate.html

Adeniran, N. N. (1991). Effects of teacher's training on children's achievement in Nigeria. *Businessmen Studies Journal, 4*(6).

Adesulu, D. (2015, Aug. 10). Breaking news: WAEC releases results, withheld 13 indebted states. *Vanguard Newspaper.* Retrieved from https://www.vanguardngr.com/2015/08/ breaking-news-waec-releases-results-withheld-13-indebted- states/

Adunola, O. (2010). The challenges affecting the implementation of universal basic education. *Ejobooster Books*. Retrieved from www.omotere.com

Agbakwuru, J. (2018). *FG spends N49bn on school feeding programme.* Retrieved November 9 from https://www.vanguardngr.com/2018/08/fg-spends-n49bn-on-school-feeding-programme-2/

Agency Report. (2018, Feb. 1). NUT threatens to embark on strike over non-payment of teachers' salary arrears. *Premium Times*. Retrieved from https://www.premiumtimesng.com/ news/top-news /257338-nut-threatens-embark-strike-non- payment-teachers-salary-arrears.html

Aissat, D., & Djafri, Y. (2011). *The role of colonial education in retrospect: The Gold Coast case in the era of imperialism.* Algeria: University of Adelhamid Ibn Badis.

Ajah, M. (2015). Religious education and nation-building in Nigeria. *Stellenbosch Theological Journal, 1*(2), 263-282. Retrieved from http://www.scielo.org.za/pdf/stj/v1n2/14.pdf

Akee, R. (2006a). *Who leaves and who returns? Deciphering immigrant self-selection from a developing country.* Unpublished manuscript.

Akee, R. (2006b). *Road to Palau.* IZA Working Paper, No. 2452. Alake, T. (2018). *No Books, No Desks, No Pay: Nigeria's Education System is Failing.* Retrieved November 8, 2018, from https://www.bloomberg.com/news/articles/2018-09-12/no- books-no-desks-no-pay-nigeria-s-education-is-failing

Amaghionyeodiwe, L. A., & Osinubi, T. S. (2006). The Nigerian educational system and returns to education. *International Journal of Applied and Quantitative Studies, 3*(2). Retrieved from http://www.usc.es/economet /ijaeqs.htm

Amaghionyeodiwe, L. A., & Osinubi, T. S. (2007). Do higher levels of schooling lead to higher returns to education in Nigeria? *Applied Econometrics and International Development, 7*(1), 157-164.

Anemelu, C. I. (2012). *Psycho-cultural Adjustment of Foreign-Born Students at Colleges in the U.S.* Germany: Lambert Academic Publishing.

Anibueze, A. U. (2013). Effects of reforms in Nigeria education sector: Voices of college staff/counseling implication. *Journal of Humanities and Social Science, 15*(6), 68-74.

Adukia, A., Asher, S., & Novosad, P. (2018). *Educational investment responses to economic opportunity: Evidence from Indian road construction.* Retrieved from http://www.dartmouth.edu/~novosad /adukia-asher-novosad-dise-roads.pdf

Aremu, O. (2017). *Nigeria at 57 and the Failure of Her Educational System.* Retrieved November 7, 2018, from https://www.tribuneonlineng.com/114902/

Asiyai, R. I. (2015). School administrators' strategies for combating corruption in universities in Nigeria. *Journal of Education and Learning, 4*(4). doi:10.5539/jel. v4n4p160

Azike, A. A. (2010). Educational reforms in democratic governance issues, challenges and prospects, presented at the 6th National Conference of the School of Education Federal College of Education, Zaria, Nigeria, 2011.

Azike, A. A. (2012). Teacher's education in Nigeria: Past, present and future, presented at the Annual National Conference of the School of Education, Federal College of Education, Zaria, Nigeria, 2012.

Azike, A. A. (2013). Historical analysis of constitutional provision for education in Nigeria (1976-2011): Implication for educational administration. *Journal of Social Sciences and Humanities, 4*(3).

Babafemi, T. O. A. (2003). *An assessment of the implementation of the 6-3-3-4 system of education in Nigeria: A case study of Ilorin, Kwara State.* Unpublished M.Ed. thesis, Department of Science and Technical Education, University of Ilorin.

Ball, C. (2013, June 4). Most people in the UK do not go to university — and maybe never will. *The Guardian Higher Education Network.* Retrieved from https://www.theguardian.com /higher-education-network/blog/2013/jun/04/higher- education-participation-data-analysis

Bamgbose, A. (1991). *Language and the nation: The language question in sub-Sahara Africa.* England: Englewood University Press.

Bauman, K. J. (2016). *U.S. Census Bureau education data and statistics.* Retrieved from https://www.census.gov/data/tables/2016/demo/education-attainment/-detailed-tables.html

Bello, I., Othman, M.F., Khairri, D., & Shariffuddin, B. (2017). Political Economy of Education Financing in Nigeria. *Asian Journal of Multidisciplinary Studies*, 5(6). Retrieved on August 6, 2018 from https://www.researchgate.net /publication/319528977_ Political_ Economy_of_Education_Financing_In_Nigeria

British Council Nigeria. (2012). *Gender in Nigeria report: Improving the lives of girls and women in Nigeria.* Retrieved from https//www.britishcouncil.org/sites/default/files/british-council-gender-nigeria2012.pdf

Butts, F. R. (1953). Our responsibility for freedom in education. *Education Leadership, 11*(1). Retrieved from http://www. ascd.org /ASCD/pdf/journals/ed_lead/el_195310_butts.pdf

Cassell, J. (2007). *Relationships between student attendance and test scores on Virginia standards of learning tests* (Doctoral dissertation). Retrieved from http://dc.etsu.edu/etd/2152. (Paper 2152)

Central Bank of Nigeria. (2011). *Annual report.* Retrieved from https://www.cbn.gov.ng/Out/2012/publications/reports/rsd/arp-2011/2011%20Annual%20Report_Complete%20Report.pdf

Centre for Public Impact. (2017). *Universal basic education in Nigeria: A case study.* Retrieved from https://www.centre forpublicimpact. org/case-study/universal -basic-education-nigeria/

Channa, A. (2014). Decentralization and the Quality of Education: Background paper prepared for Education for All, *Global Monitoring Report*, 2015. Retrieved November 9, 2018, from http://unesdoc.unesco.org/images /0023/0023 24/232418e.pdf

Chua, R. (2014, Feb. 11). Why is Singapore's school system so successful and is it a model for the West? *The Conversation.* Retrieved from http://theconversation.com/why-is-singapores-school-system-so-successful-and-is-it-a-model-for-the-west-22917

Chukwusa, J. O. (2011). Actualisation of Vision 2020: The perspective of education in Nigeria. *JOWICE, 15*(2). Jos, Nigeria: Akins Press & Services.

Conover, P. J. (2009). Citizens' identities and conceptions of the self. *Journal of Political Philosophy, 3*(2), 133-165.

Dike, K. O. (1980). 100 years of British rule in Nigeria, 1851-1957. In I. Obaro (Ed.), *Groundwork of Nigerian history*. Ibadan, Nigeria: Heinemann.

Durojaiye, F. (2017, Aug. 16). Corruption and education in Nigeria. *Sun Newspaper.* Retrieved from http://www.sunnewsonline.com/ corruption-and-education-in-nigeria/

Edelman, E. M. (2013). Psychotherapist, East Brunswick, New Jersey, re: "Babes in a digital Toyland: Even 3-year-olds get gadgets". *New York Times.*

Ejirika, P. (2014). *The need for education reform in Nigeria.* Retrieved from http://dailyposting/2014/ 09/23/perter-ejirika-need-education-reform-nigeria

Emenanjo, E. N. (1998). *Languages and the national policy on education: Implications and prospects.* Retrieved from http://fafunwafoundation.tripod.com/fafunwafoundation/id9.html

Enamiroro, P. O. (2010). Attendance and academic performance of students in secondary schools: A correlational approach. *Journal of Studies on Home and Community Science, 4*(1).

Esu, A., & Junaid, A. (2010). *Educational development: Traditional and contemporary.* Retrieved from http://www.onlinenigeria.com/links/eduadv.asp?blurb=536

Fabunmi, M. (2005). Historical analysis of educational policy formulation in Nigeria: Implications for educational planning and policy. *International Journal of African & African American Studies, 4*(2), 1-7.

Fafunwa, A. B. (1971). *A history of Nigerian higher education.* Ibadan: Macmillan & Co. Nigeria Ltd.

Fafunwa, A. B. (1974). *History of education in Nigeria.* Ibadan: NPS Educational Publishers.

Fafunwa, A. B. (1989). *Education in mother tongue: The Ife primary education research project (1970-1978).* Ibadan: University Press.

Fafunwa, A. B. (2004). *History of education in Nigeria.* Ibadan: NPS Educational Publishers.

Fafunwa, A. B., & Aisiku, J. U. (Eds., 1982). *Education in Africa: A comparative survey.* London: George Allen & Unwin Ltd.

Fajana, A. (1972). Colonial Control and Education: The development of higher education in Nigeria 1900-1950. *Journal of the Historical Society of Nigeria, Vol.VI, No.3*. Retrieved from https://www.jstor.org/stable/41856960?seq=1#page_scan_tab_contents

Federal Ministry of Education. (2000). *Education Today, 8*(2).

Federal Ministry of Education. (2015a). *Education for all 2015 national review report: Nigeria.* Retrieved from http://unesdoc.unesco.org/images/0023/002310/231081e.pdf

Federal Ministry of Education. (2015b). *Statistical report on women and men in Nigeria.* Retrieved from https://www.nigerianstat.gov.ng/download/491%20 December%202016

Federal Republic of Nigeria. (1979). *The Constitution of Republic of Nigeria*. Lagos: Federal Ministry of Information.

Federal Republic of Nigeria. (1999). *The Constitution of the Federal Republic of Nigeria.* Lagos: Republic of Nigeria Official Gazette.

Federal Republic of Nigeria. (2004a). *National policy on education* (4th ed.). Lagos: Nigerian Educational Research and Development Council Press.

Federal Republic of Nigeria. (2004b). National policy on education. *Nigerian Finder*. Retrieved from https://nigerianfinder.com/national-policy-on-education-in-nigeria/

Federal Republic of Nigeria. (2014). *National policy on education.* Lagos: NERD Press.

Fosco, M. (2018). The Most Successful Ethnic Group in the U.S. May Surprise You https://www.ozy.com/fast-forward/the-most-successful-ethnic-group-in-the-us-may-Surprise-you/86885

Freedman, S. G. (2013, Dec. 28). On religion: Mission schools opened world for Africans but left an ambiguous legacy. *New York Times*, p. A20.

Fuglestvedt, J., Berntsen, T., Myhre, G., Rypdal, K., & Skeie, R. B. (2008). Climate forcing from the transport sectors. *PNAS, 105*(2), 454-458.

Gabriel, A. (2015). Secondary School Educational Challenges in Africa during the Second World War: 1939-1945. *European Educational Research Journal* 1 (13): 1-9. Retrieved on November 5, from https://www.researchgate.net/publication/280002782_secondary_school_educational_challenges_in_africa_during_the_second_world_war_1939_-_1945

Garba, S. J. (2012). The impact of colonialism on Nigerian education and the need for e-learning technique for sustainable development. *Journal of Educational and Social Research, 2*(7), 53-61.

Ghosh, M. (2017). Infrastructure and development in rural India. *The Journal of Applied Economic Research, 11*(3). Retrieved from http://journals.sagpub.com/doi/abs/10.1177/0973 801017703 499

Global Education Magazine. (2017). *Global report on out-of-school children.* Retrieved from http://www.globaleducation magazine.com/global-report-out-of-school-children/

Gusau, B. U. (2008). *Educational reforms in Nigeria: Successive years of inconsistencies and confusions.* Retrieved from http://www.gamji.com/article6000/NEWS7831.htm

Hanushek, E. A. (1995). Interpreting recent research on schooling in developing countries. *World Bank Research Observer, 10*(2), 227-46.

Heine, S. J., Kitayama S., Lehman, D. R., Takata, T., Matsumoto, H., Ide, E., & Leung, C. (2001). Divergent consequences of success and failure in Japan and North America: An investigation of self-improving motivations and malleable selves. *Journal of Personality and Social Psychology, 81*(4), 599-615.

Hogg, M. A., & Williams, D. F. (2000). From I to we: Social identity and the collective self. *Groups Dynamics: Theory, Research and Practice, 4*(1), 81-97.

Ijaduola, K. O. (1998). *Education in Nigeria: An historical perspective.* Ijebu-Ode, Nigeria: Lucky Odoni (Nig) Enterprises.

Imam, H. (2003). A survey of pre-colonial Almajiri education in Kanem-Borno and Hausaland. *SAPHA – Journal of Historical Studies, 1*(1), 1-6.

Imam, H. (2012). Educational policy in Nigeria from the colonial era to the post-independence period. *Italian Journal of Sociology of Education, 1*.

Imoke, L. (2012). *Reforms in education: The roles of alumnus.* Paper presented by His Excellency Senator Liyel Imoke at the University of Nigeria Nsukka.

India Brand Equity Foundation. (2018). *Road infrastructure in India.* Retrieved from http://www.ibef.org/industry/roads-india.aspx

Ishaya, R. (2017). NOUN gets nod for N150 m PPP project. *Infrastructure Concession Regulatory Commission.* Retrieved from https://www.icrc.gov.ng/noun-gets-nod-n150m-ppp-project/

Jayawardane, N. M. (2018) *The very American myth of 'exceptional immigrants' It is time for more privileged immigrants in the U.S. to stop seeing themselves as more deserving than others.* Retrieved on November 12, 2018 from https://www.aljazeera.com/ indepth/opinion/ american-myth-exceptional-immigrants-180119124728058.html

Jenkin, M. (2015). Tables out, imagination in: the schools that shun technology. *The Guardian*, December 2, 2015. Retrieved on November 16, from https://www.theguardian.com/teacher-network/2015/dec/02/schools-that-ban-tablets-traditional-education-silicon-valley-london

Johnson, K., & Markham, E. (2004). Education and gender inequality: A Nigerian perspective. *Gender and Behaviour, African Journals Online, 2*, 215.

Kalu, U. (2013). Nigeria is 33rd most corrupt country – Transparency Int'l. *Vanguard.* Retrieved from https://www.vanguardngr.com /2013/12/nigeria-33rd-corrupt-country-transparency-intl/

Kazeem, Y. (2018). *Nigeria Has Become the Poverty Capital of the World.* Retrieved on October 17, 2018 from https://qz.com/africa/1421543/nigerias-poverty-crisis-is-worsening-oxfam-world-bank-data/

Khandker, S. R., Lavy, V., & Filmer, D. (1994). *Schooling and cognitive achievements of children in Morocco.* Discussion Paper, No. 264, World Bank, February.

Lebo, J., & Schelling, D. (2000). *Design and appraisal of rural transport infrastructure: Ensuring basic access for rural communities.* (World Bank Technical Paper No. 496). Washington, D.C.: World Bank.

Magazina, J. (2016, June 7). Education in Taiwan. *World Education News and Reviews.* Retrieved from https://wenr.wes.org/2016/06/education-in-taiwan

Makhubele, J. (2008). The impact of indigenous community-based groups towards social development. *Indilinga African Journal of Indigenous Knowledge Systems*, Volume 7, Issue 1, p.37-46

Mkpa, M. A. (1997). *Curriculum development at Owerri.* Imo, Nigeria: Totan Publishers Ltd.

Mahmood, A. (2014). *80% of Nigerian Youths Are Unemployed – CBN Official.* Retrieved on August 26, 2018 from http://www.informationng.com/2014/06/80-of-nigerian-youths-are-unemployed-cbn-official.html

Mohammed, A. (2015, Aug. 10). WAEC releases 2015 results, withholds 118,101 results exam malpractices. *Premium Times*. Retrieved from https://www.premiumtimesng.com/news/top-news/188139-waec-releases-2015-results-withholds-118101-results-over-exam-malpractices.html

Mukhtar, U. B. (2016). *Muslims' contribution to the study and development of sciences in 19th century Nigeria: A preliminary account.* Paper presented at the 7th International Congress of the International Society of the History of Islamic Medicine and 4th Fez Congress on History of Medicine, UK, 24th to 28th October 2016.

Murtala, A. (2017, July 25). Nigeria has the highest number of out-of-school children. *The Guardian.* Retrieved from https://guardian.ng/news/nigeria-has-highest-number-of-out-of- school-children/

Nair, K. (2018). *What we all need to learn from Finland's education system.* Retrieved from http://www.youthincmag.com/what-we-all-need-to-learn-from-finlands-education-system

Nakpodia, E. D., & Urien, J. (2011). Teacher education in Nigeria: Challenges to educational administrators in the 21st century. *The Social Sciences, 6,* 350-356. doi: 10.3923/sscience.2011.350.356

National Bureau of Statistics. (2010). *National literacy survey* Retrieved from www.nigerianstat.gov.ng/download/43 National Centre on Education and the Economy, Centre on

International Education Benchmarking. (n.d.). *Shanghai- China: Learning systems,* Retrieved from https:// ncee. org/what-we-do-/centre-on-international-educationbench marking/top-performing-countries/shanghai-china/shanghai- china-instruction

Nduka, O. (1964). *Western education and Nigerian cultural background.* London: Oxford University Press.

News Agency of Nigeria. (2018, Aug. 20). Again, Nigerian students soar at world robotics. *Vanguard.* Retrieved from https:// www.vanguardngr.com/2018/08/again-nigerian-student-soar-at-world-robotics/

Nwagwu, C. C. (2011). The environment of crises in the Nigeria education system. *Comparative Education, 33*(1), 87-96.

Obasanjo, O. (2012). *Education and development.* Lecture delivered at the 2012 Graduation Ceremonies of the University of Nigeria, Nsukka, Nigeria, January 26, 2012.

Obayan, P. A. I. (1982). *Teaching and cheating.* Inaugural Lecture delivered at the University of Ibadan, Nigeria, 1982.

Obidi, S. S. (1988). Northern Nigeria and the issue of free universal primary education, 1952-58. *The Journal of Negro Education, 57*(1), 94-105. doi: 10.2307/2295279

Obioma, G., Junaidu, I., & Ajagun, G. (2013). *The automation of educational assessment in Nigeria: Challenges and implications for pre-service teacher education.* A paper presented at the 39th Annual Conference of the International Association for Educational Assessment, Tel-Aviv, Israel, October 20-25, 2013.

Odukoya, D. (2009). Formulation and implementation of education policies in Nigeria. *Educational Research Network for West and Central Africa.* Retrieved from www.slideshare.net

Ogunbiyi, T. (2015, Sep. 4). Combating illiteracy in Nigeria. *The Nation.* Retrieved from http://thenationonlineng.net/ combating-illiteracy-in-nigeria/

Ogunnu, M. (2000). *Introduction to educational management.* Benin City, Nigeria: Mabogun Publishers.

Ojetunde, F. (2012). A critical evaluation of the implication of the Nigerian language policy at the pre-primary and primary school levels. *Journal of Education and Practice, 3*(16).

Oji, M. K. (1982). *The Nigerian ethical revolution 1981-2000 AD.* Selected Source Documents.

Okafor, F. C. (2008). *Nigeria teacher education: A search for new direction.* Enugu, Nigeria: Fourth Dimension Publishing Co. Ltd.

Okeke, V.M. (2014). Catholic Education and National Development: *Pastoral Letter 2014.* Onitsha, Nigeria: Feros 2 Limited.

Okere, T. (1990). The role of religion in moral education, Christian perspective. In A. N. Otonti & E. O. Iheoma (Eds.), *New perspective in moral education.* Ibadan: Evans Brothers Limited.

Okojie, J. (2012). *Corruption had assumed a worrisome level in education.* Paper presented at the National University Council and Independent and Corrupt Practices Commission Seminar, Abuja, Nigeria.

Okonkwo, O. (2016, Aug. 5). WAEC releases May/June 2016 results; Records 50% pass. *Premium Times.* Retrieved from https://www.premiumtimesng.com/news/top-news/208134-waec-releases-mayjune-2016-results-records-50-pass.html

Olakunle, O. (2011). *The strike and student learning effectiveness nūh.* Paper presented at Lagos State University.

Olowolagba, F. (2018, July 4). WAEC releases 2018 May/June results, reveals pass rate. *Daily Post.* Retrieved from https://dailypost.ng/2018/07/04/waec-releases-2018-may-june-results-reveals-pass-rate/

Omilana, T. (2018). Nigerian teenagers win World tech innovation challenge. *The Guardian.* Retrieved August 25, 2018 from https://guardian.ng/news/ nigerian-teenagers-win-world-tech-innovation-challenge/

Omolewa, M. (1986, Nov. 17). History of 6-3-3-4 education system in Nigeria. *Daily Sketch.*

Omotoso, S. A. (2010). Education and emancipation: An African philosophical perspective. *The Journal of Pan African Studies, 3*(9), 222-231.

Oniye, A. O. (2010). Women education: Problems and implications for family responsibility. *The Nigerian Journal of Guidance and Counseling, 9*(1).

Onuigbo, A. U. (2009). Education reforms and the merger issues in colleges of education, polytechnics and universities: Public interest. *Academic Staff Union Journal Eha-Amufu, 1*(1).

Onwuameze, N. C. (2013). *Educational opportunity and inequality in Nigeria: Assessing social background, gender and regional effects* (Doctoral thesis). University of Iowa. Retrieved from https://ir.uiowa.edu/etd/2598

Opejobi, S. (2016, Sep. 5). Nigeria one of the poorest countries in the world, over 80m living below poverty line — UN report. *Daily Post*. Retrieved from http://dailypost.ng/2016/09/05/nigeria-one-poorest-countries-world-80m-living-poverty-line-un-report/

Orji, A. S. (1992). *A historical approach to foundation of education*. Owerri, Nigeria: Vemac Publishers.

Osili, U. O. I. (2005). *Does female schooling reduce fertility? Debating and proposing policy options for national development*. Enugu, Nigeria: African Institute for Applied Economics.

Osokoya, I. O. (2002). *History and policy of Nigerian education in world perspective*. Ibadan, Nigeria: AMD Publishers.

Owenby, T. (2015, May 8). What can the U.S. learn from South Korea's education system? *World Economic Forum*. Retrieved from https://www.weforum.org/agenda/2015/05/what-can-the-us-learn-from-south-koreas-education-system/

Oyebamiji, M. A., & Omordu, C. (2011). The Nigerian system of education and the need for pragmatic approach. *World Journal of Education, 1*(2), 98-103.

Oyeleke, O., & Akinyeye, C. O. (2013). Curriculum development in Nigeria: Historical perspectives. *Journal of Educational and Social Research, 3*(1).

Oyewole, N. (2017). Two Nigerian teachers listed among top global 50. *Daily Trust*. Retrieved from https://www.dailytrust.com.ng/two-nigerian-teachers-listed-among-top-global-50.html

Ozigi, A., & Ocho, L. (1981). *Education in Northern Nigeria.* London: George Allen and Unwin Publishers Ltd.

Porter, G. (2012). *Reflections on a century of road transport developments in Africa and their (gendered) impacts on the rural poor.* Retrieved from https://journals.openedition.org/echogeo/13116

Premium Times. (2014). *UniAbuja gives breakdown of Nigerian government's N2 billion intervention fund.* Retrieved from https://www.premiumtimesng.com/news/158829-uniabuja-gives-breakdown-nigerian-governments-n2-billion-intervention-fund.html

Quatroche, D. J. (2000). Helping the underachiever in reading. *ERIC Review, 7,* 25-26.

Robinson, R., Gallagher, J., & Denry, A. (1995). *Africa and the Victorians.* London: Palgrave Macmillan.

Ross, A. (2016). *The Industries of the Future.* New York, NY: Simon & Schuster.

Sabates, R., Akyeampong, K., Westbrook, J., & Hunt, F. (2010). *School dropout: Patterns, causes, changes and policies.* Paper commissioned for the EFA Global Monitoring Report 2011.

Saghir, J. (2005). *Energy and poverty: Myths, links and policy issues.* Energy Working Paper, No. 4, Washington, D.C., World Bank.

Schiefelbein, E., Velez, E., & Valenzuela, J. (1993). *Factors affecting achievement in primary education: A review of the literature for Latin America and the Caribbean.* HRO, Working Paper. Washington, D.C.: World Bank.

Schweikert, A., & Chinowsky, P. (2013). *Re-defining "project impact": Incorporating social consideration into the rural road prioritisation process.* Proceedings of the EPOC Conference, 2013.

Shillington, K. (2005). *History of Africa* (rev. 2nd ed.). New York: Macmillan Publishers Ltd.

Shua'ibu, A. A. (2015, Jan. 9). Moral decadence amongst youth: Who is to blame? *Daily Trust*. Retrieved from https://www.dailytrust.com.ng/daily/home-front/43911-moral-decadence- amongst-youth-who-is-to-blame

Singelis, T. M. (2000). Some thoughts on the future of cross-cultural social psychology. *Journal of Cross-Cultural Psychology, 31*(1), 76-91.

Singmaster, H. (2018). Shanghai: The world's best school system. *Centre for Global Education – Global Cities Education Network.* Retrieved from https://asiasociety.org/global-cities-education-network/shanghai-worlds-best-school-system

Sulaiman, F. R. (2012). Internationalisation in education: The British colonial policies on education in Nigeria 1882-1926. *Journal of Sociological Research, 3*(2). doi:10.5296/jsr. v3i2.2222

Sule, M. N., & Bawa, A. G. (2012). 9-3-4 school curriculum in Nigeria: Verification for its accommodation of Kanuri culture in Maiduguri metropolitan area of Borno state, Nigeria. *Journal of Research in Education and Society, 3*(1), 23-24.

Taiwo, C. O. (1980). *The Nigerian educational system*. Lagos: Thomas Nelson Nigeria Ltd.

Technology and Schools: Teacher's little helper. (2018, November 17-23). *The Economist,* p. 63.

Timileyin, O. (2018, Aug. 10). Nigerian teenagers win world tech innovation challenge. *The Guardian.* Retrieved from https://guardian.ng/news/nigerian-teenagers-win-world-tech-innovation-challenge/

Toomey, S. T. (1999). *Communicating across cultures*. New York: Guilford Publications, Inc.

Transparency International. (2005). *Stealing the future: Corruption in the classroom.* Retrieved from http://www.transparency.org/ whatwedo?gcid=CPPmb3f3bM

Transparency International. (2007). *Corruption in the education sector.* Working Paper, 4, Transformation Agenda (2011-2015). Retrieved from http://www.npc.gov.ng/vault/Transformation.pdf

Transparency International. (2018). *Transparency International surveys, 21 February, 2018.* Retrieved from https://www.transparency.org/news/feature/corruption_percept ions_index _2017

Udemezue, O. (2018, Apr. 6). The tyranny of private schools in Nigeria. *Pulse Online Newspaper.* Retrieved from https://www.pulse.ng/communities/bloggers/educational-the-tyranny-of-private-schools-in-nigeria-id8214543.html

UNDP. (2015). *Human development reports*. Retrieved from http://hdr.undp.org/ed/composite/GII

UNESCO. (2012). *Reaching the 2015 literacy target: Delivering on the promise.* Action Plan of the Higher-Level International Roundtable on Literacy, Paris, 6-7 September 2012.

UNESCO and UNICEF Reports. (2014). *Global initiative on out-of-school children: West and Central Africa regional report.* Retrieved from http://www.unicef.org/education /bege_ 61659.html

UNICEF. (2011). *Equity in education to ensure all children in school.* Retrieved from http://www.unicef.org/education/ bege_ 61659.html

Van de Walle, D. (2002). Choosing rural road investments to help reduce poverty. *World Development, 30*(4), 575-589.

World Bank. (1994). *Infrastructure for development.* Retrieved from https://openknowledge.worldbank.org/handle/10986/5977

World Bank. (1997). The state in a changing world. In *World Development Report.* Oxford: Oxford University Press.

World Bank. (2012). *World development indicators 2012.* Retrieved from http://documents.worldbank.org/curated/en/ 553131468 163740875/pdf/681720PUB0EPI004019020120Box367902B.pdf

World Economic Forum. (2017). *The global gender gap report.* Retrieved from http://www3.weforum.org/docs/WEF_ GGGR_2017.pdf

World Education News and Reports. (2017). *Education in Nigeria.* Retrieved from https://wenr.wes.org/ 2017/03/education-in-nigeria

Yau, E. (2015). *Macau is becoming a higher education destination for Chinese students.* Retrieved from https://www.scmp.

com/lifestyle/family-education/ article/1736000/macau-becoming-higher-education- destination-mainland

Yomere, G. O. (2010). *Corporate culture: A bridge or barrier to organisational performance*. 21st Inaugural Lecture, Delta State University, Abraka: University Press.

Helpful Online Resources

https://africacheck.org/spot-check/yes-nigerian-americans-do-well-but-arent-most-successful-ethnic-group-in-us/

https://asiasociety.org/education/south-korean-education

http://estonianworld.com/knowledge/oecd-estonian-elementary-education-best-europe/

https://www.greaterkashmir.com/news/opinion/why-japan-s-education-system-is-unique/231058.html

https://guidable.co/education/what-can-we-learn-from-the-japanese-educational-system/

https://www.internations.org/singapore-expats/guide/29461-family-children-education/the-education-system-in-singapore-16071

http://www.itseducation.asia/article/hong-kong-education-system

https://www.japantimes.co.jp/culture/2002/01/20/books/book-reviews/redefining-the-role-of-education-in-Japan/#.W5Kznji0WUk

https://www.moe.gov.sg/education/education-system

http://www.studyinestonia.ee/education-system-estonia

http://www.studyinhongkong.edu.hk/en/hong-kong-education/education-system.php

http://www.studyinhongkong.edu.hk/en/why-hong-kong/world-class-education.php

http://www.studyinmacau.com/

https://www.studyinternational.com/news/5-reasons-finland-education-system-better/

https://taiwan.gov.tw/education.php

http://www.worldbank.org/en/topic/education/publication/how-shanghai-does-it

www.ingramcontent.com/pod-product-compliance
Lightning Source LLC
Chambersburg PA
CBHW020416010526
44118CB00010B/285